Labour
and the
British State

Labour and the British State

Barry Jones
and
Michael Keating

CLARENDON PRESS · OXFORD
1985

Oxford University Press, Walton Street, Oxford OX2 6DP
Oxford New York Toronto
Delhi Bombay Calcutta Madras Karachi
Kuala Lumpur Singapore Hong Kong Tokyo
Nalrobi Dar es Salaam Cape Town
Melbourne Auckland
and associated companies in
Beirut Berlin Ibadan Mexico City Nicosia

Oxford is a trade mark of Oxford University Press

Published in the United States
by Oxford University Press, New York

British Library Cataloguing in Publication Data

Jones, J. Barry
Labour and the British state.
1. Labour Party (Great Britain)   2. State, The
3. Great Britain—Politics and government—
1979-
I. Title   II. Keating, Michael, 1950-
324.2'04   JN1129.L3

ISBN 0-19-876187-2
ISBN 0-19-876186-4 Pbk

Set by Colset Private Limited, Singapore
Printed in Great Britain by Biddles Ltd, Guildford and King's Lynn

Preface

MUCH of the initial motivation to write this book came from our membership of the United Kingdom Politics Workgroup, from the formal debates at its annual conferences, and even more so from informal discussions which frequently ran on till the small hours of the morning. Our enthusiasm and commitment to examine the topic emerged naturally from our research into the Labour Party's policy on devolution to Scotland and Wales in the late 1970s. It seemed to us then, that fundamental questions about the nature of the British state were largely ignored by a Labour government preoccupied, and eventually overwhelmed, by short-term pragmatic considerations. In seeking to explain the failure of Labour's devolution policy, we had in effect opened a pandora's box. This book is the product of that misadventure.

Our respective geographical locations — one of us lives in Glasgow and the other in Cardiff — enabled us to examine the topic from a perspective quite different from that which is usually adopted. We are both Celts looking in on the political system from the periphery, a situation we regard as a distinct advantage. However, our two situations did cause problems, not the least of which was the difficulty of travelling back and forth between Glasgow and Cardiff. It is surely a significant comment on the nature of the British state, that we sometimes discovered it more convenient to meet in London.

The starting-point for our study was a view born of our earlier research that the relationship of the Labour Party to the form and institutions of the United Kingdom state is of great importance in the development and consolidation of the modern United Kingdom political system. Yet with the exception of some analyses bounded by Marxist presuppositons, it is a subject which has been given little attention in the large body of literature on the modern British party system. In part, this reflects the lack of thought in British political life generally about the nature of the state which, in turn, can be attributed to the British tradition of pragmatism and to the relative absence of challenges to the regime in British political history. It seemed to us that the absence of a challenge by the Labour Party was vital in accommodating the working class to the institutions of the state and thus in laying the foundations of the modern political system. We think that this absence needs to be explained. Labour's roots, unlike those of the Conservative Party, lie outside the parliamentary system and the basic form of the state was settled before Labour's appearance on the political scene and might thus have been regarded as reflecting the values of its opponents. Further, there is an implicit contradiction between the universalist and internationalist elements in Labour's ideology and support for the British state.

The underlying ambivalence in Labour's attitude to the state has been characteristic of the Labour Party since its creation but it has been brought into sharp focus in recent years by the emergence of 'the form of the state' as a major political issue in its own right. Four issues in particular are of significance: Labour's attitudes to the machinery of the state; Labour's relationship to the industrial state; Labour's identification with the territorial integrity of the state challenged by the rise of Scottish and Welsh nationalism; and Labour's response to the threats posed to the sovereignty of the state by the Northern Ireland conflict and British membership of the EEC. We explore these four issues, examine the factors which influenced Labour's attitude towards the state, and review the historical process whereby the Labour Party accommodated to the institutions of the state.

We are indebted to many colleagues for their advice and criticism on the early drafts of the various chapters: to Dave Boucher, Peter Bridger, Jack Geekie, Chris Harvie, David Heald, David Judge, Mick Ryan, and David Webster.

Our thanks are also due to the British Academy for funds which helped us overcome the difficulties which we faced in attempting to write a book while living almost 500 miles apart: to the Department of Administration, Strathclyde University and to the Department of Economics and Banking, UWIST for their continued support and to Margaret Aven, Agnes Alexander, Pat McTaggart, Ann Murphy, and Barbara Williams who typed out numerous drafts with good humour and rare patience.

Despite the help and advice we received from many quarters we alone are responsible for the book and the judgements it expresses.

Barry Jones
Michael Keating
October 1984.

Contents

	Introduction	1
1.	The state and the British radical tradition	10
2.	The emergence of Labour	27
3.	The integration of Labour	42
4.	Labour and the industrial state	67
5.	Labour's territorial strategy	104
6.	Labour and the machinery of government	140
7.	Labour and British sovereignty	163
8.	Conclusions	193
	References	202
	Index	210

Introduction

'Practical Socialism is so simple that a child may understand it. It is a kind of national scheme of cooperation managed by the State'.
                              (Robert Blatchford, *Merrie England*, 1894).

THE idea of the state is central to political discourse and practice, yet it remains one of the most difficult concepts to define and analyse. It is a descriptive concept, applying to the institutions of civil government, which can be analysed and discussed empirically; but it is also a normative concept, for in talking of the state we inevitably bring in the question of the legitimate sources of civil authority. To characterize institutions and actors as part of the 'state' is to recognize that they make a peculiar claim to legitimacy. The legitimacy of the state may not be universally accepted. Radical political movements or the leaders of newly assertive social classes or ethnic groups may challenge it and the system of power relationships which it represents; they may assert alternative principles of legitimacy, based on nation, class, or democratic choice, which the existing state does not satisfy. In most political systems, indeed, the legitimacy of the state and its institutional manifestations is, if not a subject of debate, at least a matter for analysis and explanation.

In the British and American intellectual traditions, however, the state hardly features as an organizing concept (Dyson, 1980), even on the political Left, though in both countries there is an intense and continuing debate about the place of 'government' in social and economic life. In the British case, an important reason is the continuity of political authority, the lack of a revolutionary break necessitating reformulation of principles of legitimacy. The other, and related reason, is the pragmatic tradition in both intellectual and political discourse. So the United Kingdom has seen a growth in government activity from the 'night-watchman state' into large areas of social and economic life, the construction of a multinational union and the birth and death of empire without a theory of the state to accompany them. Indeed, there is one British intellectual tradition which denies the existence of a state altogether. Ernest Barker's claim in 1930 that 'the state as such does not act in England (*sic*)' (quoted, Dyson, 1980, p. 5) is typical not merely for its ethnocentric identification of the United Kingdom with one of its consitituent parts but also in the refusal to examine the bases of political authority. As a consequence of this tradition, important questions such as the boundaries and territorial integrity of the state, citizenship, power relations among the arms of government, control over the activities of government, and the relation of the citizen to government have been neglected as subjects in their own right.

It is beyond our scope to undertake a comprehensive survey of theories of the state in the Western political tradition. Some conceptual clarification, however, is necessary. We are talking of the territorial bounds of the polity, the governing institutions within it and the scope and power of those institutions in relation to the civil society and the individual. It is these which set the boundaries of political debate and action yet are themselves part of that debate and action; for the distribution of political power and its relationship to other sources of power are important both in themselves and in the scope they give for social and economic reform through the political process. The issue is of particular importance to parties of the Left seeking both a democratization of the state machine and to use it in a progressive and purposeful manner.

If the state itself is rarely an object of analysis in the British and American political or intellectual traditions, the issues of state power and the role of government have surfaced from time to time in academic debate and have been a constant feature of political argument in both countries. In Britain, it is usually the Labour Party which is cast as the party of state power, given its programmes of nationalization, planning, and public welfare. Our argument is that it has rarely given any sustained attention to the form of the state whose power and role it is pledged to extend. Partly, we argue in the next three chapters, this is because the Labour Party itself is part of that evolution which has created the contemporary British political system. Its commitment to transcendent policy goals competes with attitudes derived from its roots in British radical traditions, defensive trade unionism, British nationalism, and the parliamentary-party model of government into which its leaders were so effortlessly absorbed. Partly, we shall argue, the neglect stems from a sheer intellectual failure on the part of Labour leaders and policy makers — a failure which persists to the present — to specify the changes in the state necessary to achieve their policy goals while preserving and extending individual and associative liberties; or to identify and frankly recognize the limits to state power.

We can clarify this latter issue by looking at the main perspectives on the state and public power which have emerged, explicitly or implicitly, from the academic debate. The social-democratic tradition, from which Labour draws so much of its inspiration, tends to emphasize the independent power of government and its dominant, or potentially dominant, position in society which allows those in control of it to impose their own policy priorities (Crosland, 1956). The state is thus the major instrument of economic and social transformation and political activity aimed at gaining control of the state apparatus the most important task of progressives. Pluralists on the other hand, de-emphasize the role of the state and government, regarding it as an arena in which policy issues are fought out among interest groups. Some American pluralists (Dahl, 1961) go on to give a positive evaluation to pluralism on the grounds that, while power might not be distributed absolutely equally, it is sufficiently widespread to prevent any group gaining dominance. Other pluralists, influenced by American experience, disaggregate the state itself into series of competing interests, sometimes allied with outside pressure groups (Richardson and Jordan, 1979). In a logical extension of their thesis, pluralists further tend to see policy as made incrementally, by a process of 'partisan mutual adjustment' (Lindbolm, 1959) rather than by radical, purposive state action. So the state, far from being a unique source of political authority and action, becomes at best one actor, or a series of actors, in a complex political system. Clearly, such a view of the political system has little attraction for a radical party intent on using the state to accomplish a social and economic transformation. Yet the pluralist dispersal of power is a widely valued feature of the British political system and one which Labour has never seriously challenged. This makes all the more necessary a clear view of how change is to be accomplished, largely through the agency of the state but while preserving the independence of private groups and associations.

As descriptions of reality, the pure social democratic and pluralist views of political power have both been widely criticized. The belief that the state, through its monopoly of legislative power, can do what it wants ignores the real constraints on public power. As government has extended its scope into new areas of social and economic policy, authoritative declaration of legal norms backed by penal sanctions is not enough to secure the implementation of policy. The positive compliance of those affected must be secured by more or less voluntary means, usually involving concessions by the state to private interests.

If social democrats are criticized for ignoring the constraints on government, pluralists are criticized for making the constraints into a complete theory, at the expense of everything else. In so far as they regard the state as a mere 'black box', the outputs to which are determined by the inputs, they fail to give due weight to the political process. Others, as we have noted, cope with this by seeing the institutions of government themselves as a series of competing groups in fixed or shifting alliances with outside interests. This, in our view, disposes of the state too abruptly. The mobilization of public power behind political purposes is a feature of all Western democracies despite the constraints imposed by external pressures; and there is a legal, cultural, and political unity to government despite the divisions within it.

Recent theories of 'corporatism' have tried to reconcile these positions by seeing public policy as the outcome of negotiation between the state and powerful interest groups. The theories are advanced in both a descriptive and normative form, as a description of the way in which western political systems were heading in the 1970s and as a prescription for overcoming the problems of 'ungovernability'. However, as most 'corporatists' have recognized, the theory requires a view as to where power lies in the relationship, or, at least, on the power resources of the various parties. Winkler (1976, p. 103) sees the state as the dominant partner, defining corporatism as 'an economic system in which the state directs and controls predominantly privately-owned business according the four principles: unity, order, nationalism and success'. He does, however, recognize other interpretations, conceding that corporatism can mean either state domination or institutionalized pluralism. Cawson (1978, p. 185) similarly notes that, as corporatism is a *method* of interest representation, there can be different types of corporate polity, with distinctions between 'state corporatism and societal corporatism, authoritarian corporatism or conservative corporatism and redistributive corporatism'. Societal or liberal corporatism focusing on institutionalized bargaining, is really 'an extension of pluralist theories' (Cawson, 1978, p. 185). In other words, to describe a political system as 'corporatist' tells us little in itself about the distribution of power or the role of the state. Certainly, Winkler (1976) puts the emphasis on state control rather than negotiation but he has been criticized (Ham and Hill, 1984; Cox,

1981) for lacking a theory of state power. The matter is of vital importance. Societal corporatism or institutionalized pluralism may be a
recipe for conservatism and immobilism in public policy as each
vested interest seeks to protect its inherited position. State corporatism, on the other hand, may — though not necessarily — be the
instrument of radical social and economic change. We trace, in
Chapter 5, Labour's attempts to grapple with the problem of
management in the mixed economy through a variety of 'corporatist'
arrangements and conclude that it, too, has lacked a clear idea of the
strengths and limitations of state power. The Labour Party, as we
shall note, is particularly prone to confuse state corporatism and
societal corporatism because of its organic links with the trade unions.
In government, there is an ambiguity about whether the unions are an
external interest group or part of the governing coalition. The issue
has often been dismissed by an insistence that unions and party share
the same socialist goals (or would do, given proper leadership). This,
as we show, is far from being the case.

Another perspective on the problem of power in the state is the élite
view which points to the concentration of power in the hands of
bureaucratic élites owing their position to their training, skills, con-
tacts, and knowledge (Sedgemore, 1980; Kellner and Crowther-
Hunt, 1980). Bureaucrats are able to exercise political power against
elected politicians in the interests of maintaining their own power and
status. This sort of theory is not difficult to reconcile with varieties of
corporatism, with the bureaucracy as a corporate interest (Sedgemore
1980). We see, in Chapter 6, however, that Labour has never developed a clear view on the nature of bureaucracy, the interests it represents and its source of power; it is not surprising, then, that it has failed
to tackle Civil Service reform when in office, while continuing to
complain of bureaucratic resistance to its radical ideas.

Given the influence of Marxism on thinking on the Labour Left, the
recent resurgence of Marxist writing on the state and power is of some
relevance to our theme. Marx's own early view of the state as the mere
executive committee of the bourgeoisie, with political power determined entirely by the economic relations of production soon gave way
to a recognition that political activity could have an independent influence. Marxists continue to believe that political power is essentially
the outcome of class relationships rooted in the ownership of the
means of production but derive this view in different ways. Miliband
(1973, 1977) points to the social composition of various public élites to

show that they derive overwhelmingly from the bourgeoisie. The difficulty with this as a contribution to theory rather than an empirical observation is that many of the leading figures on the Marxist Left have a similar social background. In any case, it is really an élite theory rather than one grounded in Marxist analysis. Poulantzas (1969), in a criticism which Miliband has come some way to conceding (indeed, it was a subsidiary theme in Miliband's own theory), emphasizes the structural constraints which force the state in a capitalist society to act in the interests of the owners of the means of production whatever the personnel of the state apparatus. This, in turn, has been critized as over-deterministic, rendering political activity futile and depriving the state of any scope for independent action. So the question for Marxists has come to hinge on the 'relative autonomy' of the state from capitalist pressures. In other words, Marxists have to face the same intellectual difficulty as other analysts in identifying the role and scope of state activity and the degree to which it is constrained by external forces. So this remains the central question in all theories.

Political debate on the proper role of the state in Britain has revolved round normative conceptions which we can characterize as liberal, social-democratic, and conservative. In the liberal perspective, the state should reduce its activities to the minimum, avoiding in particular involvement in economic and social matters, seen as a threat both to economic efficiency and individual liberty. The social-democratic view sees the state in a more benificent light, as an instrument of social and economic progress and equality, the embodiment of public, social purpose against private greed. The traditional conservative view is more complex but perhaps the most influential in the development of the British state system. The conservative is not dogmatically for or against the state, except in the fields of defence and law and order, where a strong state is seen as vital. In social and economic affairs, the conservative is prepared to use the state to rectify patent injustice and abuse but not as an instrument of equality. Rather, abuses must be removed in order to restore balance and harmony to the body politic and so preserve the traditional social order. The tradition and practice of Disraelian Conservative reformism in the ninetheeth century was one of the factors leading the emergent Labour Party to put its faith in the parliamentary system. So while social democracy in other countries rested on a revolutionary establishment of its democratic prerequisites, British social democrats (and the

Labour Party) sought to adapt existing mechanisms. Indeed, since 1979 it is the Labour Party which has been defending the state from the attacks of the new liberalism (albeit combined with a penchant for authoritarian measures in the law and order field) of the modern Conservative Party. The party, thus forced on the defensive by the populist anti-state rhetoric of Mrs Thatcher and her supporters, has failed to articulate an alternative view of a less alien, remote, and bureaucratic state and has appeared as the defender of the status quo.

Another vital element in conservative theory is the emphasis on the national family — which has never been satisfactorily defined — as the basis for social solidarity. This, indeed, partly explains the conservative readiness to use the state in the pursuit of collectivist measures and to promote internal co-operation in the interests of international competitiveness. For the Labour Party, this poses a number of problems. Its ideology and composition force it to pay some attention to the concept of class solidarity, a loyalty both narrower and wider than national solidarity, excluding compatriots of other classes but including the workers of other countries. Yet, as the quotation from Blatchford above indicates, Labour leaders have often seen national collectivism and socialism as identical. There is a further problem in the nature of the United Kingdom. The UK has never existed as a nation-state. Its emergence coincided with the imperial experience and, while Labour was of course in favour of decolonization, in the case of Ireland the line between decolonization and dismemberment of the metropolitan state has never been clear. Partly because of the imperial experience, the symbols of British nationalism have been appropriated by the Conservative Party (which even uses the national flag in its party emblem), enabling it to tap the strong nationalism in the British working class. Radical anti-imperialist nationalist traditions do exist in the United Kingdom, in the 'Celtic fringe' and in the 'little Englander' radicalism of which Tony Benn is but the latest exponent; but in the absence of a popular democratic base for UK state sovereignty, any nationalistic appeal is liable to arouse imperial passions, as the Falklands War showed. It does not help for Labour to dress up nationalistic appeals in the ideological garb of democracy, self-determination, or working-class interest, as it did over both the Falklands and the Common Market; it is the nationalist message which gets through, to Labour's ultimate embarrassment. We examine Labour's difficulties with the concept of state sovereignty in

Chapter 7 and in Chapter 5 look at its attempts to grapple with competing nationalisms in Scotland and Wales.

We have noted how difficult it is to theorize about the state in general. In the British case, the problems are compounded by the identification of the state with the institution of Parliament. The absence of a revolutionary break in British constitutional development and the failure consequently to develop a theory of popular sovereignty left Parliament as the sole repository of state sovereignty. Parliament is the only constitutional entity common to the whole of the United Kingdom and exclusive to it; its domestic jurisdiction is unlimited. So both the sovereignty of the state in its relations with other states or international organizations and the sovereignty of the state over its subjects are identified with the institution of Parliament. The workings of Parliament and, indeed, the whole parliamentary system, are in turn closely bound up with the tradition of party politics, binding together executive and legislature in a unitary system of government. This, together with the advent of universal suffrage, has led the Labour Party to see in Parliament an instrument for radical social and political change. At the same time, the parliamentary tradition is two-edged. Parliamentary government has come to be identified with single party, 'strong executive' government; yet Parliament also has the task of limiting and controlling government, of representing the diversity of the nation. Labour's difficulties in reconciling the two aspects of the same institution have led to great confusion, as we show in Chapter 6.

The Labour Party came into being at a time when the basic features of the British system of parliamentary and party government had already been established. That it failed to challenge them has sometimes been seen as a tribute to the flexibility of British constitutional conventions and the tradition of procedural consensus; sometimes as a sign of rank betrayal. It has certainly produced ideological problems for the party — for example in reconciling strong centralized government with a commitment to decentralization — as well as practical problems in achieving its policy goals. These are an important theme of our substantive chapters. We do not believe, however, that the process can be explained either by idealized versions of British constitutional practice or by theories of leadership betrayal. We have indicated that none of the general theories of the state can give us ready answers to the question of where political power lies. That must be a matter for empirical investigation — by politicians seeking to carry out their programmes as well as by academics. We have also drawn attention to some of the unique features of the British state and its historical evolution. The Labour Party, too, was part of that historical evolution and can only be understood in terms of it. Hence our methodology, historical and empirical, tracing the evolution of the Labour Party within the British political system and examining in detail selected instances when the party has been confronted with the issue of the state, its boundaries, role, and powers.

Having defined the state as vaguely as we have and indicated our concern with the distribution of power, we have opened up a vast array of historical and contemporary material which could serve to illustrate our theme. We have consequently had to be selective, choosing cases to illuminate the main areas of concern but neglecting or mentioning only in passing others equally relevant to the theme of Labour and the state, for example, civil liberties, foreign and defence policy, the management of nationalized industries, the electoral system. Our sole excuse is that one cannot cover everything and that our style of analysis inevitably involves some sacrifices of breadth for depth.

The early chapters are historical, tracing the evolution of thinking about the state in the British radical tradition and the emergence of the Labour Party from a complex of elements within that tradition. We note that much of the ambivalence towards the state derives from the complexity of the Labour coalition itself, with Fabian socialists taking the social-democratic view of the benificent purposes of state activity, union leaders exhibiting a suspicion derived from their dealings with the state and the paliamentary groups rapidly absorbing the conventions of government. Chapter 2 continues the theme, tracing the progressive integration of Labour into the institutions and practices of the British state. The next chapters review Labour's recent experience of handling four issues of central importance to our theme: management of the 'industrial state', centralization and devolution, the machinery of government, and the sovereignty of the state in relation to the Northern Ireland and European Community issues. In the conclusion, we draw together these themes and point to problems facing Labour — or indeed any social-democratic party — in the future.

CHAPTER 1

The state and the
British radical tradition

OUR concern is the Labour Party, its relationship to the British state and its perception of the manner in which the power of the state should be exercised to create a socialist society. Our approach is historical because the continuity of the British political experience is such a dominant characteristic and because the attitudes of the Labour Party cannot be evaluated in isolation. The party is itself part of the British radical tradition and traces its roots to the Lib–Labs of the late nineteenth century and beyond to various co-operative movements and friendly societies. Its attitude on a variety of political issues, including the role of the state, was influenced by its radical precursors. Thus any assessment of the Labour Party must take full account of this complex and extensive inheritance.

Throughout history, radical movements in Britain have tended to voice their demands within the framework of the existing state whose nature and structure they rarely questioned and then usually by reference to earlier historical or utopian forms. The universalist idea of 'natural rights' — the frequent resort of continental radicals — was in Britain, noteworthy for its negligible contribution to political debate. In contrast, British radicalism was characterized by a constitutionalism in theory and a pragmatism in strategy. Rooted in persistent and pervasive native traditions, political radicals in Britain exhibited a cautious conservatism in their dealings with the state, rarely confronting it and seeking incremental reform of its institutions. We can therefore identify a radical tradition in Britain in which a theory of the state is remarkable for its absence.

The word 'state', as generic term for the body politic was used by Machiavelli in the fifteenth century and was progressively incorporated into the official constitutional language of several European countries, including England, during the sixteenth century. In Europe the strength of Roman law tended to identify the concept with the public good and by the early seventeenth century the state was firmly established as a fundamental legal concept and regarded as 'the bond within society which cannot exist without it' (Dyson, 1980,

p. 27). In Europe, the state was increasingly identified with an autonomous public power, separate from, and above, mere politics and
expressed either as a detached autocracy or as a benevolent and idealistic sense of public purpose.

In England however, the term 'state' vied with the older concept of
'commonwealth' to frustrate a consistent application and a clear definition. In English history the state was never recognized as a legal
institution. Nor did it become a technically precise term in English
law — a crucial weakness, given that so much of English political
thought and action is based upon legal concepts and precedents. The
problem of defining the concept of the state in contemporary Britain is
compounded by difficulties in determining the ultimate location and
dimension of sovereignty. The sense of an autonomous public power
and authority, basic to the European concept of sovereignty, is almost
non-existent in Britain where *state* sovereignty is inter-laced with the
traditional English idea of *parliamentary* sovereignty. This in turn
depends upon an inter-relationship between such a variety of political
forces and institutions that Sir Ernest Barker (1930, p. 173) was
persuaded that:

the state as such does not act in England; there is a bundle of individual
officials each exercising a measure of authority under the cognizance of the
Courts, but none of them, not even the Prime Minister, wielding the authority
of the State.

According to Barker's assessment, the state is implicated with
government and the government machine, but this view was never
universally accepted. Burke idealized the state, made it the bearer of
all civilized values and, like Blackstone, failed to distinguish consistently between state, society, and government. Both tended to use the
term 'state' as a synonym for 'nation', a tendency still common today.
However, that usage raises a fundamental question: whether such an
entity as a British nation exists within the British state and, if so,
whether it coexists with the Irish, Scottish, Welsh, and even English
senses of nationhood? This is particularly pertinent given that the
nationalists of the Celtic nations are committed to the breakup of the
British state and, in the cases of Ireland and Scotland at least, are able
to draw on historical or contemporary examples of statehoods quite
separate from those of Britain. In Scotland, the doctrine of parliamentary sovereignty central to the English Parliament was not established before the Union of 1707. Subsequently a sense of Scottish

nationhood has been sustained and carried forward through the institutions and practices of civil society, to challange fundamentally the
equation of state with nation which is characteristic of the European
doctrine of the 'nation-state'. In Ireland, there are at least two traditions: one based upon the concept of the Irish nation, with the question of exactly who is included in this often left deliberately vague, and
the other based upon the maintenance of the United Kingdom state,
underpinned not by a doctrine of common *nationality* but by the
symbol of the Crown and by religion.

The existence of the Celtic periphery raises obvious and fundamental difficulties as regards the territorial integrity of the British
state. Lacking a clear legal concept and looking to an ambiguous
historical experience, the British state has resorted to obscurantist
compromises to resolve its territorial identity. The legal distinction
between 'Great Britain' and the 'United Kingdom' serves to show
both the weakness of the concept of the state and the imperfection of its
assimilation by British political and constitutional practices. When
constitutional doctrines have been required they have been found not
within the experience of the United Kingdom as an amalgam of
various national traditions, but in English constitutional practice.
Thus, although both Scots and English Parliaments were abolished in
1707, it is customary to trace parliamentary practice and doctrine in a
direct line back through the English Parliament to Simon de
Montfort. The rather muddled 1707 Act of Union never specified that
the doctrine of parliamentary sovereignty was to apply to the new
'combined' institutions, but practice soon established that precedents
of the English Parliament should prevail. Thus the new Great Britain
Parliament embodied the role and status of the institution which,
under Thomas Cromwell, had become not only the supreme legislator
but the embodiment of the (English) nation. The political dominance
of England and the consequent imposition of the English tradition,
ensured that Parliament became the essence of the state, a surrogate
both for a doctrine of the state and a definition of the nation.

English radicalism has itself reflected these confusions about the
nature of the state. It identified strongly with the concept of parliamentary supremacy, which it sought to enhance and legitimize by
advocating a progressive extension of the franchise. Such questions as
the role, organization, and machinery of the state remained open until
the nineteenth century and the advent of socialist philosophies.
Socialism in Britain, however, was influenced not only by the Marxist

critique but also deeply rooted in the traditions of English radicalism, from which it inherited constitutionalist attitudes towards the state. Ricardian socialists argued that labour was entitled to a more equal share of the nation's wealth but did not challange the economic system or the ruling oligarchy which proceded to dominate the parliamentary system until the last quarter of the nineteenth century. The continental debate between *anti-étatiste* Marxists and *étatiste* Jacobins was largely ignored by British socialists more concerned with immediate social problems which they presumed could be resolved without a fundamental review of the state This willingness to accept the existing framework of the state enabled early British socialists to establish understandings and accommodations with radical non-socialist groups and profoundly influenced the development of the Labour Party in the twentieth century.

To explore the origins of this attitude, we must take another step into history and the inter-linked histories of the English state and radical thought. In particular, we must examine three distinct but inter-connected factors: the strength and persistance of the medieval tradition in England; the constitutional and legal developments which lead to the establishment of the concept of parliamentary supremacy; and the emergence of a political tradition which, while utopian, looked to historical precedents for justification.

There are two major strands in the English medieval political tradition: the sense of a Christian commonwealth involving a form of community co-operation for the general welfare, and a sense of monarchical authority which was conditional on the general welfare. Wyclif, addressing himself to the pressing political and social problems of the dissolution of feudalism sought to re-establish the Christian commonwealth in which there would be equal measures of kingship and communism. A similar theme was repeated a hundred years later by Sir Thomas More in *Utopia* and it was implicit in Thomas Cromwell's efforts to establish a parternalistic authority for the Tudor dynasty. It is a recurrent theme in English history extending down to the nineteenth century and William Morris's writings and to the twentieth with Tawney's incorporation of medieval values of service and community into his nostalgic form of socialism. (Lichtheim, 1969, p. 187.)

The view that the monarch was part of the community and not above it, was particularly powerful in medieval England. Bracton in *De legibus et consuetudinibus Angliae* conceded that the king ought not to be subject to any man but argued that 'he ought to be subject to God and the Law, since Law makes the King' (Sabine, 1963, p. 220). From this emerged the idea of the institution of the Crown quite distinct from the person of the monarch. This qualified view of monarchical authority was reinforced by a variety of political and constitutional developments. The early emergence of an integrated political community under one monarch, the barons' revolts, Magna Carta, and the evolution of political process which progressively transferred power from the king to his fellow lords and, ultimately, to political institutions, all served to develop a form of political authority quite different from that of European countries.

Consequently, the medieval view of the omnipotence and egalitarian nature of law, although not unique to England, persisted longer and stronger than on the continent. English Common Law and the legal profession retained a private and autonomous existence independent of the framework of government so that the perceived role of law was to establish limits on the authority of government rather than positively to promote the concept of 'public power' as was the case in Europe. The persistence of the medieval view of law also underpinned the authority of Parliament, traditionally regarded as the supreme court which alone could clarify customary laws and give them effect; a necessary precondition for the establishment of the concept of parliamentary supremacy to which political radicals subsequently looked in their efforts to bring about social and economic change.

In the developing European debate during the sixteenth century concerning the nature of the state and its authority, there was a tendency, typified by Montaigne, to look back to a golden age to more primitve and purer societies. In England this was reinforced by powerful political myths of the sleeping hero, such as Arthur and Alfred which, more potent and profuse than their continental counterparts, subsequently loomed larger in English political ideas and actions.

England at this time also experienced a growing interest in its political history. In 1572 the Society of Antiquaries was founded with the purpose of discovering and elevating the importance of an Anglo-Saxon tradition broken by the Norman invasion and the ensuing 'Norman Yoke'. Notable in this 'new historical movement' was Sir Edward Coke who combined a respect for the past with a determination that history 'was conveniently and tidily disposed for his purpose' (Butterfield, 1944, p. 6). His primary purpose was to prove the continuity of English Common Law, thereby establishing a code which would enhance the constitutional status of the House of Commons and legitimize opposition to royal authority. To those ends he was prepared to interpret Magna Carta as an affirmation of common law rather than feudal law; to assert that the laws of England predated those of imperial Rome; and to claim that trial by jury and a bicameral Parliament existed before the Norman conquest. Despite the dubious historical basis of these propositions, Coke was able to translate the medieval limitations on monarchy into seventeenth-century terms with some success. English Common Law with its medieval values thus survived to frustrate the emergence of an absolute monarchy and a clear concept of the state.

By the early seventeenth century the persistence of the medieval tradition, the continuity of English Common Law and the predisposition to refer back to an earlier golden age of Anglo-Saxon liberties destroyed by the Norman Yoke, were all firmly established. They were part of a construction designed to counter-balance the authority of the monarchy, not with the intention of clarifying the parameters of public power but primarily to preserve private property rights. Whilst revolutionary in constitutional terms, they were socially conservative. They revealed that Englishmen 'dared not yet appeal to reason and utility alone' (Hill, 1958, p. 69) but sought to challenge authority with the counter-authority of historical precedent. Inevitably this lent credibility to those governmental institutions which were constructed on historical antecedents. It ensured that the political debate, even when it involved radical change, employed a constitutional vocabulary and largely accepted the existing constitutional structures and precedents.

These qualities were reflected by radical elements during the English Civil War. The most significant and influential, the Levellers, expressed a radicalism which was essentially retrospective. It leant heavily on Coke, an Anglo-Saxon golden age, the imposition of the Norman Yoke, and the continuity of English law. Yet under the dynamic of civil and political disorder it became creatively revolutionary (Hill, 1958, p. 64.) Thus the monarchy was unacceptable because it was descended from the 'Norman Bastard' and had been used to hold the English nation in bondage. The aristocracy's hereditary rights were rejected because they were merely 'the Conqueror's fellow robbers, rogues and thieves [who] had helped him enslave and envassalise the English people' (Hill, 1958, p. 75). The establishment Church and the professional clergy were similarly tainted by the

'Norman Connection.' They had preached obedience to the Prince, moulded the people to accept slavery, and made religion obscure to protect their monopoly of preaching. This attack on the mediating professions was extended to condemn the legal profession. The Levellers argued that the Norman Conquerer had 'elected a trade of judges and lawyers to sell justice and injustice at his own unconscionable rate'; that the localized Anglo-Saxon court structure had also been centralized by the Normans to make the law less accessible to ordinary people and that the courts used Norman French and Latin so that 'the poor might be more easily gulled and cheated' (Hill, 1958, p. 77).

This detailed critique of English political, legal and spiritual institutions did not lead the Levellers to demand a *new* constitutional settlement. According to them an Englishman's rights did not have to be established because they already existed, safeguarded by the English common law, although frustrated by its legal practitioners. As the people were sovereign, Parliament need not be destroyed but restored to them. Thus, despite the most virulent critique of the constitution, Parliament retained its central role unquestioned save for a demand that the franchise be extended, because sovereignty resided with the 'people'. For the Levellers this meant the whole adult male population and threatened the 'old constitution' based on law and property, the Englishman's birthright. The more socially radical Diggers actually advocated the abolition of private property and provided much of the inspiration for Spence and utopian socialist movements in the nineteenth century. But the strong religious emphasis of the Diggers and their commitment to communal rights, based on the Englishman's birthright of shared free land, were derived from the medieval ideas of a Christian commonwealth and firmly incorporated the Diggers into the English radical tradition. Thus both Levellers and Diggers argued their case on the basis of dubious historical precedents and shared a common presumption that an assertion of an Englishman's rights coincided with an affirmation of universal natural rights. Some Levellers were willing to discard the 'Norman Yoke' thesis. When challenged in the Putney debates on the accuracy of their history they set aside questionable historical precedents, argued on the basis of the inalienable rights of man, and suggested that customary rights and natural rights stood side by side. In justifying the political changes of the mid-seventeenth century the Levellers were prepared to invoke either the law of God, or of Nations, or of Nature, in addition to the fundamental laws of England, to advance their cause. Like the Diggers, they believed the rights of Englishmen derived from English Common Law *and* natural law, but their radicalism was so influenced by the English political tradition that they found it more congenial to operate within the framework of the constitution. Their importance to our analysis lies in the fact that they established a tradition of English radicalism that was not only pragmatic and constitutional but also national and popular.

Any review of English radicalism cannot discount the Whigs. They defended the fundamental laws and liberties against what they saw as the 'popular tyranny' proposed by the Levellers. Their constitutional perception was enshrined in the 'glorious revolution' of 1688 and introduced a view of the state and the political process which profoundly influenced the English political tradition. Butterfield (1944, p. 83) argues Whiggism

reveals the discernable implications of the Englishman's alliance with Time and History. It raises the question of the way men can best assert themselves in the historical process, the question of the most effective way of cooperating with Providence. We might say that it expresses the relations of Englishmen with their history, expresses the continuity of past and present by resolving this into a certain kind of political mechanics.

The Whig empathy for 'co-operation' and 'continuity' promoted a distaste for drastic change and a preference for political adjustment. Whig governments were inclined to compromise and, if need be, to concede radical demands rather than endanger the consitutional edifice. It is doubtful whether a consitutionalist and reformist radical tradition could have survived if it had been confronted by a series of intractable reactionary governments. Thus the two traditions may be regarded as mutually supporting. Political radicals, taking the institutions of the state largely for granted, persisted with a constitutionalist approach, a pragmatic strategy, and settled for incremental change in the fairly optimistic expectation that their rights as 'freeborn Englishmen' would be recognized by Whig governments and that concessions would eventually be made.

A radical tradition which sought justification in historical precedents or imagined historical events persisted until the beginning of the nineteenth century. It is testimony to the essential Englishness of the tradition. The continuity of the Norman Yoke thesis is equally remarkable. The anonymous *Historical Essay on the English Constitution* published in 1771 employed the thesis in its attack on arbitrary authority. Thomas Paine is an obvious departure from this tradition, arguing that common sense and reason were a more proper basis for radicalism than historical tradition and consititutionalism. Nevertheless, even he felt obliged to support his contention that the monarchy lacked legitimacy by reference to a 'French bastard landing with armed banditti and establishing himself King of England' (quoted, Hill, 1965, p. 99). The tradition of an Anglo-Saxon utopia also died hard and late. Thomas Spence and his followers, in arguing for an agrarian commonwealth, advocated the restoration of the old Saxon constitution in which 'all land, the water, the mines and the houses and all the permanent feudal property must return to the people' (quoted, Hill, 1965, p. 107). For some, including John Baxter, the Saxon precedent was interpreted as equivalent to the state of nature in a confusing mélange of nationalistic empiricism and a priori reasoning.

Even where historical events were not cited, there was a marked predisposition on the part of political radicals until late in the eighteenth century to think in constitutionalist terms. Thus Wilkes in 1776 argued for the extension of the franchise, not by an appeal to natural rights but in traditional English terms: 'to recover the pristine beauty of the form of government established by our ancestors' (Thompson, 1968, p. 91). Most radicals shared the belief that the appropriate avenue to social and economic reforms was constitutional, a view most forceably expressed by Cobbett, both a patriot and a philosophical radical. He was regarded as a rabble rouser and viewed as a dangerous revolutionary by governments of the day. However G. M. Trevelyan's (1922, p. 191) pertinent observation that 'the violence of [his] diction obscured the fact that the whole tendency of his propaganda was to avert revolution and to guide the proletariat into the paths of constitutional action' reveals how completely Cobbett fits the mould of English constitutional radicalism. This constitutionalism was integral to the English radical tradition and not, we would argue, something superficial adopted by radicals merely to present themselves as patriots in an attempt 'to take over the rhetoric of the age' (Thomson, 1968, p. 96).

The tradition of lost rights, the Norman Yoke, the restoration of traditional Saxon freedoms, and the 'true' constitution, were closely and logically linked with a nation of rural communities. Clearly the tradition ill fitted the increasingly industrialized society of nineteenth-century Britain. Yet it provided the basis for two political illusions. First, it suggested that the ills of capitalism could be resolved by an escape to a rural co-operative utopia. This belief was expressed by radicals such as Spence, Baxter, and particularly Cobbett, whose dislike of the enclosures and factories was matched by an impossible dream of a return to the yeoman world. Nor was it alien to the early socialists such as Robert Owen and William Morris. Secondly, it promoted an attitude of mind which tended to reinforce the view that economic and social reforms, no less than political, were obtainable within the framework of the English consitution. Both persisted to influence progressive thinking and political actions for much of the nineteenth century.

The modernization of this essentially backward-looking rural and utopian radical tradition took place during the nineteenth century. E. P. Thompson argues that the process was completed, at least in London, within a period of twenty years. In support of this proposition he cites the Church and King Rioters in 1791 who identified civil liberty with the constitution, rallied in support of the establishment, and attacked the reformers. He suggests London had become radicalized by 1810. The reformers no longer feared 'the mob' because of 'a major shift in emphasis of the inarticulate sub-political attitudes of the masses' (Thompson, 1968, p. 85). It is debatable whether this was true of London but it certainly did not represent the political mood in the rest of the country and one can discern elements of the 'old radicalism' in the sentiments expressed by Chartist leaders a generation later.

There is a school of thought which regards the Chartist movement as a watershed, marking the point when the industrial working classes finally threw off the tutelage of middle-class radicals and traditional English radical ideas. But such a view disregards the fact that Chartist political demands were focused on an *extension* of the franchise. Far from seeking to destroy the institutions of the bourgeois state, the Chartists implicitly accepted the parliamentary system and sought to extend its provisions and to enhance its legitimacy by making it responsible to a more representative electorate. A large part of the movement's membership, particularly those in the London Working Men's Association and the Birmingham-based Political Union, did not want revolution. They argued for moral force rather than physical force, a viewpoint dominant until the 1839 convention and one which clearly fitted the English radical tradition. Furthermore, their frequently-expressed concern with democracy and political rights of the individual, linked the Chartists more closely to that radical tradition than to nineteenth-century socialism. Lichtheim (1969, p. 106) regarded them as more 'agrarian socialists' than socialists and noted that many of the Chartist leaders thought in terms of reviving a pre-capitalist, even a pre-industrial form of economic life, an aspiration which eighteenth-century radicals such as Spence and Cobbett would have enthusiastically supported.

The Chartist movement did mark a change, however. Its 'physical force' wing threatened the structure of the state to an extent not matched since the English Civil War. In the 1840s there was talk of an enslaved working class for whom the traditional rhetoric of 'liberties under the constitution' did not apply. Furthermore, socialism, in the sense of an autonomous philosophy, was a significant fact because of 'the growing colony of foreign workers [who] impressed the Chartists with their clarity of thought', unencumbered by the confused inheritance of English radicalism (Dobrée, 1937, p. 151).

The emergence of a socialist philosophy amongst progressive reformers coincided with the establishment of a modern state structure in Britain. The passage of the Great Reform Bill in 1832 marked the advent to political power of the English middle classes whose social radicalism and Christian morality led to increased state intervention and regulation. While the 1833 Factory Act was not the first attempt by Parliament to deal with the evils of the factory system, it differed from previous attempts, in as much as it established a permanent mechanism to inspect the factories and to enforce the law. Thus a precedent for later and greater state involvement was established.

There was another side to middle-class perceptions of the state. In part it stemmed from the traditional English view of freedom from arbitrary government. In the nineteenth century, stimulated by middle-class values, this extended from economic matters and the *laissez-faire* philosophy, to political issues in which any attempt to extend the power of the state was viewed as a potential tyranny. While middle-class morality expected the state to play a night-watchman role, middle-class financial virtues determined that the state should operate with the minimum of waste and maximum efficiency. As a result of the 1835 reform, municipalities not only had fewer powers delegated to them by central government but those local initiatives which remained were stifled by dissenting shop keepers (Cole and Postgate, 1946, p. 273). The new Poor Law of 1834 was a perfect example of the conjunction of moral outrage and economic expediency characteristic of the middle class's perception of the role of the state. The law was intended to discourage improvident idleness and to allow wage levels to rise to a level determined by market forces. The intention of the law and the state's role was to create a sounder economic system which would redound to the advantage of all sectors in society. Chadwick, the law's architect, and a philosophical radical of the Benthamite school, was convinced of the law's moral virtues and long-term economic benefits. His intention was to operate the state machine in a more efficient and more centralized fashion and so obviate the need for state intervention characteristic of the old Speenhamland System; but he was oblivious to the acute social distress produced by the 'ruthless logic' of his legislation (Cole and Postgate, 1946, p. 277). Yet it was also Chadwick whose reports on urban sanitation and health were one of the most powerful engines for the growth of state functions in social welfare areas during the later nineteenth and twentieth centuries.

By the mid-nineteenth century the British state was hedged round by similar paradoxes. Its growth was the product of middle-class concerns on moral and welfare issues but it was a growth geared to 'efficiency first' principles involving the centralization of the state's administrative machinery and the consequent erosion of traditional local institutions and authorities. Furthermore, it was a growth largely promoted by those who felt that the state should have a minimal role, certainly in economic matters, and preferably in other policy areas as well.

The middle-class radicals lacked a theory of the state and were forced to create an *ad hoc* structure with the paradoxes we have noted. The Tories by contrast had a much clearer view of the state. In their eyes it was 'the organic unity of society under the Crown and the independent authority of monarchical government as the diviner of the public interest' (Dyson, 1980, p. 36). For the Tories, the state was linked precisely with those traditional institutions, customs, and relationships threatened by the radical reformers. Not surprisingly, therefore, the Tory Party and Tory democrats such as Richard Ostler and John Field, were to the forefront in criticizing the new Poor Law not simply on moralistic grounds but because it over-rode local autonomy and traditional procedures, both of which were intrinsic to the Tory perception of the state. The opposition engendered by Bentham's Ministry of Police plan revealed similar concerns for local rights and customs.

One may legitimately describe the state which came into existence during the mid-nineteenth century as a new state in as much as its involvement in social and economic life was novel and superseded procedures identified with the old state. There was, however, another novel characteristic of the new state: it was British rather than English. The distinction is not merely one of semantics. The Britishness of the modern state coincided with Britain's assumption of an imperial identity. London, for so long the centre for court and business, now became a political and administrative capital, not merely of the various nations of the British Isles (a process completed after the abolition of the Irish Parliament in 1801) but of a world-wide empire as well. The acquisition and growth of an imperial identity was a potent factor in the growth of the modern British state. It overcame a significant anti-imperial tradition which dated back to the loss of the American colonies and which as late as 1860 still regarded imperial colonies as worthless mill-stones. However, the anti-imperial tradition was progressively assimilated by *laissez faire* economics and was all but overwhelmed by the establishment of the British imperial state in the 1870s. Only in the radical politics of the Celtic periphery did it retain any coherence, a factor of some significance for the politics of nationalism and devolution in the twentieth century.

The basis of the new British state was not popular. It most closely approximated to the old Tory idea of the state with little reference to ideas of popular sovereignty. Accordingly the state was framed and justified by traditional norms. The Crown was of central importance as a focus of loyalty not only for the Kingdom of Scotland or the Principality of Wales but for the white Dominions and the Indian Empire as well. Parliament also loomed large, its political and legal supremacy confirmed and consolidated by successive franchise reforms and its status appropriately enhanced by the new parliament buildings suitably designed in the mock-gothic idiom by Sir Charles Barry. The new British state also came to depend upon a centralized bureaucracy manned by a social élite committed to the authority of the Crown and the supremacy of Parliament and which, after the Northcote–Trevellyan reforms, became increasingly professional and proficient in its duties.

The new British state was traditional and élitist but it also reflected paradoxes. The old Tory idea of the state incorporated both imperial and paternalist visions. As we have shown, the Conservative Party had never been dogmatically opposed to state power. Indeed, the state has been widely viewed in Conservative ideology as part of the traditional order and a bastion of that authority necessary if society was to survive. Nor was there always dogmatic hostility in Conservative circles to using the state to achieve measures of social welfare. Disraeli has often been credited with a vision of Conservatism which the working classes, protected by a paternalist state, could support against a Liberal Party dominated by their industrial employers. In the 1880s, Joseph Chamberlain, later to serve in Conservative Cabinets, asked 'What ransom will property pay for the security which it enjoys?' (Miliband, 1972, p. 37) and in 1895 Balfour, like other Conservatives, could see social legislation as a necessary means of maintaining the social order: 'Social legislation', he declared, 'is not merely to be distinguished from Socialist legislation, but is its most direct opposite and its most effective antidote' (Miliband, 1972, p. 37). The franchise reforms of 1867 and 1884 gave greater urgency to the need to cultivate working-class support. But the effect of this should not be exaggerated. Modern writers have decried the notion that Disraeli had a clearly developed strategy to accommodate the working class in the Conservative fold and, as Blake, (1970, p. 124) points out, this would have run into direct conflict with the demands of the middle class, frightened off by Gladstonian liberalism. In any case, the Conservative view of the state, while often free of *laissez-faire* prejudices, did not allow it a dominant role in society but merely saw it as one of a number of traditional institutions.

Nevertheless, the role of the state did expand under Conservative governments and with relatively little opposition. In the latter part of the century, this was given further impetus by, what was now, a rampant imperialism. While, as Barker (1978, p. 46) says, 'imperialism represented a territorial rather than a functional extension of state power', it did have wider implications. It was linked to the campaign for tariff reform and imperial preference advocated by Joseph Chamberlain from 1903 and which questioned many of the assumptions of *laissez-faire*; it raised the issue of national efficiency in a more acute form and in the international context; and it questioned Britain's capacity to defend itself against military as against economic threats. In Chamberlain, the various strands of the Conservative and Unionist view of the state came together in a demand for imperial preference to weld the empire together, protect it militarily and economically from American and German competition, and provide revenue for social reform (Blake, 1970, p. 177).

The state's policy objectives were strongly influenced by the Liberal Party as, during the late-nineteenth century, it moved from its traditional *laissez-faire* approach towards collectivism and expanded the state by a rather different route. The rise of Radicalism following the franchise reforms of 1867 and 1884 brought to the fore a new range of issues. Many of these concerned the destruction of aristocratic power and the advancement of democracy through reform of the franchise and the House of Lords, Church disestablishment and 'Home Rule all round'. These policies all represented attacks on the institutions of the state in their current form, in the interests of liberty and equality.

From the 1880s, however, Radicalism began to assume a more positive form. Land ownership was seen as presenting unique problems, not amenable to traditional liberal solutions. Ownership of land, given its limited and non-renewable character, could pose a direct threat to the liberty of others. Therefore land nationalization could be justified — and from the 1880s *was* justified — on liberal grounds. Other measures of collectivism and state control could similarly be justified on the grounds that the greatest liberty for all demanded restrictions on liberty for some.

In 1888, the Metropolitan Radical Federation proposed taxation-to-extinction of rent and interest, the taxation of land value and ground rent, the granting to local authorities of compulsory powers of land purchase, statutory minimum wages and maximum working days, municipal housing, pensions, and relief works to deal with unemployment (Barker, 1978, p. 17). The Liberal thinkers Hobhouse and Hobson asserted the role of the state not merely in removing the barriers to individual liberty but in actively promoting welfare. Hobhouse further justified this with the argument that state intervention, undesirable when the state was in the hands of the aristocracy, was acceptable now that the state was the agent of the whole society (Barker, 1978, p. 20). Radical liberals were able to support a wide range of social welfare measures going well beyond the institutional reforms of the Gladstonian agenda. This culminated in the Liberal government of 1906, with its legislation on old-age pensions, the eight-hour day and minimum wage for miners, National Insurance, Labour Exchanges and a series of like measures.

However these developments did not enable progressive social forces to identify with the state as such. They certainly recognized the value and utility of Parliament as a means of rectifying social and economic inequalities and of securing greater liberty for the masses;

but there was still an incomplete realization of any concept of the state as larger than merely Parliament and legitimately able to assume a positivist role. The tradition of English radicalism stretching back to the Levellers could have provided the philosophical basis for such an appreciation of state but, as we have indicated, that tradition of an 'Englishman's birthright' was identified with an English nation no longer contiguous with the political state. Thus the emergence of the modern British state effectively cut off the institutions of government from national traditions and values not only, as is usually argued, in the case of Ireland, Scotland, and Wales, but in England too. By the mid-nineteenth century then, identification of the political Left with the British state and the British nation was very weak (Jenkins and Minnerup, 1984).

British socialism as it emerged in the nineteenth century confronted acute and unique difficulties in establishing a relationship with the state. Socialists in France, because of the revolutionary nature of the French state, had few such problems during the nineteenth century when the jacobin tradition was in the ascendent. It was nationalist, secular, egalitarian, *and* centralist. In a jacobin polity where all were equal there was no need for intermediate institutions between the citizen and the state. Given the reactionary nature of the French provinces, centralization of the state was regarded by the 'jacobins' as the means for ensuring victory both of republican principles and of democracy itself. German socialists experienced a more confused relationship with the Bismarkian state because, like the British state, it possessed a continuity of, and a dependency upon, élitist institutions. But German socialists had accepted the Marxist critique of the state more completely than British socialists and what ideological problems persisted were resolved by the German revolution in 1918 and the destruction of the traditional institutions of the Prussian state. Thus socialists movements in Europe, because of their clearer concept of the state, were able to develop a *national* character and to establish an effective relationship with the state. An exceptional political tradition and different historical developments denied both to British socialism. Furthermore, the overlap of early socialists with a wide range of middle-class philanthropists and reform groups resulted in the frontiers between conservatism and socialism remaining fluid far longer in Britain than on the continent (Lichtheim, 1969, p. 6). British socialism acquired a pragmatism in its dealings with the state. While not necessarily identifying with the state, socialists were persuaded by the experiences and examples of other radical social reformers that the existing state could be instrumental in attaining collectivist ends. This largely uncritical acceptance of the state and its institutions not only rested on very dubious grounds but also promoted ominous repercussions. Whenever political events moved so as to involve the state itself, its nature, its institutions, or its role, British socialism was to display a less-than-sure touch.

CHAPTER 2

The emergence of Labour

BY the late nineteenth century, the golden age of *laissez-faire* — if it had ever really existed — was drawing to a close. But the gradual expansion of state authority owed less to general principles than to a pragmatic view of the needs of the moment, together with a weakening of ideological hostility to state action.

It was thus in a time of expanding state activity that the early moves to independent Labour representation were made. It is not our purpose to rehearse the story of the emergence of the Labour Party but rather to note the way in which the early movement regarded the institution of the state, for there was a wide range of views on the extent to which state intervention was supported; and a remarkable absence of thinking on the form of the state which would administer that intervention, beyond a repetition of the old Radical agenda of constitutional reform — adult franchise, abolition of hereditary peerage, and 'Home Rule all round'.

This is perhaps not surprising in view of the backgrounds of many of the early Labour leaders in Liberal Radicalism. Reid (1960) describes Keir Hardie's early views thus:

As Hardie saw the politics of the early 1880s, the demand for many forms of state intervention was growing in the Liberal Party. Besides prohibition of the liquor traffic and free education, nationalisation of the land was being canvassed by 1885 in those Scottish Liberal circles described at the time as 'advanced'. The best interests of the miners, Hardie believed, lay in cooperating closely with the advocates of such proposals to form a Radical wing that could push the Liberal Party's leadership forward along the road of state intervention.

Hardie, like other working-class politicians, was to find local Liberal associations less amenable to this approach and unwilling to adopt Labour men and measures; but it took a long battle to convince the leaders of late-nineteenth century trade-unionism of an alternative strategy, that of setting up a completely new party whose primary concern would be with the role and the affairs of the state.

Such a strategy presented many problems for a trade-union

movement developed under capitalism and with the prime function of bargaining 'freely' with private employers. For many unionists then — as now — free collective bargaining could only with great difficulty be separated from the market system itself. Thus state intervention in labour relations or wage determination could be interpreted as an attack on the trade union's traditional role. The 'old' unions of the late-nineteenth century were generally craft unions of skilled workers with relatively high status whose leaders were steeped in the ideology of Liberalism. As Macdonald (1976) comments:

> So far as industrial legislation was thought desirable, they were content to leave it to the 'progressives' in Parliament, especially the Liberals, and the statutory industrial reforms of the 'seventies and 'eighties owed little to pressure from the TUC or its Parliamentary Committee.

This should not be regarded as merely irrational reaction. Unions had experienced a long struggle in the course of the nineteenth century to free themselves from state regulation and their first demand was for their own independence. Although 'collectivists in practice they nevertheless were usually suspicious of state intervention lest it be turned against them' (Poirier, 1958, p. 15).

These attitudes were changed with the arrival of the 'new' unionism of the unskilled workers after about 1880. Lacking the status and bargaining power of the older craft unions, they had a greater interest in using the state to alter the balance of power, especially after the extension of the franchise in 1884. One of the demands voiced by the new unions was for a legal eight-hour day though, at the 1887 Trades Union Congress, this was dismissed by the Lib–Lab MP Henry Broadhurst:

> Congress had always stopped short at asking Parliament to protect men capable of protecting themselves . . . It had never been in the character of Englishmen, to ask for protection, except for women and children . . . Men were capable of protecting themselves by their own manhood and independence (Hobsbawm, 1948, pp. 96-7).

It was not until 1890 that the TUC was finally persuaded to vote for the eight-hour day.

While the new unions were generally more favourably disposed to political action, what finally drove the mass of the trades unions to support independent Labour representation was a series of attacks on union independence culminating in the Taff Vale judgement of 1900. This ruling, in the year in which the Labour Representation Committee

was formed, struck down the immunity which unions had previously
been assumed to enjoy in respect of actions by their members. Along
with judicial decisions in *Bradford* v. *Ellis* and *Quinn* v.
Leatham in the next two years, it has generally been credited with the dramatic
increase in affiliation to the LRC, from 469,000 to 861,000 in 1902–3
and to nearly a million by 1906–7 (Macdonald, 1976).

These adverse judgements were reversed by the Trades Disputes
Act of 1906, in which the new Liberal government acceded virtually to
all Labour's demands. The Act was a milestone in the history of
trade-unionism, but it hardly reflected the new politics of state intervention. On the contrary, it firmly established the independence of
unions from the law *and* the state. It could even be viewed as 'in
conflict with basic socialists tenets, by which the state was to be the
arbiter in fundamental matters of common concern' (Macdonald,
1976, p. 62). Thus trade unions were as yet far from accepting the
necessity for the all-powerful state as a means of securing social and
industrial gains. This much is clear from the composition, indeed the
name, of the Labour Representation Committee itself, which represented a compromise close to the unions' position with a strictly limited
role and no commitment to socialist policies.

The Fabians were the element of the early Labour coalition with the
clearest commitment to state intervention and control as an expression of their socialism. Indeed, so inevitable did they regard the
growth of state intervention that for some time they doubted the need
for a new party. As Sydney Webb wrote in the *Fabian Essays* of 1889:

Private ownership of the means of production has been in one direction or
another, successively regulated, limited and superseded, until it may now
fairly be claimed that the Socialist philosophy of today is but the conscious and
explicit assertion of principles of social organization which have been already
in great part adopted. (Webb, 1889.)

In the Webbs' *Industrial Democracy*, this form of statist socialism was
carefully distinguished from trade-unionism which was concerned
with a narrower range of affairs:

The Trades Union Congress is a federation for obtaining, by Parliamentary
action, not social reform generally, but the particular measures desired by its
constituent Trade Unions (quoted in Hobsbawm, 1948, p. 11).

Early Fabian writings, as Webb recognized later (Webb, 1920), give
scant attention to the unions whose role in a Labour alliance was not

appreciated until the early twentieth century. In so far as they do feature, they are an element of society which, like others, must be subject to state regulation and control. Sydney Webb was a signatory to the Report of the 1903 Royal Commission on Trade Disputes and Trade Combinations which found 'no more reason that [trade unions] should be beyond the reach of the law than any other individual partnership or institution' (Macdonald, 1976, p. 56). In a separate Memorandum of his own he challenged the whole basis of collective bargaining, strikes and lock-outs as 'private war' and called for a system of state conciliation and arbitration, a proposal regarded by most unions with the deepest suspicion.

At times, Webb appeared to *equate* socialism with state control, citing long lists of activities already performed by the state against 'the general failure to realize the extent to which our unconscious socialism has already proceeded' (Webb, 1889). While in the same volume of *Fabian Essays* Herbert Bland warned that 'although socialism involves state control, state control does not imply socialism' (Bland, 1889), and called for the creation of a separate Labour party, the Webbs' position was to prove a stumbling-block in the way of a clear formulation of Fabian attitudes to the state, its form and its purpose.

It is difficult to talk of a Fabian attitude to the *organization* of the state as, in the early days, this was little discussed. There was, of course, an assumption that the Fabian state would be more democratic and efficient. George Bernard Shaw in the *Fabian Essays* writes of the need to expand the franchise, sweep away privilege, and institute a competitive public service — but these are items which could find a place in any Liberal manifesto and hardly betoken a break with Radicalism.

The Webbs often showed an impatience with those who wanted to argue about general principles and this pragmatic bent extended to thinking about the state. Certainly their new state would be democratic but this view coexisted uneasily with a technocratic impulse and a penchant for bureaucracy and efficiency which was later to lead them to admiration for Stalin's Soviet Union. The pursuit of 'progress' could make them impervious to what they perceived as irrational demands which conflicted with the wider needs represented by the state. Such an attitude led them to oppose the pro-Boer Radicals. 'What' wrote Sydney Webb, 'in the name of common sense have we to do with obsolete hypocrisies about "peoples struggling to be free?" ' (quoted, Poirier, 1958, pp. 106–7). In 1900 Shaw proclaimed his view that 'the world is to big and powerful states by necessity;

and the little ones must come within their borders or be crushed by necessity' (Poirier, 1958, p. 107).

While big states were regarded as the guardians of progress, there was a recognition of the virtues of local government; but the relationship between central and local interests was never spelt out . In 1920 Sydney Webb admitted that, at the time of the *Fabian Essays* of 1889, 'we were still groping after the illuminating idea that would assign to our Local Authorities their appropriate place and function in the Social Organism' (Webb, 1920). Thereafter, more attention was given to the potential for municipal socialism. Inevitably, however, that potential was restricted because support for local *power*, as opposed merely to local *administration* would have come into conflict with the Fabian stress on rationality, efficiency, and, increasingly, equity.

Nor was a great deal of thought given to the problem of exercising power in the modern state. This is perhaps understandable given the Fabian view that society already was evolving in a socialist and statist direction and would soon be ripe for a peaceful transition. Discussing the process whereby the state would take over industry, Webb (1889) claimed that the growth of joint-stock-enterprises in place of owner-managers meant that their 'shareholders could be appropriated by the community with no more dislocation of the industries carried on by them than is caused by the daily purchase of shares on the Stock Exchange'. Similarly, Ramsay MacDonald, who for a time was an active Fabian, claimed that the growth of trusts in the United States was not to be regarded as, of itself, a regressive development. On the contrary, it pointed the way for Britain, but here 'the introduction of the Trust should be marked by public ownership' (quoted, Marquand, 1977, p. 87). As Marquand comments, 'If it had been elaborated into a systematic analysis of how and where trusts should be encouraged and public ownership introduced, it might have furnished the starting-point for an economic strategy of democratic socialism . . . But, as so often happened with MacDonald's insights, it was left hanging in mid-air, a hint and not a policy' (Marquand, 1977, p. 87). What MacDonald was clear about from an early stage, however, was that Labour must take its place *within* the state. This implied a strategy of acceptance of the existing constitutional order and the presentation of a thoroughly respectable image which was profoundly important for Labour during MacDonald's long ascendancy after the War.

In the vagueness of his visions, MacDonald was not alone. If the intellectuals of the Fabian Society gave little attention to the problem of the state, the orators of the Independent Labour Party, founded in 1893 and part of the 1900 Labour Representation Committee, practically ignored it; and this in spite of the fact that public ownership of industry and state-sponsored social welfare formed a central part of their programme. Keir Hardie impatiently dismissed the question: 'To dogmatise about the form which the Socialist State shall take . . . is a matter with which we have nothing whatever to do. It belongs to the future' (quoted, Barker, 1978, p. 40). ILP thinking on the state was consequently largely limited to support of the constitutional programme carried over by its founders from Radicalism. By the end of the century these had fallen down their list of priorities, though they rose again in importance around the First World War. Even the inaugural conference of the ILP deleted a list of 'political' items including adult suffrage, the second ballot, payment of MPs, and abolition of the monarchy and the House of Lords, in favour of a general statement about democratizing the system of government. It was not that Conference was opposed to these items — merely that it could not see the relationship between them and the members' passionately felt, but vaguely defined, socialism.

Another element in the early Labour Party was Marxism, espoused by the Social Democratic Federation of H. M. Hyndman. In the *Communist Manifesto* Marx had dismissed the state as a 'committee for managing the common affairs of the whole bourgeoisie' but he never went on to develop a throughgoing theory of the state. Indeed, his writings show a marked lack of consistency on this point. In some places, the state is regarded as mere 'superstructure' — 'the mode of production of material life conditions, the social, political and intellectual life process in general' (quoted, Miliband, 1977, p. 7). The state, if it is important at all, is merely an instrument of the ruling class; where there is no subjection of one class by another, there is no need for the state, which then 'withers away'.

In other places, Marx sees the possibility of the working class using the machinery of the state to achieve socialism:

We know that heed must be paid to the institutions, customs and traditions of the various countries, and we do not deny that there are countries such as America and England, and if I was familiar with its institutions I might include Holland, where the workers may attain their goal by peaceful means (quoted, Miliband, 1977, p. 79).

Towards the end of his life, Marx could even advocate reformist action based on survey research to improve social conditions through bourgeois government (Feuer, 1959, p. 33).

Given the basic ambiguity in the Marxist conception of the state, it was only to be expected that Hyndman and other late-nineteenth century Marxists should have been confused in their strategy; in addition they had to contend with Hyndman's own eccentric personality and the relative weakness of Marxist ideas in the British Labour movement. Socialism was certainly to be about public ownership of the means of production, and this was taken to mean state ownership, but, as Barker notes, Hyndman gave little attention to the state to which he wished to transfer so much responsibility (Barker, 1978, p. 28). In fact, the Social Democratic Federation itself was riven with dissention on political strategy and the utility of co-operating with other elements on the left, and disaffiliated from the Labour Representation Committee after a year (Bealey and Pelling, 1958, p. 168). Thereafter, Marxist ideas, and with them the concept of the overthrow of the state as a prelude to the establishment of socialism, ceased, except sporadically to feature in Labour's thinking.

Marxism, of course, was not the only revolutionary doctrine around at the turn of the century. Varieties of anarchism had their advocates, and in the early years of the century some currency was gained for syndicalist ideas. Syndicalists believed that power must be seized by workers at the point of production, through politically-conscious trade-union action. The new state would be built upon these worker-controlled industries. Although syndicalist ideology has sometimes been credited, at least partly, with the strike wave of 1910–12, there are reasons to doubt this. Often syndicalism was taken up by the old 'Labour aristocracy' as a protest against mechanization and dilution of its skills; or as a means of mobilizing workers in the pursuit of conventional collective bargaining (Barker, 1978, p. 93). Then, as now, it was easy enough for both participants and observers to confuse militant pursuit of wage claims within the existing order with a revolutionary challenge; and the *reaction* against change with change itself. To anticipate our narrative a little — and with the advantage of hindsight — the ease with which, in Britain, a series of state measures could turn 'assertion into participation, and conflict into collaboration' (Barker, 1978, p. 94), suggests the absence of a deeper revolutionary impulse. However around the time of the First World War this was not so apparent, and it must be conceded that the syndicalist inheritance has left a trace of libertarian and anti-statist ideas in the Labour and trade-union movement.

The final element in our survey of the composition of the early Labour Party is the 'Celtic fringe'. Labour in Scotland emerged separately from Labour in England, though there was contact and collaboration. The first dent in the British two-party system in the late nineteenth century was made in 1885 by the four Crofters MPs in the Highlands. Keir Hardie's Scottish Labour Party of 1888, founded after his independent candidature at Mid Lanark, drew on the support of these Highland land-reformers as well as that of other advanced Liberals disillusioned with the conservatism of much Scottish Liberalism. Consequently, it had a strong Radical tinge, campaigning for temperence, disestablishment and 'Home Rule all round' as well as on working-class issues (Keating and Bleiman, 1979). The Scottish Labour Party merged with the Independent Labour Party in 1894, but for a time the Scots were able to stay aloof from the Labour Representation Committee, establishing their own Scottish Workers Representation Committee which coexisted uneasily with the LRC until 1909.

In Scotland, Labour inherited a strong Radical tradition of support for Home Rule, fortified from time to time by distinctive Scottish issues and preferences. Home Rule was to be a significant, albeit secondary, theme for Scottish Labour up until the First World War when it became, for a time, a most insistent demand. But, whereas the party at large was quite prepared to support this in principle as an unimpeachable Radical proposal, there was little attempt to relate it to a coherent conception of the state as a whole.

In Wales, the Labour movement was 'profoundly shot through with an integrated sense of community, in some sense isolated from the English world outside' (Morgan, 1981, p. 254). It had to contend not only with the all-powerful Liberals who won 33 of the 34 Welsh seats in 1906, but also with a non-conformist culture that was still in the ascendant, and a Welsh-speaking community that accounted for almost half the Principality's population. This led to a firm support for Home Rule in the years up to the First World War. Again, this was a demand which the party could accommodate, given the vague formulation and Labour's still vaguer conception of the state; but it was to give rise to tensions later.

In Ireland, a Labour Party emerged from the trade-union movement but was from an early stage caught up in the sectarian and constitutional conflicts. Although the British Labour Party did not exclude Irish members and held its conference in Belfast in 1905, the Irish movement tended to go its own way. In 1918, it took the significant decision not to contest the election, given the primacy of the national question, so missing the chance to appeal to the newly enfranchized working classes. In turn, the British Labour Party's failure to organize in Ireland made the constitutional issue a less vital one than if it had been obliged to compete for Irish votes.

So the Labour Party from the start contained a variety of competing views about the importance, uses, and form of the state. They were neither clarified nor reconciled in the party's early years, but they did not impede its progress. As a result of the secret deal with the Liberals, the LRC was able to win some twenty-nine seats in the election of 1906. In 1909, the adhesion of the miners, who had previously doubted the need for a new party, brought their numbers up to forty. Labour thus advanced without the need to develop its philosophy, determine its political strategy, or detail its programme. It was unclear whether Labour was in Parliament to build itself up into a major party and eventually take power in the state; to adopt an independent minority role, playing the big parties off against one another in return for specific concessions; or to form a more-or-less loyal left wing of the Liberal Party. Prior to the First World War, it was able to avoid directly confronting these questions. Some significant reforms such as the 1906 Trades Disputes Act, the 1913 Act reversing the Osborne judgement, and the payment of MPs, could justly be claimed to Labour's credit. However, aside from pursuing specific trade-union issues (Beer, 1965) Labour was content to support the measures of social reform of the Liberal government. With rare exceptions, Labour MPs were unquestioning in their support for parliamentarism, their political views having themselves been formed by late nineteenth-century Radicalism rather than coming from a revolutionary background. In this, the diverse strands of the Labour movement could agree. As Howell (1976, p. 27) comments:

The Fabian doctrines provided an intellectual rationale for the instinctive attitudes of leaders. Faith in gradualism, class cooperation and the neutrality of the state came readily to many working-class spokesmen.

Labour MPs' complaints that they were ignored by the government or given less consideration than the Irish, merely emphasized their willingness to participate in the institutions of the state. There was little hint of the rejectionist or 'tribune' roles played by the French Communist Party and described by Lavan as a party

> whose function . . . is principally to organize and defend the plebeian social groups (that is to say, those who are excluded or feel themselves to be excluded from the process of participation in the political system, as also from the benefits of the economic and cultural system), and to give them a feeling of strength and confidence . . . The proposal of a political programme or the carrying out of a line of policy have less importance for this type of party in terms of what they represent in the eyes of the plebeian masses thus represented (quoted, Johnson, 1981, p. 148).

Neither seeking state power nor rejecting it as inherently alien, the Labour leadership was caught unprepared by the outbreak of industrial militancy in 1910–11. Apart from some formal condemnations of syndicalism, they had little idea how to reconcile extra-parliamentary militancy with a parliamentary strategy.

The crucial test of Labour's attitude to the British state arose in 1914. For some years Labour and socialist parties had agreed that, in the event of war, workers in the belligerent countries would refuse to co-operate and take direct action to secure peace. In 1907 the Socialist International unanimously passed a resolution to this effect (Miliband, 1972, p. 39) and in 1910 it was the British Labour contingent which proposed strengthening it. Certainly, some Labour leaders had misgivings about the use of the General Strike as a weapon against war or exploiting war conditions for revolutionary insurrection. However, apart from the odd chauvinist such as Hyndman, there was general opposition on the Left to the idea of imperialist war which would set the workers of Britain against those of other countries.

When it came to the point of decision, however, anti-war feeling all but collapsed. With the country actually at war, to have refused support to the government would be to attack some of the deepest feelings of the British working class. There was some opposition, notably from Ramsay MacDonald and Keir Hardie but, as we have seen, these were not men to draw revolutionary implications from their stance. Rather, their position and that of other Labour opponents of the war, drew on radical, pacifist, and anti-imperialist traditions inherited from advanced Liberalism and developed during the Boer War. So there was no attempt to exploit the war for Labour's 'socialist' ends. Indeed, Hardie and MacDonald themselves recognized that , in the midst of war, the troops must be supported (Miliband, 1972, p. 44).

More serious divisions arose on the issue of Labour participation in the affairs of the state. For the government, Labour's active support for the war effort was crucial in mobilizing and disciplining the industrial work-force and in 1915 the party was invited to join the Asquith coalition. In the crisis of war, it is perhaps not surprising that Labour did not choose to make this an occasion for demanding sweeping reforms of the state. Rather the question centred on tactics; whether Labour would be better retaining its independence and freedom of criticism or surrendering these to aid the common war effort. As Snowden put it:

the whole Labour movement will be united on one point — namely that it is the duty of the movement to help the nation in its present difficulties (but) . . . the point of difference is that some members think that the Labour Party can be much more useful outside the Government than inside it (Miliband, 1972, p. 49).

In the event, despite the opposition of a majority of MPs, a joint National Executive Committee–Parliamentary Party meeting decided on participation (Mackenzie, 1964, p. 401). Withdrawal over the issue of conscription was narrowly averted in 1916 and in the same year it was decided to enter the new Lloyd George coalition, a decision subsequently endorsed by the party conference by 1,849,000 votes to 307,000 (Mackenzie, 1964).

There was little attempt to extract specific policy concessions in return for participation in government, but the party did increase its representation at all levels in the state. Arthur Henderson, followed by George Barnes, sat in the Cabinet and, as Miliband (1972, p. 48) notes,

a host of Labour representatives became deeply involved in the business of the state and, with their service in the new bureaucracy that was born of the war, acquired a stake, if not in the country, at least in the country's official business. By the end of the war, a whole army of Labour representatives were serving on a multitude of official committees, commissions, tribunals and agencies.

This experience in government was to have an important influence on Labour's attitudes towards the state, as the first stage in the integration of Labour which we trace in the next chapter.

Many analyses of Labour's history have presented its strategic choice in stark terms, between 'selling out' to the capitalist system and its state or developing a 'revolutionary' strategy of a clean break with both. Such analyses too often have failed to specify what a revolutionary strategy would involve or how a post-revolutionary state could be constructed; or at what point peaceful contestation within a given political system becomes objective collaboration. We see Labour's strategic dilemmas in the years before 1918 in more complex terms. As far as the state is concerned, the question was: what features of the existing political system can be turned to Labour's advantage and to what extent must the remaining features be transformed? Apart from following behind quintessentially Liberal reforms such as the reduction of the power of the House of Lords, Labour failed to face up to this question. Even on the issue of women's suffrage, it found difficulty in agreeing on a policy line and a strategy. So if Labour is to be condemned, it is not for a treacherous 'sell-out' of working-class interests to the 'system'. Rather, it is for a failure to specify clearly what its interests were or even to *think* about the nature of the British political system. This in turn stems from its origins in the British radical tradition we have surveyed, but it was also derived from the nature of the Labour coalition itself.

As a political party, Labour has always found itself pulled three ways by the conflicting roles demanded of it. In the first place, it must operate as the political wing of the Labour-and-trade-union movement, the defender of immediate working-class interests as articulated by the industrial wing. These interests are typically seen as bargaining gains *within* the existing social and economic system and rest upon the support of an often conservative working class. Secondly, Labour must operate as an electoralist party, seeking a plurality of support sufficiently large to gain a parliamentary majority and form a government. As we shall see, Labour's expansion and the ascendancy of MacDonald in the 1920s were to give added emphasis to this role. Thirdly, Labour is an ideological party, seeking to realize a form, however vaguely defined, of socialism. In turn, while the three roles are observable throughout the party, there is a tendency for the trade unions to emphasize the first role, the parliamentary leadership the second, and the rank-and-file activists the third.

In a society in which the majority of the population consisted of working-class trade-unionists committed to socialism, reconciling these three roles would pose little problem. Class politics and majoritarian politics would amount to the same thing and the pursuit of power could be conducted in the name of socialism, through liberal–democratic mechanisms. This, however, has never been the case in Britain and was clearly not so in 1918. Yet, while the three elements of the party might have rather different aspirations, there was, from the early days, a recognition that each needed the others. The parliamentary leadership provided parliamentary representation and the prospect of governmental power. The unions provided finance and organizational backing to keep the party in existence, especially in lean times. The activists provided workers to campaign at elections and keep the party organization going on the ground.

It was this mutual dependence which was recognized in the 1918 Constitution. Sovereign power was vested in the annual conference which, in turn, elected the National Executive Committee (NEC); but the conference is made up of representatives of unions and activists, with the unions exercising a block vote corresponding to the number of members for which they affiliate. The activists, through Constituency Labour Parties, are represented in a separate section of the NEC.

A commitment to socialism was inserted to reassure the socialists — at that time represented through the socialist societies and the Independent Labour Party, rather than by Constituency Labour Parties — but, in the form of clause IV.4, was so loosely worded as to be capable of a wide variety of interpretations. It is worth quoting, given its long-standing role as token for Labour's socialist commitment:

To secure for the workers by hand or by brain the full fruits of their industry and the most equitable distribution thereof that may be possible upon the basis of the common ownership of the means of production, distribution and exchange, and the best obtainable system of popular administration and control of each industry or service.

There is no mention of the state or of nationalization and no attempt to define the relationships between ownership, control, and use of industries and services. In fact, all the problems of interpretation and implementation of the commitment in the context of a given state and society are swept aside. Only later was clause IV interpreted as meaning the nationalization of selected industries under the control of the central state; and battles have raged about whether 'popular administration and control' means the state, the workers of the industry concerned, or the consumers, ever since it became apparent that these three were not the same thing.

The parliamentary party is, according to the constitution, supposed to give effect to the programme as laid down by the conference but recognition was given to the need for flexibility in interpretation and timing, if the leadership was to play the parliamentary game and to pursue majoritarian politics. Indeed, this had been recognized as early as 1907, when Conference had accepted that 'the time and method of giving effect to [conference resolutions] be left to the Party in the House, in conjunction with the National Executive' (Miliband, 1974, p. 26). Richard Crossman's cynical view of this has often been quoted;

Since it could not afford, like its opponents, to maintain a large army of paid party workers, the Labour Party required militants — politically conscious socialists to do the work of organizing the constituencies. But since these militants tended to be 'extremists', a constitution was needed which maintained their enthusiasm by apparently creating a full party democracy while excluding them from effective power. Hence the concession in principle of sovereign power to the delegates at the Annual Conference, and the removal in practice of most of this sovereignty through the trade union block vote on the one hand and the complete independence of the Parliamentary Labour Party on the other. (Quoted, Mackenzie, 1964, p. 641.)

Labour's 'impossible' constitution has given rise, over the years, to all manner of problems; but for our purpose one is crucial: Labour's ambiguous relationship to the state. The parliamentary leadership has always aspired to power within the state and even before 1918 had assumed the form and manner appropriate to playing the parliamentary game. Yet it is allied with an activist cadre many of whom are committed to a radically different order or to policies implying such an order; and to a sectional interest group. While in any society in which class-based politics are important, one might expect parties to align themselves broadly with class-based interest groups, the organic link between party and group is unusual. It can be reconciled with the party's majoritarian aspirations only by a theory of the party representing the class and the class comprising the majority of the nation. Even then, the concept of class power fits ill with the acceptance of the existing constitution.

Two specific problems were to arise from the constitution. One concerns the role of a Labour government, representing the state and thus the 'wider interest' of society when faced with opposition from the trade unions. Should it deal with them purely as an important pressure group or recognize that, as part of the 'movement', they effectively comprise part of the governing interest? There is a similar dilemma on the part of the unions, who have insisted on retaining their autonomy in collective bargaining with employers under Labour governments while at the same time retaining their status *within* the

Labour Party and their control over its policy. In effect, they have refused to put all their eggs in the political basket, retaining their industrial freedom of action, while refusing to concede a similar freedom to the Labour Party. The second problem raised by the 1918 constitution is the difficulty faced by the party in changing its policies in response to changed circumstances. Given the importance of each of the three elements in the party and their differing concerns, any policy shift is likely to encounter the opposition of one or other of them and, effectively, be vetoed.

The constitution was made manageable only by a series of understandings and the circumstances facing the party over much of its history. By and large, the major union leaderships were prepared to support the parliamentary leadership on 'political' matters where their own immediate interests were not a stake. Militant activists could thus be kept in check. In any case, it would be an exaggeration to identify activists solely with militants. With the party open to individual membership after 1918, a significant loyalist element developed, seeing Labour's parliamentary success rather than measurable socialist achievements as the fulfilment of their dreams. When popular support for Labour has been rising and the party advancing, all three wings have appeared to march in harmony. However, at times of defeat and decline, the tensions have re-emerged. Eventually, it was Labour's attempts to manage the state, at a time when old assumptions about the tractability of the problems, the apoliticism of the unions, and the deference of the activists were all in question, which created the strains that were to destroy the 1918 consitution some sixty years later.

CHAPTER 3

The integration of Labour

DESPITE the adoption of a new party constitution in 1918 and the commitment to create a Socialist Commonwealth of Great Britain, Labour remained uncertain in its dealings and relationship with the British state. The widely contrasting wartime experiences of Labour Party members, when some had served in the War Cabinet while others had been gaoled for their pacifist convictions, compounded the party's difficulties in determining its attitude. The party required time to refine its philosophy and to clarify its strategy, to determine to what extent the British state was redeemable and which of its institutions were capable of being used for a socialist purpose. The task was uniquely urgent for the Labour Party whose historical origins were extra-parliamentary and whose political power was closely identified with the industrial wing of the Labour movement. Although the product of British society, the movement had little empathy for the institutions of the British state which pre-dated both the industrial revolution and the establishment of democratic processes.

In the first years of peace, with Parliament completely dominated by Lloyd George's coalition government, the Labour Party embarked on the process of organizational advance and ideological renewal. The non-pacifist and pacifist wings of the party were reunited with remarkably little rancour and increasing numbers of ILP branches and Divisional Labour Parties were founded across the country. The publication of the 'Constitution for the Socialist Commonwealth of Great Britain' stimulated a debate on the manner in which political power should be exercised in the British state. The Webbs and the Fabians generally, regarded the central state as the necessary agent and public ownership as the essential mechanism for social and economic change and this eventually became the prevailing orthodoxy of the Labour Party. In the early 1920s, however, the debate concerning the organization and distribution of political power within the state, and whether its dispersal should be on functional or territorial lines, was still very open. G. D. H. Cole, although beginning to move away from guild socialism, still entertained serious doubts about the growth of the

central power of the state and questioned whether this would necessarily benefit the workers (Cole, 1972, 1921). Tawney was similarly
unconvinced that public ownership could only be achieved by using
the machinery of the state. He objected to the over centralization that
would be involved and argued for an element of territorial *and* functional decentralization to involve the representation of consumer and
worker interests (Tawney, 1921). However, MacDonald, who was to
become the party leader in 1922, remained firmly committed to
gaining control of the existing state and subsequently using its institutions to distribute the fruits of production in the interests of all.
MacDonald's evolutionary brand of socialism was not concerned with
destroying the state because he rejected the concept of class war and its
corollary that the state was the instrument of one dominant class
(MacDonald, 1905). Instead he argued an expanded role for the state,
creating socialist order out of capitalist chaos. MacDonald's constitutionalist strategy of gaining control of the state by parliamentary
means, rejected any philosophy or policy which might call into question the very mechanism by which the socialist society was to be
progressively introduced (MacDonald, 1921).

While the debate was never resolved and echoes of it reverberate
through Labour Party history, it was brought to an abrupt end when
Labour was presented suddenly and rather surprisingly with the
opportunity to assume responsibility for the British state. The Fabian
philosophy of the 'inevitability of gradualness' hardly implied immi-
nence, and as late as 1923 Sidney Webb's cautious talk of Labour
coming to power 'somewhere about 1926' (Mowat, 1966, p. 53)
seemed highly optimistic. Yet within six months Labour formed the
government. Less than thirteen years had elapsed since Labour had
occupied the position of a small fourth party trailing the Irish Nationalists in parliamentary seats. The speed and the circumstances of the
advance had profound implications for the Labour Party's perception
of its relationship to the British state, an issue to which we will return.
Our more immediate concern however, lies with the explanation for
Labour's rapid rise.

The most commonly proffered reason, the internecine strife within
the Liberal Party and the personal vendetta between Lloyd George
and Asquith, is a necessary but insufficient explanation. The quirks of
the electoral system also worked in Labour's favour, as the party's
support consolidated in specific territorial enclaves; working-class
mining and industrial areas. The party began the process of occupying

the commanding heights of the electoral system. Between the 1922 and 1923 general elections, Labour increased its popular vote by a modest 120,000 but its parliamentary representation rose dramatically from 142 to 191 seats. Labour also benefited from Baldwin's quixotic decision to hold an unnecessary general election on the issue of Protection versus Free Trade which divided the anti-Labour vote on an issue which had nothing to do with socialism. Indeed it has been suggested (Cowling, 1971) that this was part of a deliberate decision by the Conservative Party to ditch the Liberals and to promote itself as the more effective party of resistance to socialism. Whatever the relative importance of these factors, the Labour Party found itself the government almost by default and before it had defined which was the appropriate role for the British state to play when governed by a party committed to democratic socialism.

The party's difficulty in deciding its relationship to the state was intensified by the divergent aspirations of the three group interests — trade-unionist, electoralist, and ideological — which make up the Labour coalition. As indicated in the previous chapter, the 1918 Constitution was designed to balance these interests and to permit the development of a cohesive party with consensual policies. However, the changed political and economic climate in the immediate post-war years created fresh intra-party tensions. Labour's electoral advance in successive general and by-elections and MacDonald's emergence as 'leader', evoked an increasingly electoralist strategy in the parliamentary party. Paradoxically, the ideological element within the party increased as more MPs were returned by ILPs and by the rapidly growing number of divisional Labour parties. A new generation of trade-union leaders who now regarded Labour as a realistic party of government produced additional pressures. While none of the group interests had clear or consistent views of how a Labour government should use the machinery of the state, all looked to the Labour government to satisfy their own particularist demands. Thus Labour's somewhat fortuitous acquisition of political power in no way clarified its view of the state. On the contrary, the sequence of *ad hoc* measures and policy expedients which the government felt obliged to take under the pressure of political circumstance further obfuscated the party's position.

For a period after the end of the war the trade-union movement gave every indication of seeking to confront the power and to threaten the structure of the British state. Army mutinies, police strikes, and a widespread apprehension of the social and economic consequences of rapid demobilization provided opportunity and justification. A sequence of industrial stoppages during 1919 and 1921, the threat of more, and the possibility that any one involving members of the Triple Alliance of miners, railwaymen, and dockers might precipitate a general strike, convinced the conservative political establishment that the state was at risk (Mowat, 1966, p. 21).

The most blatant and potentially revolutionary confrontation took place in August 1920 and focused on the possibility of British intervention in the Polish–Russian war. A joint meeting of TUC and Labour party representatives urged a change in government policy, warned the government that 'the whole industrial power of the organised workers would be used' (Bullock, 1960, p. 35), and set up a Council of Action to co-ordinate the campaign. The trade-union leaders fully appreciated the implications of their actions; J. H. Thomas of the railway workers acknowledged that what they were about represented a 'challenge to the whole Constitution of the country' (Mowat 1966, p. 41). Fortunately for the government, an almost-immediate Polish victory on the Vistula dispensed with the need for intervention and defused Britain's constitutional crisis. However, its significance for our analysis lies in the willingness of the Labour movement to exploit its industrial power to take direct political action and to confront the power of the state. Yet this was the last occasion that the industrial and political wings of the Labour movement together even contemplated such an initiative.

With the benefit of hindsight the Council of Action was quite exceptional. It is easy to misinterpret the spate of strikes in the immediate post-war period as part of a revolutionary impulse. After 1920 they increasingly reflected the traditional concerns of organized labour; wage rates and working conditions rather than political influence, a tendency reinforced by the deepening slump from 1921 on. The trade-union leadership, generally, was unwilling to threaten the state seriously and reluctant to pursue industrial action to the last constitutional ditch. Nye Bevan (1952, p. 20) describes an interview which the leaders of the Triple Alliance had with Lloyd George in 1919:

He said to us: 'Gentlemen, you have fashioned, in the Triple Alliance of the unions represented by you, a most powerful instrument. I feel bound to tell you that in our opinion we are at your mercy . . . if you carry out your threat and strike, then you will defeat us' . . . 'But if you do so', went on Mr. Lloyd George, 'have you weighed the consequences? The strike will be in defiance of the country and by its very success will precipitate a constitutional crisis of the first importance. For, if a force arises in the State which is stronger than the State itself, then it must be ready to take on the functions of the State, or withdraw and accept the authority of the State. Gentlemen', asked the Prime Minister quietly, 'have you considered, and if you have, are you ready?' 'From that moment on' said Robert Smillie (of the Mineworkers) 'we were beaten and we knew we were'.

Rather than confront the state the instinct of the trade-union leaders increasingly led them to work with, and through, the machinery of the state whose capacity to control and regulate privately-owned industries in the national interest had been demonstrated during the war.

   In the immediate post-war years, faced with mounting industrial unrest Lloyd George set about exploiting this instinct. The Sankey Coal Commission (1919) and the National Industrial Conference (1919–21) were created with the intention of buying time but they had a more profound effect. The industrial wing of the Labour movement was incorporated into the consultative procedures of the British political system, and the authority of the state consolidated. Revolutionary rhetoric was replaced by reasoned debate, physical confrontation by intellectual interrogation and, because of the publicity attracted, trade-unionists were obliged to present their sectional interests so as neither to alienate public opinion nor to conflict with the popular perception of the national interest. The trade unions were thus redirected into constitutional paths which, with one notable exception, they subsequently followed.

   With MacDonald as leader, constitutionalism became the Labour Party norm both in the country and in Parliament. Communist Party attempts to affiliate in 1921 and 1922 were rejected by Labour's NEC and annual conference. It became increasingly apparent that the Labour Party was no longer the all-embracing alliance of working-class organizations envisaged by Keir Hardie and which before the First World War had tolerated revolutionary elements such as the British Socialist Party within its ranks. The party was now committed to the task of electoral victory, winning the support of erstwhile Liberals and accepting the conventions of the parliamentary system (Brand, 1965, p. 86). It could no longer contemplate association with those political groups which fundamentally questioned the structure of the state. Thus Labour's electoral strategy was not based on an appeal to transform society but to govern it more efficiently and humanely. The socialist commonwealth was on the far distant horizon. Meanwhile the Labour Party was intent on proving itself a legitimate and responsible party of government.

Consistent with this intent the new Labour government immediately declared itself to be a national rather than a class government (V. L. Allen 1960, p. 232). Its actions were also consistent with preserving and protecting the interests of the British state. Defence spending was maintained despite the protests from the pacifist wing of the party and Britain's imperial inheritance was preserved; Labour's colonial secretary expressed his desire to promote its welfare by drawing closer the ties that bound it together (Brand 1965, p. 103) and left-wingers in the party began to talk about the British Empire as a 'lever for human emancipation' (Lyman 1957, p. 217). However, more significant for the trade-union interest was the Labour government's willingness first to invoke the Emergency Powers Act and on several occasions to threaten its use. Industrial disputes which confronted the sovereignty of the state were to be dealt with as any other government might.

Labour in office was thoroughly constitutional and responsible and not simply because the government's minority position precluded any socialist measures. None were attempted as Labour's immediate aim was to prove itself capable of running the state and finally to destroy the Liberal Party's claims to be regarded as an alternative government. Consequently the first Labour government's policy was, in that limited sense, successful. The real loser in the 1924 general election was not Labour, but the Liberal Party, which lost one and a quarter million votes and three-quarters of its parliamentary seats. Criticisms that Labour failed to grasp its opportunities between 1923 and 1924 are therefore mis-directed. Those opportunities in any case were limited and Labour's primary objective, the demotion of the Liberal Party, was largely successful. But Labour's concentration on short-term electoral pragmatic considerations carried a cost. Labour's experience in office in no way clarified its thinking on how the state should be used; it merely familiarized the leadership with the levers of power. The fundamental predicament of the party's long-term role remained:

Capitalism was the cause of the country's ills, and so socialism was the cure. Yet precisely how the socialist cure was to be applied remained unclear. Was it to be by using the power of the state to create work? The idea propounded by J. M. Keynes of a major public works programme aroused only derision in the Labour ranks. Was it to be by using taxation to take from the rich and give to the poor? Was it to be by the public ownership and control of certain industries — the notion of 'planning' which was to be so beloved of progressive politicians in the 1930s? Eight months in office exposed to the Labour Party the flaws in its thinking, its preparations and its programme (Roberts, 1980, p. 112.)

Uncertainty concerning the manner in which the power of the state should be used persisted until the outbreak of the Second World War. However, Labour's first experience of office convinced the party that the British state in all its majesty could and should be used by a Labour government. From this viewpoint the General Strike in 1926 was not the watershed in Labour Party history. It merely confirmed Labour's existing commitment to constitutional action using the machinery of the state. In the days leading up to the strike the parliamentary leadership acted as an intermediary between the government and the trade unions to head off the strike. Henderson led a PLP delegation which negotiated with Baldwin throughout the night of 3 May. According to Clynes, Labour MPs counselled moderation and strongly advised the unions to keep within the law and to have a care for 'the well-being of the nation' (W. D. Muller, 1977, p. 40). J. H. Thomas expressed the opinion that 'in a challenge to the Constitution, God help us unless the Government won' (Mowat, 1966, p. 319). Nor was the parliamentary party alone in its abhorrence of anything which endangered the stability of the state. Once the trade-union leaders realized the revolutionary possibilities of the strike they were impatient to end it (Mowat, 1966, p. 321). In Bevan's (1952, p. 25) opinion 'they had forged a revolutionary weapon without having a revolutionary intention'.

The failure of the General Strike persuaded the trade-union movement to look towards the parliamentary option to create a legal framework within which the trade unions could discharge their industrial functions. Further evidence of the retreat from direct action came from the growing practice of consultation with employers' associations which became the *modus operandi* of the union leadership. However, the approach failed to clarify trade-union perceptions of the role which the state should play. The trade unions were primarily concerned with industrial matters and the position occupied by the Labour Party, while crucial, was nevertheless subordinate. Bevin, with the experience of the first Labour government fresh in his mind, explained that the Labour Party was an auxiliary to the trade-union movement (Allen, 1960, p. 226). The trade unions expected Labour to play the parliamentary game, to win office, and to exercise the power of the state to remove the legal restrictions under which the trade-union movement was obliged to operate; the repeal of the 1927 Trades Dispute Act was a priority in this context. But the trade-union movement was not prepared to brook any interference in its activities by the British state, even when the state was administered by a Labour government (Miliband 1972, p. 109). The trade unions expected the state to hold the ring while they and the employers' associations performed their traditional functions, bargaining about wage levels and working conditions. Thus the state was to be captured, its powers exercised to produce a more sympathetic environment for trade-union activities and then restored to a limited and largely non-interventionist role. Far from welcoming an expansion of state authority, many trade-unionists were distinctly apprehensive that the development might limit their freedom of action. The left-wing shop-stewards' movement regarded the collectivism of the First World War not as part of the inevitable gradualness which would lead to socialism but as a stage in the construction of state capitalism (Finley, 1980, p. 57). Yet, as affiliates to the Labour Party, the trade unions also subscribed to the policy of public ownership and nationalization which, enunciated by Webb and developed by MacDonald, clearly envisaged state ownership and control. Furthermore, union leaders and rank-and-file members quite genuinely and vigorously advocated public ownership for their respective industries. However, just how the nationalization of basic industries was to be squared with a minimal regulatory role for the state was not explained; still less how a trade union should operate in an industry owned or controlled by the state. While encouraging the Labour Party to pursue its parliamentary strategy and to win control of the state, the trade unions were unable to give a clear directive as to how its power should then be exercised.

A similar confusion was found within the ranks of the parliamentary party, although electoral considerations and a preference for constitutionalism loomed larger. After 1918 the leadership was increasingly committed to parliamentarianism but there was a significant and vocal tendency within the parliamentary party urging more radical socialist policies which inevitably would have impinged on the structure of the state. The Clydeside group of MPs led by Maxton and Wheatley had always advocated full-blooded socialism. Following the defeat of the Labour government in 1924 and the inevitable post-mortems, they assumed a dominant position in the ILP which they used to demand a policy of 'socialism now'. The ILP report, *'Socialism in our Time'* (1925) envisaged substantial positive state intervention in financial, industrial, and welfare fields but it did nothing to stimulate debate within the party as to the proper role of the state because it was largely interpreted, particularly by MacDonald, as an attack on the parliamentary leadership. Nevertheless it had some effect. The publication of *Labour and the Nation* in 1928 could be construed as a limited and tardy response, but while it reaffirmed the party's attachment to public ownership it did little to explain how in practice that policy was to be implemented. In the socialist scenario envisaged by the party the British state had a role but its precise moves had not been finalized nor its dialogue decided. The obscurity on this point may be judged from the following extracts. The Labour Party declared its aims as 'the organization of industry — in the interest — of all who bring their contribution of useful service to the common stock' and its socialism as 'a conscious, systematic and unflagging effort to use the weapons forged in the victorious struggle for political democracy to end the capitalist dictatorship'. But there was no indication of how industry should be organized in the 'interest of all'; no attempt to evaluate the relative importance of worker and consumer interests; nor of how the state, which in a socialist democracy represents the interest of the whole community, would relate to either. The report was similarly uninformative as to the nature of 'weapons forged in the victorious struggle'. Were they all constitutional or were some extra-parliamentary; and were they compatible with the traditions and *mores* of the liberal-democratic state? The policy statement failed to resolve any of these dilemmas. *Labour and the Nation* was pre-eminently a propaganda exercise to attract popular support for socialism as a form of secular morality (Roberts, 1980, p. 118). It is a measure of its success that in the 1929 election Labour attracted three million additional votes and became the largest single party in the House of Commons. However a document whose staple fare consisted of statements of socialist belief and outrage could not, by its very nature, provide the new Labour government with a blueprint for socialist action and organization. The second Labour government, therefore, was no clearer on how precisely the state might be employed to implement socialist policies than the first Labour government had been.

There was another similarity between the two governments. Their greatest success came in the field of foreign affairs, where they could simply slip into the traditional mould of a British government protecting the interests of the British state and its citizens within the framework of the international community of nations. The instinctive patriotism of the Labour leadership, so often inhibited by class loyalties in domestic matters, was able to find full expression in this policy arena. Snowden held up agreement on the Young Plan — scaling down German reparations because it reduced the percentage of repayments to Britain — and became a national hero; the 1930 Naval Treaty between Britain, the United States, and Japan was widely regarded, even in the Tory press as a personal triumph for MacDonald (Brand 1965, p. 141); and Henderson in a difficult and deteriorating international situation, emerged as a Foreign Secretary of transparent honesty and integrity.

The Labour government's most serious weakness, and one which caused its eventual downfall, lay in its inability to get to grips with the economic crisis. There was nothing exceptional about this. Most governments were undermined and toppled by the world slump. Labour failed, however, because it was unable either to perceive or to exercise those powers of the British state which could have staved off the worst effects.

In constitutional matters the continuing and deepening depression induced a conservative reaction both within the parliamentary party and amongst rank-and-file activists. The greater the economic crisis the greater it appeared was the need for the state to administer a policy of redistribution to alleviate the most excessive social and territorial inequalities. A single central control to co-ordinate the various functions of individuals and groups within the state was increasingly accepted as a basic tenet of socialist philosophy. A similar conservatism was apparent in the Labour government's economic policies. There were elements both inside and outside the Labour Party which appreciated that the impending crisis in international capitalism demanded bold and radical solutions. As the crisis deepened in 1930 the left-wing members of the Economic Advisory Council — Tawney, Cole, and Bevin together with Keynes — urged that the resources of the state should be used to produce a planned economic expansion. A similar demand was voiced by Maxton and the ILP. The Mosley Memorandum also advocated an expansion of purchasing power through increased benefits and allowances, controls on imports, and public control of banking and industry. Inevitably such policies would have required a vast growth in the responsibilities of the state, creating new ministries and increasing the level of recruitment to the public service, the establishment of new public bodies to adminster novel functions not previously the concern of government and, finally, the careful development of the appropriate relationship between the new and expanded public sector and Parliament. In short, economic innovation was linked to, and dependent upon, constitutional engineering. For the Labour government to assume such a task would have required a detailed blueprint of the state's role in running a socialist economic system and developing a socialist society, but this the Labour government lacked. Even if such a blueprint had existed it is highly doubtful whether the 'constitutionalist' leadership of the party would willingly have embarked upon the programme such was its uncritical acceptance of the constitutional process which had brought them to power.

Instead, the Labour government attempted to deal with the growing crisis using the existing institutional framework and conventional policies. A special Cabinet committee chaired by J. H. Thomas attempted to rationalize British industry; a Development Act made £25 million available for public works; Thomas promoted British exports in Canada; and Lansbury proposed schemes of colonization in Western Australia. However, Snowden's financial orthodoxies, which were given full rein and support in the Treasury, frustrated most initiatives and he remained convinced (until he was part of a national government) that ending free trade and coming off the gold standard would lead to chaos. In fact Snowden believed the state could do very little to resolve the crisis; private enterprise would have to be the primary factor in any recovery (Brand, 1965, p. 149). It is clear that the government as a whole had limited expectations of what state intervention could achieve and reverted to exercising those responsibilities which the nineteenth-century state had progressively assumed; easing the lot of the most seriously disadvantaged in society through social welfare legislation. The Pensions and Housing Acts, although important in themselves, were mere palliatives in face of the deepening recession but so far as the Labour government were concerned they possessed two distinct and fortuitously linked advantages. They were constitutionally conservative and they provided help for Labour's working-class constituency on whose loyalty depended the party's electoral strategy.

We have no desire to delve into the circumstances leading to the formation of the national government; that has been dealt with in considerable detail elsewhere. However, from the point of view of Labour attitudes towards the British state it is significant that the party's leader and the three Labour ministers who followed him into the national government were prepared to put at risk their political careers and to respond to the call, whether expressed by the King alone or in conjunction with the leaders of the opposition parties, to form a national government with a mandate to preserve the fabric of the state. The circumstances betoken a scale of priorities curiously out of place in a party whose *raison d'être* was opposition to the political establishment and whose origins were extra-parliamentary. It would be convenient to characterize these constitutionalist and statist sentiments as unique to the author of the great betrayal. However, MacDonald's romantic sense of socialism with 'too great a sense of history, too great a respect for convention and constitutional forms' (Skidelski, 1967, p. 80) was not exorcized from the party despite the trauma of 1931.

Throughout the inter-war years the Labour party displayed a singular reluctance to countenance tinkering with the institutional structures of the British state. The objectives of creating a comprehensive welfare system and transforming the nature of society, represented radical enough departures from the norms of the early-twentieth century but an implicit understanding pervaded the party — and certainly its leadership for much of the twenties and the early thirties — that the machinery of the state could be redirected in some undefined way from defending the interest of capitalism to creating the conditions for socialism. Given this assumption there was little need to be concerned with reforming the institutions of the state. There are other explanations for Labour's relative inactivity in this area. Both Labour governments in the inter-war years were minority governments, dependent upon Liberal support and goodwill. Labour had no wish unnecessarily to alienate either. Nor did it desire to raise doubts in the mind of the British electorate about its fitness to govern by any action which might be misconstrued as even mildly revolutionary. Electoral pragmatic tendencies of the party therefore precluded an expression of radical zeal in constitutional matters, but it is doubtful whether Labour with a clear parliamentary majority would have initiated a programme of constitutional reform. Lacking a detailed and coherent philosophy of the state, Labour was particularly receptive to pragmatic considerations. The party's experience in government persuaded it of the merits of the traditional procedures and institutions of the British state. We can trace the development of Labour's constitutional inhibitions in four specific areas; the emergence of the party

leader, the role of the House of Lords, the issue of proportional representation, and the policy of Home Rule all round.

As Labour acquired first the status of official opposition and then, a
year later, of Government, the position of Chairman came to resemble
the role of 'Leader' in the other two great parties (MacKenzie, 1964,
p. 307). Despite the counter-balancing provisions of Labour's constitution, MacDonald in 1924 and again in 1929, was permitted to act
exactly like any other party leader in forming his government.
Although leading members of the party discussed the situation, the
party had evolved no clear principles to guide its deliberations and
eventually it was decided to follow Webb's advice and adopt 'the usual
constitutional practice' (MacKenzie, 1964, p. 308). MacDonald's
defection in 1931 provoked a series of attempts to limit the singular
powers of the party leader by means of consultative procedures
incorporating the collective leadership in the shadow cabinet and the
parliamentary party. Attlee's election as leader in 1935 was interpreted as another stage in the campaign to frustrate the emergence of
an autocratic leader. For much of his early period in office Attlee
showed deference to conference decisions but his explanation that
conference was the final authority while the parliamentary party was
supreme in its own sphere (Attlee, 1937) was deliberately confusing.
As he confided later: 'the Party's passion for definition must always be
resisted' (Harris, 1982, p. 131). During the 1945 election Attlee cate-
gorically rejected Churchill's accusation that a Labour Cabinet
would be at the beck and call of the NEC and subsequently set about
constructing his government like any other previous prime minister.
The safeguards constructed in the 1930s were ignored or forgotten
(MacKenzie, 1964, pp. 321–3). The parliamentary embrace proved
too seductive.

Labour's policy on the House of Lords was similarly transmuted by
its experience of government. Reform of the House of Lords was part
of Labour's radical inheritance but the party as a whole lacked a clear
view of the priority that should be accorded to the reform and of its
precise nature. Tactical considerations again intruded. A House of
Lords reform package could have been worked out with the Liberals
and would have attracted popular support without injuring socialist
sensibilities, but neither of the Labour governments in 1924 and 1929
desired to embark on a course of action which might reflect credit on
the Liberals. Furthermore Labour was unclear whether or not it
wanted complete abolition. The 1918 Conference was opposed to the

House of Lords and *any* form of second chamber but the subsequent policy document, *Labour and the New Social Order*, limited its opposition to a second chamber based on the hereditary principle. During the second Labour administration the Lords fatally weakened the Coal Mines Act and effectively killed off the Alternative Vote Bill, but Labour's 1931 manifesto made no mention of abolition and merely declared that it would not tolerate opposition from the House of Lords.

In the aftermath of MacDonald's departure Labour adopted more radical socialist positions on a whole range of issues. The publication of *For Socialism and Peace* in 1934 marked the party's first serious attempt since before the First World War to consider the role of the state in creating a socialist society. It accepted that 'socialist reconstruction was not possible without adapting the machine of government to its purpose' and it specifically identified the hereditary House of Lords and the old-fashioned procedure of the House of Commons. However radical the diagnosis, the prescription offered was constitutionally bland. The procedural reforms advocated for the House of Commons were no more than 'an extension of existing constitutional tendencies or of long standing suggestions for political and administrative reform' (Miliband, 1972, p. 208). In the case of the House of Lords, it was to be abolished 'as a legislative chamber' implying that it might continue in some other role. However, even this limited form of abolition was absent from Labour's 1945 manifesto which simply repeated the ritual phrase of not tolerating obstruction of the People's will by the House of Lords. With this background the 1949 Parliament Act can hardly be interpreted as part of a long-term strategy of institutional reform. It was a pragmatic response to the problems posed by the passage of the Iron and Steel Bill and reflected Labour's most persistent characteristic: an unwillingness to think and act on institutional matters except when obliged to by political circumstance.

A similar retreat from a thoroughgoing reform directly influencing the workings of the supreme institution of the parliamentary state, was evident on the issue of the electoral system. The 1919 Labour Party conference had reaffirmed its belief in the principle of proportional representation and in 1921 the Parliamentary Labour Party voted in favour of a Private Member's Bill introducing the Single Transferable Vote by 25 votes to 5. In 1923 two other bills seeking to reform the electoral system for local government and Parliament attracted the support of the overwhelming majority of Labour MPs. However the following year a Labour government was noticeably cooler towards the whole idea of electoral reform. It refused to support the Liberal bill in favour of the single transferable vote and decided to deny the bill facilities if it passed its second reading. Labour members divided 90 to 28, the majority voting with the Conservatives against the proposal, thus denying the bill its second reading.

The traditional explanation advanced for Labour's pauline conversion is partisan self-interest. It has some force. The Labour Party was the chief beneficiary of an erratic electoral system in 1923 and even more so in 1929 when with 1.2 per cent fewer votes than the Conservatives it won 28 more seats (Butler, 1963, p. 173). It is arguable that but for the electoral distortions Labour would never have gained office during the inter-war years. So considerations of electoral advantage were certainly a factor. However, there were other considerations which revealed the extent to which Labour was becoming integrated into the governing system of the British state and was progressively abandoning the postures of a minority anti-establishment party sniping from the sidelines. By 1924 the Labour Party was sensitive to the benefits of stability in the governmental process. Herbert Morrison went so far as to express a preference for a bad, logical government to a well-meaning but unstable one and suggested that the electoral system's weakness was not so serious that it would not soon be cured by the disappearance of the Liberal party. (Butler, 1963, p. 45). The Labour Party was coming round to the view that the traditional institutions of the parliamentary state should be preserved; that stability depended upon a strong government confronted by a coherent opposition; and that polarization of the vote between the Conservatives and Labour would redound to Labour's advantage. The view which tacitly accepted the traditional two-party system as the appropriate mode for running the state was confirmed by MacDonald, paradoxically while speaking in support of electoral reform (Butler, 1963, p. 68). Whatever enthusiasm there had been for electoral reform in Labour ranks, most of it evaporated after Labour's abbreviated experience of office in 1924. It is difficult to interpret the moves to reform the electoral system between 1929 and 1931 as other than a rather cynical expedient to keep the Labour government in office. Thereafter as Labour consolidated its position as a party of government, it showed little interest in electoral reform until the 1970s when political circumstances again obliged it to consider the issue.

The anti-statist tradition within the Labour party which, as we have shown, made it so receptive to Home Rule was another casualty of Labour's increasing familiarity with government. The change was not immediately apparent. Labour's annual Conference in 1918 debated constitutional devolution and resolved that 'there should be constituted separate statutory legislative assemblies for Scotland, Wales and even England' (Labour Party, 1918, p. 70). In Scotland after the First World War socialism 'was not the doctrine of the state planned economy which it has since become' (MacCormick, 1955); traditional radicalism and the new industrial militancy were allied within the Labour Party to produce a brief upsurge of support for Home Rule.

However by the mid-1920s pragmatic class and electoral considerations became more important. The interests of Labour supporters, concentrated in regions of deprivation, and the party's need to expand its electoral base pointed towards central economic planning. The shift was assisted by the effects of the post-war depression which undermined the confidence of the Scottish and Welsh Labour movements and contributed to establishing the conventional wisdom within the party, that the economic problems of the peripheries were to be solved only by gaining access to United Kingdom resources. The partial solution of the Irish problem which removed the most significant nationalist force from British politics, rapidly followed by Labour's parliamentary breakthrough in 1922, concentrated the party's attention on Westminster. Labour's Scottish and Welsh seats made a vital contribution to its parliamentary strength and the party leadership impressed by the logic of the electoral and parliamentary arithmetic, thus acquired and developed an interest in maintaining a unified parliamentary system. Attempts by Scottish 'home rulers' to influence the Labour governments in 1924, and between 1929 and 1931 were simply stone-walled as Labour turned to central planning as the solution to Britain's economic problems (Keating and Bleiman, 1979) and as the basis of its electoral appeal.

The electoral disaster which overtook Labour in 1931 had important implications for the party. It raised doubts about the parliamentary strategy which had presumed the 'inevitability of gradualness' and it prompted a reappraisal of Labour's ideology. On both counts the nature of the existing British state was called into question. Those on the left wing of the party adopted a recognizably Marxist position identifying the state, its machinery and ethos, with the dominant economic class. Laski in particular criticized those in the party who had 'assumed the absolute validity of the form of the political state regardless of the economic character of the society it was supposed to represent'. He asserted that 'in a capitalist society sovereignty belonged to the owners of capital; and custom was registered, legislation made, in their interest also' (quoted, Wright, 1983, p. 123). Others in the party argued that the traditions of 'relative civil liberty' associated with the bourgeois British state might be exploited to frustrate and overthrow a socialist government (Strachey, 1936) and that it might be better and more conducive to the general peace and welfare of the state for a socialist government to establish a temporary dictatorship (Cripps, 1933).

Although significant, these views failed to find general support within a party which was endangered by Communist infiltration at home and confronted by Fascist dictatorships abroad. The party leadership still adhered to what was essentially a liberal-democratic view of the state and its role. The state's prime concern was 'to prevent oppression of an individual by others and to secure that the liberty of one does not restrict that of others or conflict with the common good of society' (Attlee, 1937, p. 141). However, such well-meaning aspirations hardly clarified the precise role which the state was to play under a socialist government. Tawney (1934) concluded that this deficiency reflected Labour's lack of a political creed so that it did not achieve what it could because it did not know what it wanted. Skidelsky (1967, p. 433) reached a similar conclusion in ascribing the failure of the 1929–31 Labour government to an immature doctrine:

[The Labour Party] believed that socialism was the cure for poverty, of which unemployment was simply the most vivid manifestation. It thought in terms of a total solution: but socialism would clearly take a very long time, for it would not be established until the majority of people were ready for it. In the meantime the Labour Party simply did not know what to do .

According to both interpretations Labour's deficiency lay, not in the quality or the intensity of its commitment to a socialist philosophy but in a coherent set of short-term policies by which the party could approach its long-term objective.

We have argued that during the course of the 1920s and 1930s this void was occupied by the traditional norms, procedures, and institutions of the British state as Labour emerged as one of the two major parties. Logically the process would have fitted the Labour party securely into the consitutionalist mould of most radical reform movements in British history. However, as we have seen, the norms of the

British state were never universally accepted by all levels of the party and its insitutions. There were those, and not all Marxists, who questioned the legitimacy of the British state. During the 1920s the theory of the manifesto was deployed to sustain the sovereignty of the party's annual Conference and to control the leadership of the parliamentary party. It made 'no concession of principle to the parts of the British constitution which emphasize the right of the cabinet to coordinate policy'. In Drucker's (1979, p. 92) opinion it was 'an outsider's ideology — a populist ideology'. It was this view rather than the Marxist analysis which gained strength in the wake of the 1931 electoral disaster. However, the shift in the balance of power within the party, far from resolving Labour's confusion as to the role of the state, merely perpetuated the party's ambivalence.

This ambivalence was reflected in the rhetoric employed by the leadership. The party's commitment to untrammelled socialism was regularly reaffirmed. In the 1920s the party leadership talked 'not of patching the rents in a bad system but of transforming capitalism into socialism' (MacDonald, 1928); the failure of the Labour government in 1931 was ascribed by MacDonald to the capitalist system which was 'breaking down' (Skidelski, 1967, p. 270). In 1934, *For Socialism and Peace* prophesied 'a rapid advance to a socialist reconstruction of national life' while the party's 1945 manifesto proudly proclaimed 'a Socialist Party [whose] ultimate purpose is the establishment of the Socialist Commonwealth of Great Britain' (Beer, 1965, pp. 136-7). All implied that the existing economic and political system of the British state was defective and breaking down. However, the only detailed policies to emerge which approximated to the socialist rhetoric were central planning and nationalization. During the 1930s they were established as basic tenets of Labour's socialist belief and were increasingly regarded as the practical and intermediate stage in the establishment of socialism. As such they appeared to provide a legitimate socialist role for the state. However there was an inherent ambiguity in the policy of nationalization. It was expected to fulfill two functions. First, it was regarded as the key to effective planning which would ensure greater efficiency and expansion. In *Let us face the Future* (1945) Labour argued: 'It is either sound economic controls — or smash'. Secondly, socialist benefits were also presumed to flow from the policy, most notably the equalization of wealth and industrial democracy. Nationalization and central economic planning, however, were not logically dependent on socialist ideology (Beer, 1965, p. 190);

an enhanced role for the state did not necessarily connote a socialist role.

The immediate task of developing the administrative machine for public ownership confronted Labour with several problems. The model eventually adopted was based on Herbert Morrison's 1931 bill to reorganize London's transport services with a single independent public corporation; it attracted criticism from different sectors of the Labour party. It was based on the administrative precedents set by a Conservative government (the Central Electric Board and the BBC in 1926) and left-wing critics considered it 'a constitutional outrage [that] a member of parliament should be expected to defer to a non-elected person' on the board of a nationalized industry (Bevan, 1952, p. 98). The kind of persons nominated to the board also provoked debate. Morrison was utterly opposed to the specific representation of sectional interests, including trade unions; the final test of appointment should be individual capacity and the national interest. (Pelling, 1954, p. 300.) This represented the somewhat naïve belief on Morrison's part that an individual could be divorced from sectional interests; it led to the exclusion of board members representing the interests of the workers. Trade-union leaders were particularly critical that the concept of the independent board would fail to follow socialist lines and would stratify industrial society by assuming the permanency of the purely commodity status of labour. Their main apprehension — that Morrison's nationalization plan would create an efficient state bureaucracy with no effective check on it — (Pelling 1954, pp. 300–1) once again revealed the traditional trade-union aversion to the over-powerful state.

Nevertheless, despite these pertinent criticisms, the public corporation model was accepted by the party. Nationalization and central planning became the dominant features in Labour's socialist programme and with it the whole concept of state collectivism was incorporated into the party's conventional wisdom (Cole, 1935). For the vast majority in the Labour party, and even more so for its critics, state collectivism became synonymous with socialism and Attlee could measure the progress of the Labour party by the extent to which the whole conception of state planning had become part of the assumptions of the ordinary man and woman (Pelling, 1954, p. 329).

When Labour entered the 1945 general election campaign, state planning, nationalization and state welfare provisions constituted the core of its electoral appeal. In its first year in office Labour introduced bills to nationalize the Bank of England and the mines, to create a National Insurance scheme and to set up a National Health Service. In response to the desires of the trade-union movement as well as the Labour Party's self-interest, the Trade Disputes and Trade Union Act of 1927 was repealed. The following year the railways were nationalized. These measures represented the very least that could be expected of a Labour government. All the bills related to policy issues which had formed part of the political dialogue since the 1920s and, if not positively welcomed by the official opposition, they escaped the unqualified hostility subsequently directed at the Iron and Steel Nationalization Bill. However, the fact that the legislation had been passed by the House of Commons and implemented by the Civil Service appeared to confirm the prevailing view amongst the parliamentary leadership that the state's apparatus was essentially neutral.

Looking back on the activities of the Labour governments between 1945 and 1951, the predominant feature which emerges is not so much socialism as *statism*. The promise in Labour's manifesto *Let us Face the Future* to build a new Socialist Commonwealth was quietly forgotten as the party moved 'towards an acceptance of the welfare state and the managed economy as the basic structure of policy within which the party would pursue its aims' (Beer, 1965, pp. 189–90). The ethical side of Labour's ideology was progressively subordinated to considerations of efficiency and prosperity. The shift was facilitated and, we would argue, largely determined by the techniques of national income analysis and physical planning controls developed during the Second World War by the coalition government. Socialism became what the Labour government had done (Donoughue and Jones, 1973, pp. 515–16). However, what the Labour government actually did between 1945 and 1951 was to become immersed in the administration of the British state. Techniques of central economic planning which had been created to meet war-time conditions were developed and refined by Stafford-Cripps; the government frequently invoked the war-time spirit of 'national unity' to exhort its supporters and to justify its actions. Nationalization increasingly was presented in a less idealistic tone, as a means of ensuring that basic industries were efficiently run rather than as vehicles for shifting class power either within the particular industry or the state (Coates, 1975, p. 51).

The nationalization of the basic industries by the Attlee government has traditionally been regarded as the jewel in Labour's crown; although the programme has been subjected to increasing criticism that Labour lost the opportunity to shift fundamentally the distribution of social and economic power (Coates, 1975 and Miliband, 1972). We would argue, however, that the significance of Labour's post-war programme lies in the relationship of the nationalized industries to the state.

Despite moves towards workers' control in the 1930s, the Morrisonian model was the one finally adopted. This involved a Board of Directors appointed in their capacity as 'expert' managers who would be responsible for the running of their respective industry to Parliament; the custodian of the popular will and the repository of the sovereignty of the nation. The nomenclature was also important. Morrison (1959, pp. 257–61) referred to the public corporations he was creating as 'socialized' industries. Nevertheless, the commonly adopted term 'nationalized' more accurately reflected the role they were expected to perform. National criteria, national interests, national requirements, and national priorities were the considerations which enveloped the nationalized industries. Nationalization was undertaken to ensure that those industries basic to the national economy were modernized or rationalized, that industries which private capital had failed to sustain should benefit from public capital investment programmes to secure the national interest.

Given such national objectives, the prime concern of Morrison and the rest of Attlee's Cabinet was not to socialize British industry, still less to create alternative political and economic power centres exterior to Parliament, 'but to control it and to bend it to the government's purpose' (Miliband, 1972, p. 290). Thus there was no question of workers' control. The Fabian tradition was, according to Dahl (1974, p. 877), a significant factor:

Two features of the Fabian conception of state and government led inevitably to the rejection of workers' control. The first was the acceptance of parliamentary supremacy as an expression of the general will . . . the other determining feature of the Fabian conception of government was an uncommon respect for the expert.

Nationalization, therefore, failed to advance the cause of socialism and, because of the central directive role played by the nationalized industries, supported the capitalist economy. Miliband (1972, p. 288) argues that this was their sole purpose. Although this is a matter of some conjecture and one which we would not completely accept, it is indisputable that the programme of nationalization increased both government control and the ultimate authority of Parliament although effective procedures for parliamentary accountability were slow to develop. The identification of nationalized industries with central state control, with rundown industries and with disillusioned workers who discovered that Labour's belief in the expert had left most management structures and personnel intact, meant that nationalization ceased to be a policy that could evoke either popular enthusiasm or support.

Miliband (1972, p. 272) has described the 1945–51 period as the 'climax of Labourism' but the evidence suggests a party uncertain of what its role should be. Admittedly there was a strong trade-union element within the parliamentary party (over a third were trade-union sponsored MPs) and the government was anxious to protect the interests of organized labour, as its repeal of the 1927 Act indicated. However, that legislation and Bevin's formidable presence in the government, was used to ensure trade-union co-operation in maintaining industrial discipline on which Labour's programme of state planning depended. When that was not forthcoming the Labour government was quite willing to use the full power of the state, including troops, to break strikes. The government's increasingly statist position also made it sceptical of workers' control and industrial democracy. The scope of joint consultation procedures was as narrow as it had been before the War. The Labour government seemed intent not so much on nationalizing British industry in the socialist sense as ensuring that it was controlled by the state.

The Labour government's statist posture had a significant impact on local government. Labour's commitment to local government and local democracy extended back to the early Fabians who had been municipal socialists because they believed that the state machine was in a process of disintegration under the strain of spreading democracy (Shaw, 1904). The Webbs (1920) in their *Constitution for a Socialist Commonwealth of Great Britain* had indicated a preference for municipalization rather than nationalization because the incentive for efficiency was more likely to come from a sense of community feeling than from the more nebulous concept of the national interest.

After the First World War Labour expended considerable efforts at the local government level with growing success. In 1919 it won control of Durham County and Monmouthshire; Merthyr Tydfil was captured in 1920, and Sheffield in 1926. In 1934 Labour won a majority on the London County Council. By 1939 Labour controlled

4 county councils, 18 country boroughs, 24 non-county boroughs, 17 London boroughs and 100 district councils (Keith-Lucas and Richards, 1978, p. 114).

At one level Labour's involvement in local government marked the ultimate stage in its integration to the British state. The local authorities possessed very limited executive powers and to administer their functions in a legitimate fashion could be construed as an acceptance of the ultimate authority of the parliamentary institution of the British state. Many Labour councillors were content to accept this role because it lent status to the Labour party and enabled them, in a limited fashion, to translate socialist theory into practice. Throughout the inter-war years a succession of Labour back-benchers introduced private member's bills to extend the powers of local authorities and to enable them to engage in commercial ventures. However the other parties were less than enthusiastic in giving additional powers to what Tawney had described as the 'little republics' of Birmingham, Manchester, and Leeds (Tawney, 1921) and none of the enabling bills were passed. There was a general concern in non-Labour ranks that the contagion of 'poplarism' should not be encouraged. However the roots of 'poplarism' although deep were not widely spread. During the inter-war years very few Labour councillors regarded themelves as, in the words of George Lansbury, 'clear class conscious Socialists working together using the whole machinery of local government and parliament for the transformation of Capitalist Society into Socialism' (Keith-Lucas and Richards, 1978, p. 69). The majority were prepared to criticize, to lobby and generally to exert pressure, but in the final analysis, to work the system. By 1951 however, much of that system had disappeared. Labour's nationalization programme which deprived local authorities of their hospitals and their electricity and gas services, placed greater emphasis on state efficiency than local democracy.

A similar set of priorities was displayed in Labour's dealings with the Celtic peripheries of the British state. We show elsewhere (in Chapter 7) how the Labour government was predisposed to preserve and even consolidate the border between Northern Ireland and the newly declared Republic of Ireland, in 1949. In the case of Scotland and Wales all party campaigns for devolution were launched in the late forties. Not only were they peripheral to Labour's major concerns but they were also antipathetic to the party's developing attachment to state planning and economic centralism. The Scottish Convention of the late 1940s gained widespread support within the party in Scotland but its activities were soon interpreted as attacks on the Labour government. The Labour Party's Welsh Council of Labour expected the Labour government to satisfy their longstanding demand for a separate Welsh Office with a Welsh Secretary of Cabinet rank. However, Morrison's total opposition and Bevan's apprehension that devolution of authority 'would divorce Welsh political activity from the mainstream of British politics' (Griffiths, 1969, p. 161) frustrated any constitutional reform. By 1951 the Labour government was firmly identified with the centralized British state.

Labour betrayed a constitutional conservatism in its reform of parliamentary procedures. The rules of the House of Commons were amended to make it more efficient, to make it a workshop as well as a talk shop (Morrison, 1964, p. 254). The reforms facilitated the flow of legislation which benefited the government but no move was made to change radically the imbalanced relationship between the executive and the legislature. Labour again refrained from taking action against the House of Lords. As noted earlier, the pledge to abolish it had been dropped from the 1945 manifesto and replaced by a declaration that Labour would 'not tolerate obstruction of the people's will'. When obliged by the Iron and Steel Bill veto to introduce reform, Labour's bill was determined by short-term tactical considerations. In only one area was the Labour government prepared to countenance radical institutional reforms. Granting India independence precipitated the constitutional process which led to the end of the imperial epoch, so while Labour failed to create a Socialist Commonwealth in Britain it could point to the Commonwealth of Nations.

After six years of majority government, Labour was firmly established as the party of the British state. It was identified with state intervention, central economic planning, and nationalized industries, the symbols of state collectivism. Its actions in government had associated the party with the constitutional status quo and the preservation of the central power of the state. It was either suspicious of, or openly hostile to, demands which questioned the authority and the structures of the British state. Part of the reason was Labour's reverence for the British constitution (Harris, 1982, p. 134), a characteristic which, as we have shown, Labour shared with many radical movements in British political history. Labour's attitude was also the product of its experiences in government, in the war-time coalition as well as the 1945–51 government. By 1951 state power and intervention were regarded as indispensible elements of socialism. However, Labour operated in a highly competitive party system and was not exclusively responsible for setting the political agenda. Both major parties contributed to the political dialogue which developed during the 1920s and 1930s; expanding the role of the state was by the 1930s part of a political consensus. S. H. Beer (1965, p. 27) said of the Conservatives:

In their reassertion of state power over the operation of the economic system as a whole they not only broke with fundamentals of British policy in the previous hundred years but also created many patterns of government action which, in spite of important modifications, have been followed since that time.

A similar extension of the responsibilities and powers of the state was not only implicit in Keynes's economic prescriptions and Beveridge's welfare plan (Barker, 1978, p. 127), it was the obvious conclusion to be drawn from Britain's experience in the Second World War. Labour's identification with the British state thus was only marginally connected with socialism. It is, therefore, ironic that for many of its supporters and critics, state centralism became synonymous with socialism and that a quirk in the electoral system, one of the institutions which Labour had studiously refrained from reforming, should force it from office and into thirteen years of opposition.

CHAPTER 4

Labour and the industrial state

STATE involvement in economic and industrial affairs is a feature of all industrialized societies and, in Britain, has been pursued by Conservative and by Labour governments. Such a development might have been greeted by the early Fabians as a vindication of their belief in the inevitability of socialism. We have seen that state planning, albeit vaguely formulated, was one of the main elements in the party's platform since the 1930s, providing a way of transcending capitalism and realizing public as against private goals. It provides, too, a means of promoting economic and social equality through redistributing resources and emphasizing the needs of the needy. In fact state intervention has brought the party 'to a series of crises and raised fundamental questions, as yet unanswered, about its ultimate purposes.

At the centre of Labour's problems is the relationship of economic and political power and of public and private purposes. Middlemas' (1979) view of the party's early leaders as tied to the 'nineteenth-century constitution' and a strictly party view of government could, as Chapter 6 shows, be extended into the contemporary period. But management of the modern industrial state requires an appreciation of the constraints on state power and the limitations of traditional constitutional doctrines in the face of corporate power. The problem is compounded by Labour's commitment to the 'mixed economy', allowing a large scope for capitalist enterprise. Support for the mixed economy stems partly from a respect for the potential of private capital to create economic growth but, perhaps more importantly, from the commitment to government by consent and political pluralism. This involves at least an implicit acceptance of market criteria for allocating resources and retention of the profit motive as the principal means of economic incentive. It is customary for Marxists to argue that this necessarily obliges Labour governments to act in the interests of capital accumulation and thus of the capitalist class. Failure to do so will undermine the profitability of capitalism, prevent the accumulation and reproduction of capital and so, eventually destroy the system. Social expenditure can only be increased to a certain point without killing the goose that lays the golden eggs (Offe, 1983). This argument we would reject as too simplistic, for three reasons. Firstly, it assumes that there is a single capitalist class interest which is knowable. The very different behaviour of governments which we could assume, *a fortiori* on this argument to be favourable to capitalists' interests — for example the Macmillan, Heath, and Thatcher governments — must put this in doubt. One cannot, indeed, assume a priori, that state expenditure and intervention are either good or bad for private capital. The most commonly held Marxist position at present is to believe that, the state being the servant of the dominant classes, all interventions must be in their interest, if only by 'legitimating' the system and stifling unrest, but that, at some point, social expenditures will overwhelm it (Offe, 1983). However, attempts to separate conceptually the 'productive' and 'consumption' activities of the state, whether from the Left or from the Right, have had little success; the relationship between state activity and private sector profitability is more complex than is allowed for either by most Marxist writers or by the anti-state liberals of the new Right (Heald, 1983). Secondly, the argument too often assumes that 'capital accumulation' is a feature specific to capitalist systems, whereas, in fact, what distinguishes capitalism is the *private ownership* of capital, not its accumulation which, under the name of investment, would presumably be a feature of any economic system committed to growth. In a state-controlled economy, or under a system of workers' control, for example, there would be the same imperative to divide resources between investment and consumption and between individual and collective ends. Thirdly, there is the weakness of much of British capitalism this century and, particularly, since the Second World War, which undermines the argument that it is predominant in the making of state policy. Of course, there is an argument to the effect that the weakness and failures of British capitalism are precisely what have necessitated calling the state in aid, but the causal mechanisms whereby a debilitated capitalist class can subordinate the state to its interests have never been adequately specified. We do not accept, therefore, that the policies of Labour governments must necessarily be predetermined by capitalist class interests. We do concede that their acceptance of a mixed economy does impose constraints on the scope of their activities and the instruments which can be deployed in the pursuit of these. It is our argument that these constraints have never been properly explored by the party, though at times halting moves have been made in this direction. For this reason, the party has failed to appreciate both the strengths and the weaknesses of the state as an instrument of economic intervention.

Labour's relations with organized labour pose another set of constraints on its freedom in government. The trade unions' compliance with state policy under Labour governments must be regarded as largely voluntary, for both practical and principled reasons. In practical terms, it is not possible to coerce organized labour and achieve industrial success, as various governments have discovered. For a Labour government, coercion contradicts one of the basic tenets of its ideology and runs up against interests rooted in the party itself. Some Marxist writers have interpreted Labour's political role as serving capitalist interests by defusing the demands of the organized working class. Panitch (1976), following a long tradition of Marxist analysis, emphasizes the influence of the party on the trade unions, rather than the reverse, and sees Labour as an 'integrative party', reconciling organized labour to the needs of the capitalist order. The main intellectual problem with such an argument is its purely functionalist basis, the integrative role , which is itself inadequately specified theoretically, being seen as stemming from the necessary operation of the state in the interests of 'those who own and control industry' (Panitch, 1979, p. 172). Such a formulation tells us little about how Labour came into being as a political movement or how and why it adopted its 'integrative ideology'. Indeed, by describing Labour's integrative role as an 'ideology', Panitch undermines his own functionalist argument by implying that the party's adoption of policy positions may have been the result of deliberate choice. Yet, to concede this would be to make the implausible claim that Labour has set out to subordinate the interests of the working class to capitalist oppression. The alternative, according to Panitch and other Marxist writers, would be for Labour to become a purely class party, dedicated to the attainment of working-class hegemony and thus socialism, by identifying with, and encouraging, trade-union wage militancy. This is to confuse the very issues which Labour as a political movement is obliged to reconcile.

These are, firstly, the needs of economic management in a mixed economy, which require governments to have policies on prices, wages and industrial relations. In full employment, this implies restrictions on free collective bargaining and a strengthened state role in the allocation of resources. Secondly, there are the social consequences of industrial disputes, which often have repercussions well beyond the immediate parties, by affecting the provision of public services and the employment of workers in other industries. The inter-dependence of economic activities as well as the size and significance of the public sector itself mean that disputes frequently raise issues of public policy. Thirdly, there are the ideological goals of the Labour Party itself. Definitions of these are legion but all emphasize the pur-suit of economic and social equality and the role of public policy in achieving it. This implies a commitment to a form of income determination freed, at least to a degree, from market criteria, whether through incomes policy or taxation. Finally, there are the demands of the trade unions, organically part of the party but with their own concerns and priorities. These are essentially related to the practice of 'free collective bargaining' under capitalism, though in the case of the public sector unions these terms have to be stretched con-siderably to fit. Of course, many trade-union leaders profess a belief in socialism but, as Jenkins (1970, p. 9) points out, this is a 'poor guide to their behaviour when they have on their negotiating hats'. Indeed, as we have noted, the constitution and practice of the Labour move-ment make clear the demarcation between the political and industrial spheres, with the unions taking a patchy interest in the former and the party largely banned from the latter.

For Panitch (1976) and other Marxists, this is a false problem. Trade unions are objectively obliged to pursue socialist aims by the very fact of their being working-class organizations. The problem of equality of incomes 'within the working class' is seen as secondary to equality between classes, which is what Labour should be pursuing. What the working class is, in this formulation, is not defined. Some-times, it appears to equate to everyone belonging to a trade union; at other times, to all non-owners of means of production. In either case, it must include an extraordinary range of incomes and encompass groups which by no stretch of the imagination could be seen as 'working class'. The problem is that Marxists' obsession with the question of ownership of the means of production tends to blind them to the fact that this is but one cause of inequality in modern industrial society. Further, expropriation of the means of production by the state, however justifiable on other grounds, would by no means neces-sarily produce equality of income. Given the continued needs of investment, appropriation would yield little surplus for redistributive consumption. Nor is Panitch justified in equating wage militancy with the pursuit of socialism. He rejects the Wage Fund theory — that there is a fixed amount available in the economy — on the authority of Keynes. Apart from the inconsistency of a Marxist calling on Keynes for authority, this ignores the fundamental Keynsian distinction between bargaining in a recession and conditions of full employment. In the latter, the effect of free collective bargaining can simply be to cause inflation, with no increase in real incomes.

There are others on the Left who argue that incomes policies might be acceptable under socialism but not under the present regime in which overwhelming power is held by employers. In some cases, this is little more than an augustinian postponement of socialist virtue, for, to be consistent, these critics should specify what a socialist society would look like and how incomes would be determined in it. In particular, they should spell out what the role of trade unions would be under socialism and how wage bargaining would be conducted. This, however, would break the tactical alliance between those who support free collective bargaining under capitalism only, and would be prepared to see greater state control under socialism, and trade-union leaders who are concerned to maintain free collective bargaining as a principle. The problem is not helped by there being no examples of command economies in which free collective bargaining and free trade-unionism exist.

This is a problem to which we return below. We see an important theoretical and empirical distinction between Labour's political objectives, derived from its complex ideological and electoral requirements and the industrial demands of the trade unions as expressed in collective bargaining. We also see a distinction between the trade unions' collective bargaining role under capitalism — their primary role — and the pursuit of socialism. This distinction is obscured by the subscription of many union leaders to socialist ideals in theory — but this political dimension has only occasionally been an important influence in industrial affairs rather than a legitimizing principle in serious industrial disputes. Most of the time, the pursuit of socialism has explicitly been seen as the province of the political wing of the movement, acting through the institutions of the state.

The consequence of all this is that Labour governments, like other governments in this century, are obliged to work through the institutions of 'corporate bias', a term coined by Middlemas (1979) to describe the process whereby the large interest groups of labour and capital are co-opted into the 'extended state'. The rather vague term 'corporate bias' indicates the weakness of the state in the bargain.

While state corporatism involves the subordination of voluntary organizations to the needs of state policy, modern British practice is for the state to bargain with interest groups, exchanging favourable policies for political and industrial consent. But there are at least three distinct modes of state behaviour in such a system. The state can act as mere 'ringmaster' between labour and capital, without a fixed policy line of its own; it can take the side of one or the other, seeking to change the conditions of collective bargaining; or it can see itself as a distinct third party, with its own views and priorities. The last need not necessarily be some disembodied view of the 'public interest' or the 'national interest', concepts which have rightly been criticized widely. It could, instead, be a commitment to a specific set of political goals not identifiable with the immediate aims of either management or unions. The achievement of such transcendent goals requires both that the Labour Party consider itself an institution distinct from the trade unions — a difficult task when the unions are constitutionally an integral part of the party — and that the state should acquire real levers of control over the private sector, within a mixed economy. There are many who would argue that the 'contradictions' of this render it a priori impossible. We argue that what it requires is a more sophisticated understanding of the nature of the state and the political system than the Labour Party has shown itself capable of attaining.

We shall examine the issue by looking at key developments in Labour's industrial and economic strategies from the 1960s to the 1980s.

Labour, the trade unions and incomes policies

Labour has consistently tried to resolve these dilemmas by striking bargains with the trade unions whereby, in return for wage restraint, the state will deliver non-wage benefits to union members. This not only allows it to bridge the ideological and interest divisions within the movement itself; it also gives the party a special claim to government in its ability to secure industrial peace through its links with the unions. Such bargains have equally consistently broken down as both sides have found it impossible to deliver. We would argue that an incomes policy is a necessary condition for price stability and growth at full employment; it is not however a sufficient one and Labour governments' over-reliance on it in unfavourable conditions has brought its relations with the unions to some very low points. On the union side, there remains the historic unwillingness to surrender free collective bargaining or to bring its activities within the purview of the state.

In the years before the 1964 election, Labour gave a great deal of attention to the problem. Indeed, by 1964 there seemed to have been established a substantial consensus between the two wings of the movement. In 1963, the TUC voted for economic planning, covering salaries, wages, profits, and the 'social wage' (Middlemas, 1979), though narrowly endorsing another resolution expressing 'complete opposition to any form of wages restraint' (Howell, 1976). That year's Party Conference also pledged support for 'an incomes policy to include salaries, wages, dividends and profits' in the context of an expanding planned economy. It was a formula on which agreement was not difficult to reach. There was considerable support on the Left for incomes policy as a means of socialist redistribution in 1964 as earlier in 1945 (Panitch, 1976). On the Right of the party there was a strong belief in indicative planning; and in the trade unions, which had recently agreed to participate in the National Economic Development Council at the behest of the Conservative government, there was an expectation that rather better terms for such institutional representation would be available from a Labour government. The ambiguity of these various commitments was to become apparent only later.

In December 1964, two months after Labour's election victory, George Brown at the new Department of Economic Affairs was able to get TUC and employers' agreement to a *Joint Statement of Intent* on incomes policy. This was followed by a White Paper on *Machinery of Prices and Incomes Policy* proposing the establishment of the National Board for Prices and Incomes (NBPI). So far, the approach was explicitly voluntary but already doubts were arising as to what voluntarism meant in this context. The TUC apparently had in mind a tripartite system in which the National Economic Development Council (NEDC) would set wage and price guidelines for the NBPI to monitor (Panitch, 1976). Harold Wilson and George Brown, however, seem to have envisaged the government setting the guideline, according to its view of the national interest. As for the operation of a voluntary policy, this could mean at least two distinct things: that compliance with the policy on the part of unions and employers was voluntary, which comes close to saying that there is not really a policy at all; or that the policy would be policed by the trade unions and the TUC themselves, rather than by the state. In either case, radical changes would be needed in the way in which trade unions saw their role and operated.

Time was not to be given for the unions to make this adjustment as, under the pressure of deepening economic crisis, the government moved rapidly towards a statutory policy. A White Paper of November 1965 was followed by a bill empowering the government to delay wage settlements while reference was made to the NBPI, though this was lost with the 1966 general election. The bill's reintroduction in the new Parliament was rapidly followed by the deflationary package and wage freeze of 20 July, to be implemented through a new clause tacked onto the bill. There followed three years of statutory incomes policy, with further legislation in 1967 and 1968, and relations between unions and government coming under ever-increasing strain.

The trade unions, meanwhile, having conceded from 1963 that there was a public interest in wage settlements and that unrestricted free collective bargaining would have to go, were struggling to reconcile this with their traditions and structure and with the implications of wage bargaining entering into the field of public (and therefore state) policy. Several distinct points of view emerged. The TUC narrowly accepted the proposals for statutory control in 1965 and even the freeze in 1966, though out of loyalty to Labour rather than conviction. In 1967, as statutory control continued, Congress narrowly voted against government policy and by 1968 was firmly opposed. At the same time, however, it continued its search for a non-statutory alternative. One answer was a strengthened TUC which could itself patrol a wages policy. George Woodcock, as General Secretary, had long favoured more powerful central control of the movement and as early as 1964, the TUC had set up its own committee to vet wage claims. Though this does not appear to have been very effective, it continued until 1969. A notable convert to this point of view was Frank Cousins, who had resigned as Minister of Technology in 1966 because of the introduction of statutory powers. Now he saw the solution in national bargaining between the TUC and employers to set the basic terms of pay policy. What was objectionable to Cousins was not incomes policy *per se* but state intervention in collective bargaining. In 1966, he told the TUC, 'If the trade unions themselves are going to surrender their authority, I suggest that they will want to surrender it to this body here and not to a Government' (Stewart, 1968). This approach was even taken as far as holding talks with the CBI, with agreement between the two sides, in the words of John Davies, the CBI's Director General, on the need to avoid 'the feeling that we were constantly subject to comment, disagreement and correction by the Government' (Stewart, 1968, p. 175). However, the proposal for the TUC to take on the role of running an incomes policy to have regard to the public interest in wage bargaining ran into two obstacles. It had no means of determining where the wider social interest lay in any given claim; and it lacked control over its own membership.

Other leaders opposed all forms of incomes policy albeit sometimes with an augustinian 'not yet'. This soon became the policy of the Labour Left. While Richard Crossman was discovering the virtues of incomes policy as a socialist instrument, supported by the *New Statesman* (9.9.66), Tribune MPs were declaring that it would be tolerable only in a totally planned economy, where the state controlled prices, investment and production. It took Eric Heffer to (implicitly) point out the ambiguity in this tactical alliance of trade-unionists and state socialists by arguing that, even in a publicly owned economy, trade unions would have to be free 'to defend and develop the interests of their members' (Panitch, 1976).

The question of the trade unions' relationship to the state was raised again by the report of the Donovan Commission on Trade Unions and Employers' Associations and the subsequent proposals of the White Paper, 'In Place of Strife'. Donovan's (1968) report was firmly in the voluntarist tradition. Much attention was given to the fact that two systems of industrial relations had developed, the 'formal' system based on official negotiating machinery at national level and the 'informal' system of bargaining at plant level, with a key role for the shop stewards. Order was to be restored in industrial relations by bringing the two together. The public interest in industrial relations and wage bargaining was recognized, incomes policy was seen as having 'an outstanding contribution' to make to economic growth and the promotion of collective bargaining seen as part of 'public policy'. This did not, however, mean that state regulation was necessary. Rather, an orderly system of collective bargaining should be promoted through voluntary persuasion. Jenkins (1970, pp. 22–3) pointed to a fundamental weakness of this approach in ignoring wider social concerns: 'Modern industrial society contained a public conflict no less troublesome than the private conflict between the "two sides of industry"'. The conflict was between governments, charged with managing the economy so as to produce rapidly-rising prosperity, and wage and salary earners, whose dissatisfactions seemed to grow rather than diminish with prosperity and which were finding a more and more disorderly expression'. It is not quite true to say that Donovan totally ignored this question. In defending its opposition to penalties for trade unions and employers ignoring good industrial practice, the Commission stated, 'The intention of the (proposed Industrial Relations) Act is to promote the reform of industrial relations by establishing a system of registration which will enable society's expectations in the field of industrial relations to be brought home clearly and unambiguously to the boards of companies and trade unions' (Donovan, 1968, p. 51). 'Society' here is a carefully ambiguous term. Either it is assumed, quite unwarrantably, that 'society' has a clearly expressed interest which is knowable and unified, or else the social interest must be expressed authoritatively by the one institution in a position to do this — the state. It was this question which Donovan avoided facing. In a *Note of Reservation*, Andrew Schonfield argued the case for state involvement. While in the past it may have been justifiable to leave trade unions outside the ambit of the law because of their weakness and the possible prejudice of the judiciary, they were now large and influential bodies whose activities had wide social repercussions. So they should be legally regulated, with collective agreements made legally enforceable and restrictive practices controlled. Schonfield's objectives did not diverge fundamentally from those of his fellow commissioners. The vital difference lay in the role of the state in achieving the desired ends.

It was the absence of a clear philosophy of the place of the unions in a democratic society which seems to have concerned Barbara Castle on being given responsibility, as Secretary of State for Employment and Productivity, for implementing the report. Her alternative was to encourage the expansion of trade unionism and an enhancement of union powers in return for a clear framework of union responsibilities. With a wider conception of their goals and duties, unions could become 'a fit partner for a Labour Government engaged in the task of constructing a Social Democracy' (Jenkins, 1970, p. 27). For Harold Wilson, there were more immediate concerns. Strikes were damaging Labour's popularity and there was a need to find something to replace the statutory incomes policy which was coming to an end. In the autumn of 1968 a series of unofficial strikes had gained much publicity, with an adverse effect on both domestic and international opinion. So the White Paper, 'In Place of Strife' appeared early in

1969 with, in addition to many of the Donovan proposals, three 'penal clauses'. These were to give the government powers; to declare a twenty-eight day 'cooling-off' period in industrial disputes; when voluntary procedures failed, to order a settlement in demarcation disputes; and to order a strike ballot in certain circumstances. The proposals had a rough reception in the Cabinet. Several ministers foresaw a major row with the unions, while Anthony Crosland, from the intellectual Right of the party, thought that either Donovan's voluntary approach or (preferably) Schonfield's comprehensive scheme would be preferable to the proposed measures, which would antagonize the unions for little gain.

The story of the defeat of the proposals in the face of union and parliamentary opposition has been told elsewhere (Jenkins, 1970). Part of the reason was, no doubt, Wilson's insistence on a short bill to bring in the main provisions, including the 'penal clauses' in the 1968–9 session, in order to shore up confidence in the government as the incomes policy ended and to restore the authority of the party leadership after the fiasco of the Parliament No. 2 bill (on the reform of the House of Lords). More fundamentally, however, it demonstrated the difficulty for the Labour Party of combining its role as a party of government pursuing clear political goals, with its role as part of the wider 'Labour movement'. The unions had once again insisted upon the assymetry of the relationship. As a constituent element of the party, they could influence political affairs, but intervention by the political wing in industrial bargaining was ruled out. The alternative, as in the case of incomes policy, was organized co-operation. If state intervention to ensure the public interest in industrial relations was ruled out, then perhaps the unions could police themselves as an independent estate. This would involve a strengthened TUC with powers and sanctions over its members. Wilson fought hard for this solution when it had become apparent that the proposals for state intervention were going to be defeated, and, in the TUC *Programme for Action*, he could claim that he had obtained it. But, while the TUC had indeed come a long way in recent years towards being the voice of organized labour, it was ill-fitted to occupy the role of guardian of the public interest. This was, firstly, because it lacked the power and authority to discipline its own members. As George Woodcock, generally a supporter of a stronger role for the TUC, put it, 'The TUC cannot become an agent of the government because the unions cannot become agents of the TUC. Trade unions are essentially representative bodies ultimately responsible to their members' (Panitch, 1976, p. 193). Secondly, it is arguable that it is no part of the proper function of trade unions in society to act as custodians of the general interest. They exist to serve the purposes of their members, working within the legal and economic system which exists. To do this, they need to be independent of both employers and the state, though bargaining with both and undertaking contractual obligations to both, including those which the state may express on behalf of the social interests.

Following Labour's defeat at the 1970 general election, moves were quickly made to re-establish the party's close links with the unions. A Labour Party–TUC Liaison Committee was established, bringing together the National Executive Committee (NEC), the parliamentary leadership, and the General Council of the TUC. It was through this mechanism that the party negotiated the 'social contract', apparently a corporatist deal between a future Labour government and the unions, covering the main elements of economic policy. Already in 1970 the NEC and the Parliamentary Party had agreed on total opposition to the Conservative Industrial Relations Act, promising its repeal and replacement with a scheme based on the Donovan Report, with safeguards against unfair dismissal, disclosure of information, and compulsory recognition of unions. The 1971 Conference went further, calling for repeal of the Act and rejecting any 'state inter-ference with the independent operation of trade unions' or 'legal sanc-tions against trade unions or trade unionists in the field of collective bargaining'. This restatement of the traditional union claim to stand outside the framework of the law and public policy caused some prob-lems for the party side of the Liaison Committee as it appeared to rule out not only the Industrial Relations Act and 'In Place of Strife' but also much of Donovan, for example on the registration of unions and an independent Review Body to promote reform. The party represen-tatives expressed concern that a *laissez-faire* stance towards trade unions was inconsistent with the party's general interventionist posi-tion, that there was still public concern about trade-union power and that, without an independent review body to vet union rule-books, monitor election practices, and adjudicate on cases where individuals were in dispute with their unions, justice would not be seen to be done (RD:333/April 1972). So the NEC–PLP side of the Liaison Committee stuck to the view that the proposed Conciliation and Arbitration Service should have these tasks as well as that of arbitrating in indus-trial disputes. The argument rumbled on for a year until gradually the party side conceded the unions' case. By May 1973 it was agreed that the TUC would set up a review body under its own auspices, consisting of an independent chairman and two union members to examine alleged malpractices, breaches of election, rules and individual cases. Individuals would also have the right to go, first, to a mediator appointed by the Conciliation and Arbitration Service, but it appears that his rulings would be advisory only, with the review body as the final court of appeal (RD:782/May 1973). Policy was at this stage of development when the 1974 election came.

Agreement on other aspects of the 'social contract' proved easier, though only with some fudging of the issues. The main instrument of anti-inflation policy would be price controls and subsidies on basic foods. In this context, Labour would 'seek to conclude with the Trades Union Movement a new wide-ranging social contract designed to curb increases in the cost of living' (Labour Party, 1973, p. 11). That this coded language was indeed a reference to the need for incomes policy was confirmed elsewhere in the same 1973 document. With the Industrial Relations Act out of the way and policies for economic growth and social justice being pursued, the way would be open for a Labour government 'to sit down with the trade unions to hammer out an agreement for the orderly growth of incomes with stable prices' (Labour Party, 1973, p. 24). A standing Royal Commission on Income Distribution would be established without statutory powers to establish a factual basis for discussions about fairness in pay. On its side, the party promised a series of measures on price control, pensions, prescription charges, taxation, housing, land, transport, regional development, industrial training, public ownership, control of private firms, the Common Market, and industrial democracy which, as well as being desirable in themselves, were seen as contributing to a climate in which the unions could exercise moderation in wage claims.

The collapse of the Heath government in the midst of the industrial troubles of 1974 gave Labour the opportunity to put its new schemes into effect and there began an unprecedented period of close co-operation between unions and the state. Early concessions to the unions included the repeal of the Industrial Relations Act and the Housing Finance Act and new legislation giving increased rights to trade unions and greater employment protection and providing for sexual equality and equal pay. New agencies in the employment field, the Manpower Services Commission, the Advisory, Conciliation and

Arbitration Service, and the Health and Safety Executive were established, with trade-union involvement in their running (Coates, 1980). Subsidies were introduced on food and rents were frozen. Union leaders were consulted about government policies as part of the renewed corporatism of the 'social contract'. The other side of the coin was the continuing need for a governing Labour Party to have a policy for incomes — still seen as an inescapable necessity for economic management in a social democracy. However, the mechanism by which state concessions on trade-union powers and the 'social wage' were to be traded for incomes restraint had been specified in only the vaguest terms. The Heath government's Pay Board had been abolished and ministers disclaimed any desire to impose 'wage restraint'; a return to statutory incomes policy had been ruled out by the experience both of the 1960s and of the recent Conservative government. Instead, ministers and union leaders continued to believe that, by changing the political climate and creating a measure of greater social justice, they could induce changes in bargaining behaviour. As Jack Jones put it, 'Provided we get Government action in things like prices, rents, and so on . . . then there will be reaction at the grass roots level' (quoted in Coates, 1980, p. 60). This was in reality far from a corporatist deal, being much more in the tradition of the Donovan report, concerned with good industrial relations on the shop floor but failing to link this to central questions of state economic management. If it could work at all, it would only be in the long term and, even then, the reconciliation of pay bargaining and national economic policies would be, at least, problematic. Of course, it was not given to the government to await the long-term. The inflationary spiral of 1974 and 1975 called for an immediate response. Both union leaders and ministers were alarmed at the prospect of hyper-inflation and the threat to the future of the Labour government which it posed; rank-and-file opinion, too, was ready for emergency measures. These came in the form of the flat-rate £6 limit sponsored by Jack Jones, a piece of 'rough justice' which could be defended as egalitarian as well as counter-inflationary. The universal acceptance of this was followed by an agreed 4.5 per cent norm the following year, which also gained general acceptance.

All that this showed, however, was that wages policies could be made to stick for short periods in an emergency, a finding already known from previous experience. What was not clear was how this co-operation could be translated into longer-term arrangements for reconciling wage bargaining with the social and economic priorities of a Labour government, or with the constraints imposed by the imperatives of running an open, mixed economy. By the time the government proposed a third stage of the policy, voluntary compliance was diminishing and all that could be obtained from union leaders, faced with rank-and-file unrest, was an undertaking on the 'twelve month rule' between settlements. Determined to persist with pay policy, the government was now at a loss for a means to enforce it. The full statist approach of statutory policy was rejected as unworkable, even if the necessary legislation could have been got through Parliament. So government was forced back on those instruments which were at the disposal of the state, notably public sector wage settlements and the blacklisting of firms in the private sector which settled above the targets. Such firms would not receive government contracts or other forms of discretionary help, such as export credit guarantees. The breakdown of the policy during stage three and the collapse of stage four in the 'winter of discontent' have been well documented elsewhere and a variety of explanations put forward. Writers on the Left (e.g. Coates, 1980) have emphasized the government's failure to deliver its side of the contract. Real incomes fell during the course of the policy, unemployment rose, subsidies were phased out and, following the IMF crisis of 1976, public expenditure programmes cut back. Conservative writers attribute the failure to the excessive power of trade unions, encouraged by deference to them on the part of the Labour government.

A balanced assessment of the failure of the 'social contract', however, must examine separately the concessions made by government to trade-union status and influence and the concessions made in material matters; and must distinguish the reactions of trade-union leaders from those of the rank and file. The concessions made to trade unions' status and the recognition of their role in public life were considerable and were adhered to until the end of the government's term. There is little doubt that this helped create the climate in which the TUC and major union leaders were prepared to accept stages one and two of the pay policy. On the other hand, developments since the 1960s had continued to shift the focus of power within unions to the shop-floor and it was here that discontent with the squeeze on real wages was most felt. So élite bargains, the essence of the corporatist approach, between TUC leaders and ministers could not, in the long run, secure shop-floor compliance. Concessions to the status of union leaders, receptions at Downing Street, and memberships of new quangos were of little relevance at the grass roots and, in any case, the supply of these was running out by 1976. More material concessions would be needed if union leaders were to be able to keep their members in line and this was incompatible with the government's judgement that, following the oil crisis, reductions in living standard would be necessary. Nor is it adequate to argue that, had the 'social wage' been protected and increased, compliance with wage restraint could have been secured. However desirable increased social expenditure might have been for a more socialist programme, and however unjustified on social and economic ground the IMF cuts of 1976–7, it is clear that the groundswell of discontent against the incomes policy was directed towards increases in private incomes. Indeed, experience since has shown that the political beneficiary of this has not been left-wing socialism but the acquisitive individualism of Mrs Thatcher's Conservative Party.

Nor can we simply argue that, had Labour pursued a class-based strategy of distributing wealth and income in favour of the 'working class' there would have been plenty available for private and public consumption. The struggles of the late 1970s were about the distribution of incomes within the wage-earning section of the population, exacerbated of course by the lack of overall growth in the economy, but presenting problems to be faced in virtually any economic climate. Indeed, another finding of experience since 1979 is that it is a great deal easier to obtain wage restraint in a climate of recession and high unemployment than in the conditions of growth to which Labour governments aspire.

So once again we must draw the conclusion that there is a major potential conflict between Labour's tasks as a government and the immediate interests of trade-unionists and that this would apply even if a Labour government were pursuing a more radical socialist strategy. Indeed, it would be more so if the state were the predominant employer or, in a planned economy, alone determined the distribution of rewards. The public sector strikes of 1978–9, affecting not private capitalists but ordinary people, at a time when other workers were complaining of the burden of high taxation, provide an indication of the conflicts which would have to be reconciled in a socialist state, whoever owned the means of production and to which Labour has yet to face up. The emergence of the 'social contract' and the concept of the 'social wage' in the early 1970s suggested that the

Labour movement might at last be confronting some of these issues but its inability to reconcile its roles in government or to develop the machinery of a truly 'corporatist' state shows how far it was from success.

Managing the Economy

We have noted Labour's traditional reluctance to spell out the desired end state of its policies, the balance between public and private sectors which would prevail in the ideal 'socialist' economy, or the relationship between long-term goals and short-term management. The Attlee government had inherited the mixture of views which had characterized the inter-war period. Then some Labour thinkers, such as the Webbs, despairing of the ability of capitalism to reform itself as predicted by early Fabian theory, had opted for state-imposed planning on the Soviet model. Others took up the milder 'indicative planning' much favoured by 'middle opinion' in all parties, often combining this with the ideas of Keynes, whose work seemed to offer a method of economic management avoiding both the economic waste of unregulated capitalism and the political repression of Soviet Communism. Keynes, however, was no socialist and a deep suspicion remained of his ideas as mere financial tinkering with capitalism, no substitute for direct measures of physical intervention (Winch, 1972). Under the Attlee government, much use was made initially of physical planning instruments inherited from the war, but from about 1948 the focus shifted towards Keynsian macro-economic management of a type largely indistinguishable from that pursued by the Conservatives on their return to power in 1951. Certainly, Labour had put through an ambitious programme of nationalization but this mostly affected declining basic industries and public utilities and, with the exception of iron and steel and road haulage, provoked little opposition. Apart from the Bank of England, whose ownership was transferred to the state, the financial sector was left untouched. Nor were the newly nationalized industries used as the instruments of purposive planning. In accordance with Morrisonian doctrine, they were endowed with considerable independence, their boards filled with private industrialists. Leruez (1975) points to the reluctance of trade-union leaders to take positions of responsibility in the nationalized industries for fear of prejudicing their bargaining role, and to the lack of public officials with the requisite skills to take on management roles, bringing the objectives of state policy more directly into their affairs. Even the physical planning of the early years is seen by Leruez less as an extension of state power in the economy than as an extension of business influence in the state.

> even if they [the Labour Government] were not going to change the actual machinery they would at least have shown more concern for safeguarding the rights of the state. Paradoxically, not only did nothing of the kind happen, but if anything the involvement of business intensified (Leruez, 1975, p. 63).

So nationalization was not used as a means of transferring power in society or as the instrument of a radically different economic policy.

The move away from planning was opposed by the Left who continued to argue the case for nationalization and stronger public intervention into the 1950s. They were opposed by the 'revisionists' like Crosland and Gaitskell, who believed that Keynsian macro-economic policies with only broad-scale planning could permit economic growth and expanded social services, with the market determining the pattern of private consumption. In *The Future of Socialism*, Crosland (1956) argued, in a way reminiscent of the early Fabians, that social, economic and political change had already laid the foundations of a socialist society. Capitalism had been transformed by the growing economic power of the state, the power of trade unions and a shift of power within industry from owners to managers and technical experts. In 1937, Laski had written, 'Whatever the forms of the state, political power will, in fact, belong to the owners of economic power'. Now, according to Crosland, that should be turned on its head; 'whatever the modes of economic production, economic power will, in fact, belong to the owners of political power' (Crosland, 1956, p. 29). In 1956, Crosland could write as though the problems of production had been all but solved. Economic growth and full employment were assured by the mixed economy, neither capitalist nor state socialist; the state had the means to ensure its fair distribution and division between private and social consumption. Gaitskell took his revisionism to the point of attempting to remove from the party constitution the famous clause IV (4), the ambiguous commitment to the 'common ownership of the means of production, distribution and exchange, and the best obtainable system of popular administration and control of each industry or service'. His defeat led to a stalemate between the revisionists and traditionalists which was resolved only temporarily by the commitment to 'planning' in a form which could be sold to both sides.

While Labour were still debating the meaning of planning, their clothes were stolen by the Conservatives who, in 1962, announced their conversion to indicative planning and established the tripartite National Economic Development Council (NEDC or 'Neddy') along with Economic Development Councils ('little Neddies') for major industrial sectors. Neddy planning was a very mild form of corporatism, involving the concertation of action by the three parties to identify obstacles to growth and create a climate of confidence. It did, however, mark a recognition by the Conservative government that Keynsian macro-economic policies combined with industrial *laissez-faire* were not sufficient to allow Britain to keep pace with the industrial growth of its competitors. The 'stop-go' cycle produced by periodic balance of payments crises was damaging the country's prospects for long-term growth and only a more concerted approach could reconcile the needs of industry, unions and the state.

For Labour, the need to achieve steady economic growth was even greater, as it had not merely to show greater competence than the Conservatives in the efficient management of the economy, but also to finance its ambitious social programmes. The formula of a partnership between state and private sector was ideal for this purpose though for doctrinal as well as practical reasons it was necessary to deride the Conservative exercise as 'toothless' and to promise firmer, more interventionist measures, with the planning function brought into government itself. *Signposts for the Sixties* (Labour Party, 1963) promised a National Plan, with targets for each sector and a National Industrial Planning Board to 'ensure speedy and purposive industrial investment'. There would be new tax and financial policies to encourage investment and 'greater control over pension funds and private insurance companies'. Public ownership would be extended to acquire a stake in the growth points of the economy, to control industries which relied on government assistance and to counterbalance the power of the giant corporations. On its return in 1964, Labour duly set up the Department of Economic Affairs under George Brown, which immediately started work on the National Plan, this being published in September 1965 with considerable fanfare.

For all the rhetoric about planning with 'teeth', Labour's approach to its plan did not differ fundamentally from that of the Conservatives. The National Plan was 'indicative', based, essentially on the belief that, if all parties can be convinced that a given rate of growth is going to take place they will plan accordingly, so giving rise to the growth itself. The Plan's role is to set out the prospects for growth, the main priority areas, and the principal bottlenecks to be tackled. It was a non-zero-sum game in which, by concertation of their activities, government and private sector could attain faster growth than would otherwise be possible, so providing the resources both for increased private consumption and for Labour's ambitious social programmes. The reconciliation of state and private interests would be helped, of course, by the renewal which Wilson wanted to see in company boardrooms as in the personnel of the Civil Service. Ambitious young meritocrats of the type which Crosland (1956) and later J. K. Galbraith (1967) claimed were already the dominant influence in public and private sectors were to be given their head, sweeping away the 'deadwood' of the past.

There was a great deal of wishful thinking involved in the National Plan. The starting-point was the target of a 25 per cent growth rate by 1970. Firms were asked what the implications of such a rate would be; as most of them could be expected to reply that, in that case, they could expand, there was an element of circularity in the exercise. On the other hand, where firms indicated that their expansion would be at a lower rate, the Government had few powers or resources to change this, at least during the time-scale of the plan. It is true that the little Neddies continued to work with individual industries, seeking to remove obstacles to expansion but, as Brittan (1971, p. 318) comments, they 'had neither direct powers over the industries concerned nor incentives to offer them . . . the government's mistake was to exaggerate both the magnitude of their influence and the speed with which it could take effect'. Another piece of wishful thinking was the treatment of the balance of payments constraint and the 'manpower gap' identified in the plan which, effectively, amounted to an admission that the target was unattainable. Most observers now agree that a devaluation was an essential precondition for the Plan but Harold Wilson consistently ruled this out, partly to avoid Labour being branded as the party of devaluation but also because he seems to have seen it as a phoney solution, avoiding the basic structural problems, which required a 'direct physical intervention' (Brittan, 1971, p. 293). This reassertion of the traditional Labour preference for physical measures of planning and distrust of mere financial tinkering might have had some force (though as a complement to devaluation rather than a substitute) had such direct intervention been taking place. Instead, the means of intervention, with a few exceptions, were the same as those available to the Conservatives.

Then there was the fatal split between long-term planning and short-term financial management, between the DEA and the Treasury. The rationale for this was unclear. George Brown appears to have desired a predominant role for the DEA as economic 'over-lord', with the Treasury and Board of Trade in decidedly subordinate capacities. Harold Wilson, on the other hand, saw value in a 'creative tension' between the two, which would bring the debates about economic strategy into the Cabinet. In practice, the agreed division of responsibilities was that the DEA would look after long-term planning and the allocation of physical resources, while the Treasury looked after financial policy and short-term management (Budd, 1978). The result was an acute conflict between the Plan and the needs of short-term stabilization policy, with conflicting signals being sent to the private sector. Even before the Plan's publication, expenditure cutbacks in June and July 1965 had made the achievement of its targets unlikely (Leruez, 1975) and it was finally killed by the deflationary package of July 1966, intended to stem the balance of payments crisis and so head off devaluation.

Some of these weaknesses in the Plan could have been avoided with more thought and a greater willingness to face up to difficult choices. For the purposes of our argument, however, the key weakness was the failure to assess the possible scope of national planning and the powers of the state in relation to its realization. Much of the theory of indicative planning was imported uncritically from France, with its powerful statist tradition and relatively weak capitalism and trade-unionism. The state in France has long been a major motor of industrial growth and possesses the personnel and instruments for intervention and joint activity with the private sector. Britain's Labour government, on the other hand, could but rely on the powers of persuasion, acting for the most part indirectly through representative groups from private industry. At the same time, subject to a crippling balance of payments constraint and speculative pressure against the pound, it was not even in a position to secure implementation of its side of the bargain so that the theory of indicative planning as confidence building did not have a chance to work.

The reluctance of the government to assume greater powers of state control is striking. Earlier proposals for greater control over the finance sector, for example for the direction of pension and insurance funds into investment, were dropped, doubtless from fear of the effects on confidence in the City at a time of continuing weakness for the pound. Work was started on proposals for the use of state purchasing power as a lever for industrial modernization but all that emerged by May 1967 was a notably weak White Paper disclaiming any intention of wielding the big stick (Davis, 1968). A report produced by Robert Maxwell for the Parliamentary Labour Party proposing a Public Sector Purchasing Board to secure value for money, and encourage exports, technological change, observance of the prices and incomes policy, structural reorganization and regional development, gathered dust. The Industrial Expansion Bill, allowing the state to take equity shares in companies, was toned down after protests from the CBI and presented largely as a tidying-up measure.

Nationalization under the 1964–70 government was limited to iron and steel and parts of the transport sector. As with the earlier national-izations, little attempt was made to use it as an instrument of state economic control — the 'commanding heights' theory. Rather, there was continuity with the Conservative policy stemming from the White Paper of 1961 (Posner, 1972), with the government seeking to create a framework in which the industries would be able to perform as 'normal' commercial operations. In practice, the government con-tinued the practice of informal interference in their management while officially subscribing to the 'arm's length' theory of control.

One interventionist device which was introduced, and on which the government placed great hopes, was the Industrial Reorganization Corporation. This represented an attempt to intervene at the level of the individual firm, precisely the type of 'direct physical intervention' on which much of the party had set store. There was also the feeling that British private industry was lacking in entrepreneurial spirit and that the state, in collaboration with the more dynamic new managers, should make up the deficiency. At the same time, a more selective approach to intervention would be less costly, less bureaucratic, and more effective than nationalization on the Morrisonian model. After the collapse of the National Plan, this became the main strand of long-term economic policy (Young, 1974). Yet, apart from believing in the necessity for industrial modernization and international com-petitiveness, Labour had, at the outset, very little idea of what the IRC should or could do. It was inevitably attacked by the Conservatives as 'backdoor nationalization'; nothing could have been further from the truth. Its first director, Grierson, was said by Davis (1968, pp. 53–4) to have seen the IRC as 'a forum where directors of large companies could discuss their ideas for mergers and reorganizations without the feeling that they were talking to the Government but knowing that public money would be forthcoming'. This gave way to a more active approach under the influence of Lord Kearton after Grierson had resigned because of differences with the interventionist ideas of ministers. But still the emphasis was on encouragement of private enterprise, Kearton making 'no secret of his dislike of nationalization . . . and his belief in efficiency and profit' (quoted in Young, 1974, p. 48). There were no government representatives on the Board, which consisted almost exclusively of industrialists, and Sir Joseph Lockwood, the second chairman, declared, 'I don't want anyone who could remotely be described as a backdoor nationaliser' (Young, 1974, p. 49). Further, although it was meant to supply loans only where other finance was unavailable, it had to earn a commercial rate of return on its capital (and did so). In the event, the IRC concentrated on encouraging mergers and rationalization in industry with the consent of the firms involved, relying largely on persuasion and only rarely on the use of its market powers. Its activities were not related to other strands of government economic policy. It did not even have a staff of economists to work out sectoral strategies and did not come into operation until after the effective collapse of the National Plan (Graham, 1972); and there was no attempt to cater for the social consequences of rationalization with its frequent job losses. So, while the IRC may have played a modest role in encouraging the modernization of British industry and certainly, for good or ill, was the catalyst for a number of major private-sector mergers, it cannot be seen as a significant extension of state power in the economy or a means of bringing the private sector in behind strategic public policy objectives. This was a source of grievance to the Labour Left, who continued to demand a politically informed strategy, directed by ministers and not administered by industrialists themselves.

Labour's 1970 defeat produced a swing to the Left in industrial policy as in other fields. This took the form, partly of a reassertion of traditional nationalization measures but also of a search for means by which state economic planning could be made more effective. Under the influence of the Sussex economist, Stuart Holland, the National Executive Committee, through its working parties, came to adopt large parts of what was later to be known as the Alternative Economic Strategy. We have noted the difficulty of the 1964–70 government in affecting industrial change at the level of the firm and the consequent dependence of its plans on voluntary compliance through exhortation and the use of intermediaries. Holland's analysis pointed a way out of this problem by concentrating on the meso-economic sector, the small number of very large firms which accounted for the bulk of industrial production, jobs, and exports (Holland, 1975). Control of these enterprises would provide the link between macro and micro-economic policies and give the state direct leverage on industrial decision-making. Such control could be achieved by a combination of public ownership, selective intervention through a National Enterprise Board — a powerful state holding company — and 'Planning Agreements' with the major firms. These ideas duly appeared in 'Labour's Programme 1973', proposing a massive increase in state control and direction of the economy. The major proposals were:

(a) A system of Planning Agreements with all major companies, including the largest hundred or so manufacturing firms laying down objectives in employment, investment, prices, exports and regional development. Selective assistance to industry would be channelled through the Planning Agreements, though the programme was carefully vague as to whether all assistance would be dependent on the signing of a Planning Agreement, as demanded by the Left.

(b) An expansion of Public ownership to include North Sea Oil, the docks, shipbuilding and possibly aircraft manufacture, pharmaceuticals and some financial institutions.

(c) The establishment of a National Enterprise Board to take over existing state holdings in some industries and to establish a large state holding across a wide field of industry. Early in its life it would acquire some 25 of the largest firms and would go on to take a controlling interest in all firms in which it intervened. Clearly, it was intended here that the NEB should seize, in the old phrase, the 'commanding heights' of the economy. It would also establish new enterprises to compete with existing firms in sectors lacking in dynamism and entrepreneurship.

(d) A new Industry Act which would incorporate these measures and give increased powers for the state to obtain information from companies, to take shareholdings and to prevent foreign takeover of British companies.

Even in 1973, these proposals provoked some opposition within the party. While the idea of selective intervention and planning agreements of some sort were widely supported — and indeed their proponents could point to working parallels in France and Italy — wholesale nationalization horrified the 'revisionists' who saw it as unnecessary, unpopular and ineffective as a means of economic planning. Wilson himself insisted on removing the reference to the nationalization of the top twenty-five firms at the 1973 Conference, a move widely regarded on the Left as the first step to the new betrayal. The nationalization proposal, however, was more of a gesture towards Labour's traditional gods than part of a new economic policy. We have seen that Labour has had little idea of what to do with the nationalized industries other than run them as commercial enterprises under business leaders. Of much more interest were the proposals to exert the force of state policy over the whole of industry, both public and private, and the marshalling of the power resources which the state possessed to do this. It was still unclear whether the party at this time regarded private industry as a powerful enemy to be overcome with superior force or as a broken army, to be retrained and re-equipped by the state which, in return for its help, would demand its utter loyalty. The reality, of course, is that there were strong and weak industries, rising and declining firms, and that a coherent industrial policy would have to address itself to both, in appropriate terms.

After Labour returned to office in 1974, however, the radical *dirigiste* elements in the strategy rapidly gave way to the more familiar style of tripartite compromise. Initially, with Tony Benn and Eric Heffer at the Department of Industry, ideas were floated for firm planning agreements, with all financial aid to top firms to be made dependent on them (Coates, 1980). Already in 1974, though, Benn was being kept on a tight rein and at a crucial stage Wilson himself took charge of the White Paper preparations. The consequence was that when this appeared as *The Regeneration of British Industry* planning agreements were to be voluntary, with state aid not tied to them; nor were the unions to be party to them, as proposed by Benn and the Left. The National Enterprise Board was to have power to take stakes in industry and to give priority to projects in assisted areas, to reducing monopolies, to exports and import substitution, and to extending industrial democracy. To this extent, it represented a more inter-ventionist instrument than the old IRC. On the other hand, there was no suggestion that it was to be the predominant force in the industrial economy envisaged in earlier Labour plans. As the proposals moved on from White Paper to the stage of a bill, they were further modified under fierce pressure from the CBI. Responsibility for its drafting was removed from the Department of Industry altogether and placed in the Cabinet Office under the personal supervision of the Prime Minister (Shanks, 1977). The resulting Industry Bill further limited the NEB's terms of reference and removed the unions from any role in planning agreements, which were now seen as an adjunct to conventional sectoral planning and not as a substitute for it. Following the defeat of the Left in the EEC referendum in May 1975, Benn and Heffer were removed from the Industry Department which, under Eric Varley, moved still closer to the position of the CBI, itself still lobbying vigorously against any extension of state control of industry. Further concessions were made at the Committee stage of the bill so that, according to Wilks (1981, p. 405) the planning agreement, originally a means by which government could gain control over corporate interests, had strangely reversed its flow of influence. In the words of the Department of Industry discussion document, 'one of the principal benefits of Planning Agreements is likely to lie in the opportunity they will provide the government across the whole field of its activities to attune its policies to the needs and plans of industry' (Wilks, 1981, p. 405).

This drift of policy back to the tripartite consensus is not to be seen simply as the result of business interests forcing a Labour government to do their bidding, though it is undoubtedly true that the influence of the CBI remained very strong and increased significantly around 1975. It also reflects an unwillingness on the part of the Labour government and the trade unions to take the path of state control of the industrial economy, with all its implications. Despite the rhetoric of the social contract, indeed, there remained much common ground between the CBI and the TUC on the role of the state in industrial matters. The CBI moved away from its support for state regulation of industrial relations, as its Director General indiscretely revealed during the February 1974 general election campaign; and in a series of unpublicized meetings, the two organizations had reached a sufficient degree of consensus by 1975 to put in a joint paper to the NEDC calling for a return to tripartite indicative planning, with macro forecasts provided by the Treasury and detailed sector forecasts prepared by the EDCs (the little neddies). The unions had, in fact, never been enthusiastic supporters of state-directed planning agreements (Wilks, 1981) seeing them as an intellectual abstraction and, in their left-wing form, a recipe for increased shop-floor power. National-level tripartitism was a more familiar role for the unions and one which closely parallelled their contemporary initiatives on incomes policy.

This approach was followed in the 'industrial strategy' initiative, launched through the NEDC in November 1975. This was a tripartite agreement to give priority to industrial investment over consumption and social expenditure, with action to ensure the necessary profits, improved manpower policies and greater disclosure of information (Budd, 1978). A new National Plan was rejected as too inflexible but use was to be made of the National Enterprise Board and Planning Agreements. The Chancellor was to take account of the industrial strategy in making his budget judgement and for the first time an Industrial Policy division was established in the Treasury. The principal mechanism for implementing the strategy, however, was a series of Sector Working Parties (SWPs), of which there were soon thirty-nine, some drawn from existing little neddies and others newly established.

While some sectoral aid under the 1975 Industry Act was allocated in accordance with SWP priorities, the strategy was to have very little by way of 'teeth', so repeating the experience of the 1960s. The only Planning Agreement actually signed was with the American car firm Chrysler, following a state rescue in contradiction to the strategy for the industry. The NEB was saddled with some very large 'lame ducks', notably British Leyland and Rolls Royce, which absorbed a great deal of finance and attention; for the rest, it concentrated on small and medium firms where its limited resources could have some impact. There was no question of taking the 'commanding heights' of the economy or acting in an aggressive, entrepreneurial manner. Rather, the state continued to look after those declining industrial sectors unable to compete internationally but regarded as essential for social or economic reasons while leaving the modernization of industry to a system of voluntary co-operation in which the state was but one party. Once again, there was no attempt to strengthen state control of the finance sector. The poor record of British financial institutions in putting money into industrial investment was recognized as a major concern but here too the approach was resolutely voluntarist, with Finance for Industry being set up by the City itself at the urging of Harold Lever who, as Chancellor of the Duchy of Lancaster had a roving ministerial responsibility for financial institutions. There was no question of direction of investment finance, let alone state ownership of the major financial institutions.

Why should the two Labour governments have adopted such a weak stance towards private industry? Certainly, they were subject to considerable pressure from industrial groups, notably the CBI, but why should the state accommodate industrialists' pressures so readily? We have already indicated our dissatisfaction with the Marxist view that the state is necessarily constrained to act in this way; so left-wing criticisms of leadership weaknesses are at least partially justified. On the other hand, we see considerable force in Lindblom's (1977) argument as to the predominant weight of business influence in the politics of market economies. By presenting their demands as essential for the attainment of consensus goals such as economic growth and employment, business leaders can endow them with a legitimacy denied to other groups. Their interests become identified with those of workers and with the general interest. Union leaders, seeing their role as that of extracting for their members a share of corporate profits, have a vested interest in the maintenance of profitable industry; as we have seen they are often little interested in ownership or control. Thus they are often willing to accept management's view of what is 'good for industry', while of course dissenting from individual actions where these adversely affect jobs or wages. Hence their willingness to accept the Industrial Strategy's emphasis on industrial investment at the expense of social expenditure, based though it was on the dubious notion that it is 'productive' manufacturing industry which supports the 'non-productive' service sector. So, while the unions certainly had their own distinctive concerns in the fields of incomes policy and industrial law, they could not be expected to constitute a counter-vailing force to business in exerting pressure on central economic policy-making.

Industry's pressure on government was, it appears, rarely accompanied by overt threats; though this did happen, as in the Chrysler case in 1976 when the US multinational threatened to close its British operations unless given state help. Rather, the climate in government is such as to be receptive to business demands accompanied only by implied threats in the form of an indication of the inevitable consequences of failure to provide the right sorts of incentives. Lindblom (1977, p. 179) claims that governments do not usually 'enter into an explicit exchange with businessmen. Mutual adjustment is often impersonal and distant. It operates through an unspoken deference of administrations, legislatures and courts to the needs of business. And it relies on a multitude of common understandings shared by the two groups of leaders, business and governmental, with respect to the conditions under which enterprises can or cannot profitably operate.' British Labour governments in the 1960s and 1970s entered into more explicit exchanges than this implies but the mechanism of influence is the same, based on shared values and criteria for policy. Undoubtedly, too, the majority of civil servants in the main economic departments, themselves generalists, saw industrial issues through the eyes of businessmen, the 'experts' in the subject, rather than from a distinctively state perspective. One must also allow that the 1974-9 government's parliamentary position was parlous in the extreme and that public opinion was by this time very hostile to measures which smacked of 'nationalization'.

To challenge this would require not only more political will than those governments showed but also a more careful consideration of the relative place of political authority and market criteria in industrial policy. In the 1960s, Labour sought a convergence of the two with indicative planning which would reward the efficient in private industry and achieve public goals at the same time. Failing to equip itself with the necessary tools and allowing itself to be blown off course by short-term crises, it succeeded in neither. In the 1970s, it moved towards a stronger statist stand but in government reverted to a voluntarist policy in which industry was helped and encouraged to put its own house in order but the legitimacy of private business leadership was not challenged.

Meanwhile, in the course of the late 1970s, the party itself was moving to adopt the 'Alternative Economic Strategy' (AES) — an elaboration of the pre-1974 interventionist ideas — as the centrepiece of its policy platform, despite the lack of success in convincing the government of its merits. The 'AES' is often presented as a single, agreed strategy for the economy; in fact there are several versions and emphasis is put on different aspects by its various exponents. What all have in common is the use of increased state power to overcome the constraints on the attainment of full employment and economic growth. These constraints are seen as stemming from the state's dependence internally and externally on capital.

As outlined by the Conference of Socialist Economists (CSE, 1980 p. 6), the main elements are:

— A policy for expansion aimed at restoring full employment and raising living standards, based on a planned reflation of the economy primarily through increases in public spending.
— Planned controls on foreign trade and international capital movements to protect the balance of payments and prevent the flight of capital.
— An industrial strategy based on extending public ownership (including financial institutions) and planning at the level of the firm through Planning Agreements tied to an extensive network of industrial democracy.

— A national economic plan co-ordinating macro-economic policies with industrial planning.
— Control of inflation based on price control.

As adopted by the party in the course of the 1970s, the AES contained three key themes, planning, nationalization, and import controls. Planning was now seen not in the consensus terms of the 1960s but as a means of increasing state control and reducing the power of the private sector. To this end, control would have to be exercised at the level of the individual firm, rather than at the level of industrial sectors as in the past. So, instead of industry being relied upon to respond to government policy in its own self-interest, it would be made to respond, even against its own interests. Effectively, this meant moving from the weak societal corporatism implied in the concertation approaches of the past to a form of 'state corporatism' in which the state was clearly the senior partner. The main target would be Holland's 'meso-economic' level, between the 'micro' and the 'macro', comprising large firms whose activities could significantly affect government economic management policies. Control at this level would provide direct influence on investment, growth, and employment. The principal means of such control would be strong planning agreements, with all state aid to large firms channelled through them.

The nationalization proposals were the most ambitious to which the party had ever committed itself. They included the acquisition of a successful company operating in each of the key sectors of industry and commerce, to be controlled by the NEB and other public holding companies; priority action for a major public stake in pharmaceuticals, construction and building materials; diversification of existing nationalized industries such as the National Coal Board and British National Oil Corporation; a significant stake in the financial system; agricultural land and land required for development; a major stake in the fishing industry; North Sea Oil; and municipal enterprise. The purpose was to take public ownership beyond the basic industries of the past into growth sectors and into manufacturing and services, to provide a competitive stimulus to other firms and to ensure control of the commanding heights of the economy.

Import controls were adopted following the recommendation of the Cambridge Economic Policy Group, who had pointed to the difficulties in a Keynsian reflation, given Britain's propensity to suck in imports and the weak competitive position of its industry. Following the IMF crisis of 1976, they became a major part of the Left's strategy for breaking out of Britain's international constraints.

The AES was a set of policies devised by the party's intellectuals with appeal to various sections of the movement but it has been promoted not as a shopping list of items for a future government but as a strategy for the movement, linking its political and industrial wings and harnessing the power of the state to that of organized labour. As such, it depends vitally on its internal coherence and the ability of each of its elements to support the others. It was also seen by its progenitors as a break with capitalism, 'substituting social for market forms of control' (CSE, 1980, p. 8), loosening Britain's ties with the market order of world capitalism (Gamble, 1982). There are tremendous intellectual difficulties with this, hinging precisely on the role of the state and the potential for using it to effect a radical shift in power through the mechanisms suggested. The planning agreements recommended by Holland (1975) and others as a means of controlling the meso-economic sector must, if they are to be agreed, involve some give-and-take by both sides. Multinationals are unlikely willingly to co-operate in their own euthenasia. So in reality the AES represents a recognition of corporate power and the need for the state to treat with it and, presumably, modify its policies to take corporate concerns, particularly on profitability, into account. This may well be the only practical way to achieve economic planning in the modern mixed economy but it is a long way from the radical break with capitalism and social democracy hailed by the CSE (1980, p. 8). Such corporatist arrangements have long prevailed under right-wing governments in countries such as France and Japan. Nor is the role of nationalized industry in the AES clear. In places, it appears that the aim is state capitalism to give the dynamism lacking in British entrepreneurs. This is the rationale behind the proposal for a state firm in every sector. Yet, to provide the necessary competitive spur, such state enterprises would have to be efficient in conventional financial terms and profitable — there is no suggestion that they would be subsidized in order to undercut the private sector. In that case, they cannot represent a move from market to social criteria for success. This problem is recognized in a slightly different way by the CSE (1980) who express their doubts about the policy of setting up state industries to compete with private firms in key sectors.

We have characterized the AES as a corporatist approach. Its supporters, of course, would deny this and are at pains to insist that it is not merely a means of managing capitalism but a radical alternative to it, a means of establishing working-class hegemony in economic decision-making. Yet its practical expression consists of a series of state policies. Its political strategy in consequence rests uneasily between the social-democratic view of the state as planner and redistributor, coexisting with capitalist enterprise, the Marxist view of a unified working-class interest which will come to supersede both state and capitalism, and a slightly confused version of corporatist theory, one which fails to specify the power balance so crucial to the characterization of different types of corporatist arrangement. The idea appears to be that the state will be one of the mechanisms by which the working class will come into its own, proceeding then to impose its own alternative criteria for production and distribution. In the course of the argument, however, the nature of the state itself as an institution and set of relationships tends to get lost — it warrants a mere one and a half pages in the 1980 CSE book. Yet, clearly the state is central to the whole enterprise, as the body to be invested with massive new powers. The transformation this would require both in the state and in existing working-class institutions has been neglected in favour of an assumption that both would be responsive to radical policies emanating from the political wing of the Labour movement.

Little thought is given to the machinery of government. Most versions of the AES include provision for a National Planning Commission but the vital question of whether this is to be an arm of the state or a tripartite institution is left unsettled (RD:822/April 1981). So the extent of trade-union and employer veto power over planning proposals is unknown. Certainly, most of the advocates of AES see a need for reform of the civil service on the lines examined in Chapter 6 but the assumption often made, as we note, is that the recruitment of more civil servants of working-class backgrounds will do the trick. The issue of the need to train public-sector managers to run public enterprises is another neglected issue, often dismissed when the question is raised as mere old-fashioned Fabian managerialism.

It is only relatively recently that advocates of the AES have begun to take seriously the criticism of its centralizing bias. From the beginning, certainly, the proposals for massive increases in state power were offset by rhetorical commitments to workers' control; but no attempt was made to face up to the contradictions in the two ideas. It was merely assumed that the policies advocated by the Labour Left would be supported by the 'working class' so that increases in shop-floor power would reinforce the socialists state rather than act as a constraint on it. When it comes to practical proposals, it is the centralized perspective that is dominant. Thus, in a 1981 paper (RD:680/Jan. 1981) Stuart Holland writes that 'Central Government should in principle be concerned essentially with *strategic* planning issues; individual enterprises and local government can feasibly be concerned with the *tactical* planning of implementation', though he recognizes that the frontier between strategic and tactical issues is not rigid. Of the three levels of planning — macro, meso, and micro — local government, Holland considered, could be concerned with the latter. Such a hierarchical vision is a long way from the workers' control philosophy which is the AES' subordinate theme.

A familiar criticism of the AES is that it amounts to an advanced programme of British nationalism as compatible with a right-wing corporatist regime as with a socialist reconstruction. Jenkins and Minnerup (1984, p. 130) describe it as a strategy for a 'state-regulated, national-capitalist siege economy' while from outside the Labour party, Nairn (1981, p. 394) clearly sees the AES as a 'programme of nationalist reindustrialisation'. While granting that such a programme 'viewed in the abstract' is neither revolutionary nor socialist, he insists that in the British context it must be so, presenting, as it does, a frontal challenge to the internationalization of capital. We can agree that the implications of advanced versions of AES may be revolutionary in implications. Whether they are necessarily socialist and in what sense, however, will depend on the very questions about the distribution of power and income which the alternative strategists avoid. Few of them would, in any case, follow Nairn's logic, insisting rather on their internationalism as the response to the charge of parochialism, in the same way as workers' control is put forward as the answer to charge of statist centralization.

A great deal of argument in this respect has taken place over the question of import controls. Critics have claimed that these will hit foreign exporters, hurt the Third World and the working class of other countries and invite retaliation. Some of these criticisms are probably misconceived. Import controls may be no more than a means of allowing reflation of the economy without running into balance of payments deficit and as such could be less harmful to other countries than competitive deflation. Yet the Left have proved remarkably sensitive to this criticism and so, instead of going for general import controls (for example by auctioning foreign exchange), have proposed selective controls and a general system of planned trade, with import levels for each industrial sector. In the CSE version (1980) these could be negotiated on a tripartite basis, with any threatened sector allowed to apply for protection. It is difficult to see how this would lead to anything but a system of protection for existing producers incapable of competing on world markets, unless the state was prepared to over-rule both employers and unions to impose a run-down of declining sectors. At the same time, selective protection of uncompetitive pro-ducers is precisely the type of policy most likely to provoke foreign retaliation.

These criticisms are all directed at the intellectual formulation of the AES and its practicability as a programme for government. Its more immediate problems, however, lay within the Labour movement itself, where it has never been adopted wholeheartedly, though parts of it have appealed to parts of the movement, giving the appearance of commitment to the package as a whole; and unless the strategy is seen as a whole then it loses much of its purpose in the eyes of its progenitors.

We have noted that the AES was formulated on the Left of the party and gained increasing support in the NEC as the latter moved to the Left in the 1970s. The parliamentary leadership, in government at the time, paid it little heed and, when the time came to draw up the manifesto for the 1979 general election, most of it was excluded at the insistence of James Callaghan, the Prime Minister. Items missed out included the extension of public ownership into banking and finance, the economic and industrial plan and planning agency, the strengthening of powers over industry by giving government the right to issue directives to companies and put in a trustee to any company failing to meet its responsibilities, the specific powers to enforce plan-ning agreements, and the public ownership of named industries of North Sea Oil and of agricultural land (RD:58/Sept. 1979). Instead, the election was fought largely on the government's record. After the election, with the change in the Labour leadership and the weakened position of the Parliamentary Party, more general support was given to the AES, though the arguments about the meaning of various commitments continued.

The unions, too, were far from being committed to the full alterna-tive strategy and, indeed, there were a number of ambiguities about their role in it. As Gamble (1982, p. 191) puts it 'trade unions would have to be fully incorporated into the national planning system, surrendering their privileges and powers as independent organisations in return for participation in the making and implementation of economic policy'. None of the designers of the AES have been so frank (or tactless!), though Holland (RD:680/Jan. 1981) wrote of the 'social negotiation by trade unions of the use of resources at company level, and their involvement in planning as a process of social negotiation of changed options for the use of resources in the economy', which presumably means moving from a concern merely with pay towards non-pay issues. There is little evidence that the trade-union leaderships were greatly interested in such a new role, bringing them further within the embrace of the state; nor could the political wing of the movement put much pressure on them to respond, given the conventions about the relationship between the two wings.

Apart from the general objections of the trade unions to being co-opted into the state, there were specific features of the AES which they found unacceptable. One was the implicit commitment to incomes policy as an inescapable element of national planning. Strenuous efforts were made to accommodate union objections to formal incomes policy and to maintain the alliance between the Labour Left and the unions. It was argued by some (Holland, 1975) that faster economic growth would deal with inflation by reducing the gap between rises in output and rises in earnings. Others argued for stiff price controls as the answer to inflation but it did not escape union attention that firms subject to price controls would be less willing and able to concede wage increases (RD:900/May 1981).

A more surprising casualty of union opposition was the proposal for bank nationalization. Clearly, public control of the finance system would have to be a central element in a state-controlled economy and the National Executive Committee's 1976 programme, accepted by Conference, proposed the nationalization of the four big clearing banks, the major insurance companies, and one merchant bank. Consultation with the relevant trade unions produced a flurry of protest. The National Union of Bank Employees claimed that the alleged shortage of investment funds was not a real problem and that nationalization could mean lending to unprofitable ventures and government control over wages and conditions (RE:1011/Feb. 1977). USDAW (Union of Shop, Distributive and Allied Workers) criticized the nationalization of banking and the ill-thought-out nature of the proposals; they supported nationalization of insurance in line with longstanding union policy but wanted firm assurances about the rights of employees and policy-holders after a state take-over (RE:1013/Feb. 1977). The most virulent opposition recorded was from the National Union of Insurance Workers (Prudential Section) who denied that there was a shortage of investment funds and feared that if nationalized firms were forced to lend to unprofitable industries they would be unable to compete with private ones and so their staff would inevitably suffer (RE:1015/Feb. 1977).

In view of this opposition, the NEC climbed down, withdrew the nationalization proposals and contented itself with proposals for strengthening the existing public banks (Giro and the National Savings Bank) and for establishing a separate National Investment Bank.

Union concerns were most effectively expressed through the Liaison Committee, whose proposals were much less radical and far-reaching than those of the full AES, reflecting a lesser commitment to the expansion of state power and a greater emphasis on tripartitism. The 1978 Liaison Committee document, *Into the Eighties* (Liaison Committee, 1978, p. 7) spoke vaguely of 'additional statutory powers' to support planning agreements, of the need to be 'ready to use selective and temporary import controls if these prove to be necessary', of a 'considerable expansion of the role and significance of the NEB in the economy'. It was almost as vague on the methods of improving investment, with no suggestion of the nationalization of institutions.

So, while the NEC and Party Conference were by the late 1970s committed to a radical Alternative Economic Strategy involving substantial increases in state power, it is difficult to argue that the party as a whole was so committed, given the hostile or at best lukewarm attitudes of the PLP and union leaderships. Following the election defeat and the subsequent weakening of the parliamentary leadership, however, the AES became more generally accepted as the basis of Labour's economic policy. The major practical difficulty remained that of incomes policy. The 1980 Conference unequivocally rejected any incomes policy but at the same time passed a contradictory resolution looking to a voluntary agreement with TUC. The 1980 NEC statement on 'Peace, Jobs and Freedom' and the draft manifesto of the same year promised an anti-inflation strategy but said nothing on incomes policy. In May 1981, however, the TUC–Labour Party Liaison Committee coined the phrase 'National Economic Assessment' and agreed to discuss further how to reconcile free collective bargaining with the need for a government view on public sector pay

(RD:859/May 1981). Eventually this was to grow into a replacement for the old Social Contract, appearing in the 1983 manifesto as the last item in the counter-inflation strategy.

The other item subject to some reconsideration was the centralist nature of the AES, with the beginnings of a recognition that it could involve massive increases in bureaucracy and controls. Proposals from 1980 began to recommend a move away from total reliance on an imposed National Plan, towards 'market-oriented planning', improving, anticipating and 'fixing' the market (Labour Research papers, 1980). These ideas at last faced the crucial question of the relationship between state control, the market system, and private power and the meaning of state socialism in a pluralistic society. Unfortunately, for the next three years the party was to be so beset with its internal power struggle that policy development was neglected. So the 1983 manifesto was in effect an updated version of the 1976 programme, with most of the vital questions and dilemmas unanswered.

CHAPTER 5

Labour's territorial strategy

IT is clear from our earlier discussion that the Labour Party has never been able to work out a coherent and agreed political strategy; so perhaps to talk of its territorial strategy would be an exaggeration. Yet there are identifiable elements in the Party's approach to territorial management which recur through its history and present it with continuing dilemmas. By the post-war period it had finally laid the ghost of the old Home Rule tradition — formally abandoning Scottish Home Rule in 1958 (Keating and Bleiman, 1979). On the Left it became fashionable to believe that working-class unity was incompatible with any concession to peripheral nationalism, and required centralization. It is typical of Labour's failure to examine seriously its assumptions about the state that most left-wingers went on to see the existing British state, shorn of its imperialist elements, as the arena in which this working-class unity could best develop. On the Right, the Morrisonian vision of large-scale state industries prevailed and in all sections of the party there was a belief in the need for centralization in order to redistribute in accordance with Labour's priorities.

Territorial Management in the 1960s

The party did not and could not, however, commit itself to a purely assimilationist strategy for the periphery. Distinct political agendas existed to be addressed in Scotland and Wales, key areas of Labour support. Regional development became a major issue in England in the early 1960s; and local government reform, seen in both major parties as a vital element in the modernization of Britain, raised important questions of partisan advantage as well as the territorial distribution of power.

There is very little tradition in the Labour Party of regarding local government as a source of political authority, or a basis of power. Rather the party has assimilated the practice of its opponents in emphasizing Parliament as the unique source of authority, with local councils serving, essentially, as administrative agencies. This distinction is reinforced by Labour's practice of separating its local and national élites for, although a large number of MPs are former councillors, they almost invariably resign on election to Parliament; and local government figures rarely gain election to the National Executive Committee. So it is not surprising that the party saw local government reform in the 1960s as part of the strategy of national modernization rather than in terms of the dispersal of power.

The 1964 Government came to power with no firm proposals for local government and it was only frustration with the slow progress of the Boundary Commission inherited from the Conservatives which brought Richard Crossman round to the need for a radical shake-up. At the same time, like other members of the Cabinet, Crossman (1975, p. 440) saw the antiquated local government system as an obstacle to building the new Britain; 'the dynosaurs', he said, 'would have to give way to modern animals'. The issue was effectively shelved by the appointment of the Redcliffe-Maud Commission for England and the Wheatley Commission for Scotland and when they reported in 1969 the Government promptly accepted their recommendations. While differing considerably in their detailed prescriptions, the two reports shared an underlying philosophy. Local government structures were outdated, boundaries no longer reflected the facts of modern social and economic geography and there was difficulty in recruiting the 'right calibre' of councillor. Larger units were needed in the interests of planning and efficient service delivery while greater power and responsibility would attract a better type of councillor. This sort of thinking has been powerfully criticized by Dearlove (1979) who has pointed out the shaky intellectual foundations on which notions of efficiency were built. Nor does the rhetoric of the Commissions on the need to re-establish the independence of local government fit easily with the substance of their recommendations, hemmed in as they were by their terms of reference which limited them to considering the existing functions of local government. The proposals of the Wheatley Commission, indeed, reproduced faithfully the suggestions made to them by the Scottish Office. As one civil servant involved in the exercise has subsequently revealed (Ross, 1979), these were intended to create a local government system which, while powerful enough to do what central government wanted it to do, would not establish an independent power centre. Clear signs that Labour was not intent on a territorial dispersal of power were the refusal to contemplate a 'general competence' power for local authorities (allowing them to do anything not specifically prohibited by law), the refusal to consider new functions (for example in health or economic development) and the refusal to reform local government finance.

While the technocratic view of local government's status and purpose characterized the Labour Government, a more political perspective was forced on it after 1970. The incoming Conservative administration largely proceded with the Wheatley recommendations for Scotland, but overturned the Redcliffe–Maud proposals for reasons of partisan advantage, creating a two-tier system in which the shire counties, with the predominance of functions, would be overwhelmingly Conservative and the metropolitan counties, where Labour stood more chance, drawn tightly around the conurbations. This turned local government structure in England into a partisan issue, as it has remained since. At the same time, in defiance of the party leadership, a number of Labour-controlled councils challenged the housing legislation of the Conservative Government to the point of breaking the law. The espousal by the councillors of Clay Cross of the pre-war tradition of 'Poplarism' was a cause of deep embarrassment to the parliamentary leadership who consistently counselled obedience to the law and respect for the sovereignty of Parliament. The ensuing battles revived interest in the institution of local government, particularly on the Left, with important results, as we shall see.

Issues of power were encountered earlier on in the debate over regional government and the position of Scotland and Wales, in the United Kingdom. The strategy which emerged could be summed up as 'regional development, yes. Regional government, no'. The only concession to peripheral autonomy was support for the limited scope of the Scottish Office in social and environmental policy and a promise of a similar office for Wales. Even this aroused some opposition among the most passionate centralizers. Nye Bevan was an early sceptic, as James Griffith recalled:

Nye's doubts about the wisdom of the creation of a Welsh Office went beyond considerations of administration. He has related how he came to realise that if he was to achieve his objectives and his burning desire to create a socialist society, it was imperative to reach out from the valley, and beyond the country, to the centre, where the levers of power were operated. He was impatient of nationalism which divided people and enslaved nations within their narrow geographical and spiritual frontiers. He fears that devolution of authority would divorce Welsh political activity from the main stream of

British politics, as he felt was already happening in Scotland (Griffiths, p. 162).

The main significance of the promotion of the Scottish and Welsh Offices, however, was to lie in their role in lobbying for material benefits. They represented a privileged channel of access to the centre for Scottish and Welsh interests so that Labour politicians in the periphery came to oppose Home Rule the more strongly in that it might put these privileges at risk.

For the English regions, the strategy was summed up by Michael Stewart in a debate on the Buchanan Report in 1964, before the general election:

> What we are driven to is that somewhere in our structure of government there has to be something which is not there already — really effective operation of regional representatives of central government. We can leave open the question of whether they should be politicians or regional ministers . . . or whether they should be highly placed officials . . . My other reason for rejecting building up from the local authorities is that, in the regions we are executing national policy.
>
> (Hansard, vol. 689, col. 141, 10 February 1964).

Essentially, Labour reduced all territorial issues to economic ones, attacking the Conservatives for their neglect of regional development and promising that, with planning and economic growth, they could do better. If the underlying economic causes of discontent could be dealt with, it was assumed, Scottish and Welsh nationalism would not be a problem. On the other hand, if Labour failed to deliver the economic goods, its electoral punishment might be the more severe for its having raised expectations too high in the first place. Labour's strategy, far from denying the relevance of territory to politics, raised its salience by stressing its economic aspect while trying to deny its constitutional one.

Like its national economic plan, Labour's regional economic strategy was based on the assumption that consensus could be built around the requirements of faster economic growth. In turn, growth would allow the range of sectoral and territorial expectations which the party had built up to be satisfied. A regional incentives policy owing a great deal to previous experience but expanded in scope, could operate as a 'non-zero-sum game', bringing jobs to the depressed regions while relieving overheating in the expanding ones and adding to national output in a non-inflationary way.

The system of regional planning established in 1964 under the DEA and the Scottish and Welsh Offices was intended to provide a regional perpective to national planning and to bring together physical and economic planning behind the implementation of the National Plan. The machinery had two main elements — the Economic Planning Boards and the Economic Planning Councils. The boards comprised senior civil servants in the region. The Economic Planning Councils were advisory bodies with members drawn from industry, commerce, local government, and the universities. Their original terms of reference were 'to assist in the formulation of regional plans having regard to the best use of the region's resources, to advise on the steps necessary for implementing the regional plans on the basis of information and assessments provided by the economic planning boards and to advise on the regional implications of national planning policies'. The system was rooted in assumptions from the consensus model of planning and failed to provide mechanisms for resolving inter-governmental and public–private conflict. Specifically, they suffered from crucial weaknesses in terms of their functions, their powers and resources, and their political status.

The old functional conflict between economic and physical planning was not resolved by the system. The term 'economic' had been inserted in the titles of the boards and councils precisely to calm the fears of local councils and the Ministry of Housing and Local Government that this represented a trespass on their territory; but unless physical infrastructure planning was part of the system, regional plans could not be implemented.

The powers and resources of the boards and councils were practically non-existent. The whole system was advisory, based on a rather weakly thought-out version of indicative planning in which consensus would be achieved through accelerated economic growth.

Closely related to this was the problem of the status of the new bodies. Some, including, it seems, George Brown, saw them as the embryo of a future system of regional government which would impose its priorities for growth and development. Others, following Michael Stewart's earlier line, saw them as executive arms for the implementation of national policy. Yet others saw them as a means for local interests to influence national and regional policy — hence the representation of local government on the councils. In other words, it was unclear whether they represented a national, a regional, or a local constituency. One way or resolving this was to regard the system as a

'corporatist' forum in which these various interests could reach negotiated solutions. But this was specifically ruled out by the government,
which insisted on viewing the members of the boards as individuals
rather than representatives of interests.

This role ambiguity is reflected in the uncertainty of the relationship between the councils and the boards. Originally it had been
intended that the boards should draw up the plans with the advice of
the councils, but in 1966 responsibility for preparing the plans was
transferred to the councils themselves. This may have been to enable
the government to avoid being committed to the plans (Lindley,
1982). However, the separation was far from complete, as the councils
had no separate staff and so relied on the boards for information and
servicing. The role ambiguity was intensified as the regional civil
servants, as representatives of central government, now had to pro-
nounce on plans drawn up by the councils with their own assistance
and advice.

Only by continued rapid economic growth could the tensions
inherent in the strategy be overcome. This would allow the channelling of extra resources to poorer regions without depriving others,
the funding of expanded social programmes, and a continued overseas
role without reducing private consumption and the retention of confidence in the centralized state. By 1966 the strategy appeared a bril-
liant success. Labour's *Plan for Expansion* for the Scottish economy
published in January 1966 promised lavish publish investment; the
Welsh Office had been established and was gradually assuming
increased functions, and in the English regions preparations were
under way for their own development plans. In the March general
election the strategy won triumphant vindication at the polls, particularly in Scotland and Wales where Labour won 46 out of 71 and 32 out
of 36 seats respectively.

The Challenge from the Periphery

It was not long before the first blows fell. In July 1966, an emergency
deflationary package raised a question mark over the National Plan,
which was finally killed by the devaluation the following year. From
the summer of 1966, the balance of payments took priority over
growth or regional development and short-term considerations over
the long term. National planning was discredited as an idea and,
despite some efforts in the late 1960s, the regional planning system

never recovered. While Labour remained committed to a regional economic policy, it was of a much less ambitious kind. The failure had several consequences. It led a number of people within the party to question the efficacy of centralized policies. In a time of boom, regional development was in the interests of all, helping the deprived regions while reducing congestion in the others and contributing to the national good by bringing resources into use and reducing inflationary pressures in the overheated regions. In a recession, however, regional development could be a zero-sum game, with gains for one region being at the expense of others. Some Labour MPs and activists in Scotland and Wales began to ask whether different constitutional arrangements might not be a better guarantee of their future. These, however, were a minority. The overwhelming bulk of the party and, particularly, the trade unions, still put their faith in centralized solutions.

A further incentive to rethink the strategy came from a series of electoral shocks. It was only four months after Labour's 1966 general election triumph that Plaid Cymru captured the seat at Carmarthen. The following year, the SNP won Hamilton, overturning a massive Labour majority. Although it is possible to argue that special factors were present in both constituencies, they were nevertheless evidence of better organized and more assertive nationalist movements on Labour's flanks. Plaid Cymru had already made some advances in local government in the early 1960s, capitalizing on popular disenchantment with Labour rule and the SNP had made inroads into the Labour vote at several by-elections since 1961.

The party's reaction to this challenge was mixed. The predominant view in Scotland and Wales was that the discontent was basically economic and that it would be alleviated by a return to growth and better regional policies. Both implied continued centralization. From the government came a more pragmatic response. After considerable internal argument (Crossman, 1976) a Royal Commission on the Constitution was established. While some Ministers, such as Richard Crossman saw this as a means of facilitating a policy change to accommodate Scottish and Welsh constitutional demands, most clearly saw it as a means of buying time until economic conditions improved and the nationalist threat faded away.

The evidence of the Scottish Council of the Labour Party to the Commission put the centralist case. A Scottish Assembly, it was argued, would have a divisive effect on the UK Parliament and carry the danger of economic separation. 'Any form of assembly with substantial legislative devolution', would, it was argued, 'be a slippery slope towards total separation, or at least a form of separation which would set up divisions within the United Kingdom'. The only way to solve Scottish problems, the Council concluded, was to have a Labour government at Westminster but even a UK Conservative government would be preferable to a devolved assembly (Keating and Bleiman, 1979, p. 157). This view, however, was not unanimously held. In 1967 and 1968 considerable support for an assembly had resurfaced at Labour's Scottish Conference, and in 1969 the Scottish Trades Union Congress had favoured a legislative assembly, though it later toned down this proposal to an assembly with executive powers only. This support for devolution reflected both the residual Home Rule tradition in the Scottish Labour movement and the renewed concern about economic development.

By comparison with Scotland, the Labour Party in Wales responded more rapidly and sympathetically to the nationalist threat. The Labour Party's dominant electoral position in Wales with wide support from all areas and social groups enabled it to be more immediately aware of shifts in the Welsh political mood. In the 1950s the Labour Party had replaced the Liberals as the vehicle for traditional Welsh radicalism, a development recognized and welcomed by James Griffiths (1978, p. 57):

I feel that Labour has a duty to join with others in Wales to preserve our language and the culture that derives from it. The Radical Liberal forces of the nineteenth century nurtured the Democratic Radicalism which we have inherited. Expressing it in political action fell mainly to the Labour Party then as now. There is much to be done at home and in the wider world, and in this a strong British Labour Movement can play a decisive role. The strength of that Labour Movement depends on the strength of the Welsh Labour Movement. To my comrades in Wales — who through the years have been so generous to me — my message is 'Guard our Inheritance'.

The Labour Party in Wales had thus acquired a sensitivity to the concerns of such diverse groups as Welsh speakers, farmers, middle-class professionals and other sectors of society not immediately associated with the Labour cause but which had come to support Labour because of its identification with the traditional aspirations of Welsh radicalism.

During the early sixties the Welsh Executive of the Labour Party became increasingly identified with specifically Welsh issues and in 1965 proposed an elected Welsh Council which subsequently was endorsed by Welsh Labour's Annual Conference in May 1966. The nationalist threat posed by the Carmarthen by-election thus gave added keenness to an existing enthusiasm which was reflected in the preparation of evidence presented by the Labour Party to the Royal Commission on the Constitution.

In April 1969 a working party given the task of preparing the evidence had produced a provisional report of an unmistakably federal nature suggesting a Welsh senate with legislative and economic powers. The proposals provoked a storm of controversy in the Welsh Labour Group. The Secretary of State, George Thomas, was totally opposed not only to federalism but also to any form of legislative devolution and, together with a substantial number of Welsh MPs, was hostile to any form of a directly elected Assembly. In the face of this opposition the Welsh Executive progressively modified its proposed evidence eliminating quasi-federal features and any suggestion of legislative powers which 'would reduce the effectiveness of Welsh MPs and the influence of Wales in the UK, and would jeopardise the unity of the country as a whole'. However the Welsh Executive maintained the central prop of its devolution policy and reaffirmed its support for a directly elected assembly. The policy eventually presented in the Welsh party's evidence was justified by four considerations, only one of which was specifically related to devolution. The other three reflected more acceptable Labour Party concerns, local government, democracy, and administrative efficiency.

The preparation and presentation of evidence to the Commission on the Constitution induced severe internal strains within the Welsh Executive. Its views were criticized and opposed by the Welsh Office ministers and practically half the Welsh Labour Group. Furthermore, it was pressured by Transport House to modify its evidence and bring its proposals into line with those presented by the Labour Party in Scotland which was total opposition to an elected council. However, although much was conceded, the central principle of a directly-elected council was maintained, a fact of considerable significance in light of subsequent events.

The discovery of North Sea oil dramatically altered the economics of independence and, by implication, devolution for Scotland. While the official view, that oil was a UK resource to be used for the benefit of all parts of the country, was generally accepted, there was a widespread feeling that some way should be found of channelling at least part of the revenues into development in the deprived regions. Possibly most important, however, was the psychological effect of removing the perception of Scotland's economic dependence on England. The implications of this for constitutional change were as yet unclear and confused. After all, Scotland would only be able to stake a claim to the oil revenues if she became independent, which few in the Labour Party were yet prepared to contemplate. Specific proposals tended to favour an oil fund for all depressed regions or managerial devolution by means of a development corporation or agency to be financed with oil revenues. In 1973, the Party's Scottish Executive proposed a Scottish Enterprise Board to work in conjunction with the proposed National Enterprise Board. (This proposal later bore fruit in the form of the Scottish Development Agency.) Nevertheless, thinking on these lines could not be divorced completely from the constitutional issue and was one of the elements prompting a reconsideration of the latter.

EEC entry had a similar ambiguous but noticeable effect. The implications of EEC entry were far from clear and the issue was by no means resolved as far as the Labour Party was concerned. However, it affected attitudes in at least two ways. Firstly, it represented a major breach of the doctrine of the sovereignty of Parliament and thus of the foundations of the British State. As we show in Chapter 7 the fact that entry took place under a Conservative government left the Labour Party in the position of defending the sovereignty of the state. This a large section of it continued to do, but for others the EEC produced a second effect.

It led some politicians in Scotland to question whether the London link would in future be less important than direct access to Brussels. Again, there was confusion surrounding the issue. Only sovereign states can be directly represented in the EEC and few Labour devolutionists seriously contemplated Scotland becoming a sovereign state. In any case, the argument for direct representation in Brussels at the expense of links with London presupposed an EEC more powerful than it was, or was likely to become, in either the short- or midterm. Nevertheless, one or two pro-EEC MPs were beginning to think along these lines and the case was strongly taken up by the antimarketeer Jim Sillars. By 1973, Sillars favoured withdrawal from the EEC and a Scottish Assembly with limited powers but argued that, if Britain were to remain in the EEC following a referendum or other test of opinion, Scotland should have sufficient autonomy as was necessary to give her separate representation in Brussels. In the same year he founded the Scottish Labour EEC 'watchdog committee', a group of MPs to monitor developments in the Common Market as they affected Scotland and to ensure that Scottish interests were not neglected. In July 1973 a *Scotsman* editorial noted that support for devolution was building up among influential bodies and individuals in Scotland as a result of EEC entry.

The arrival of the Conservative government in 1970 at first had seemed to herald the end of the nationalist question. Both nationalist MPs lost their seats and the general public's attention turned to major issues such as the Industrial Relations Act and, later, the energy crisis. However, the national question remained present in the background and was given added significance by the fact that, in Scotland and Wales, solid Labour majorities of MPs faced a Conservative government dependent on English votes. Like the two issues above, this was not one whose lessons were obvious. Labour, committed still to the British state and to its own return to power at Westminster, did not — indeed could not — question the legitimacy of Conservative rule in Scotland and Wales. It had to assume the task of opposing the government with considerable care, in view of its dual role as the 'official' national opposition and, by its electoral position, as the defender of Scottish and Welsh interests. Its difficulty was highlighted in the attitude adopted to the controversial Housing (Financial Provisions) (Scotland) Bill. This Labour opposed, partly on the same grounds as the equivalent English measure, that it was unfair and ideologically unacceptable but, in addition, on the grounds that its proposals would eventually assimilate the Scottish system of housing finance to the English. As Willie Ross accused the Secretary of State:

The whole tradition of Scottish housing finance, which it should have been the Right Hon. gentleman's responsibility to safeguard, has gone (Hansard, vol. 827, col. 978, 6 December 1971).

However, Labour could not as yet follow this line through to its logical conclusion and demand Home Rule for Scotland. Nor could it make this sort of argument too prominent a part of its campaigning, for fear of giving ammunition to the nationalists. It was perhaps fortunate for Labour that the SNP, preoccupied with its own ideological tensions, virtually ignored the housing finance issue.

In Wales, the presence of a Conservative Secretary of State, particularly one representing an English constituency, served to reinforce support for the policy of limited political devolution already adopted. Here the relative weakness of the nationalists and Labour's continuing support in all parts of the country and from a wide variety of social groups, enabled Labour to project itself as the party of Welsh interests.

Another significant development in Wales was the foundation of the Wales Trades Union Congress in 1973. This grew out of a reorganization of the Transport and General Workers' Union which in 1969 had replaced its two Welsh areas with a single structure. At the same time, a new generation of trade-union leaders in Wales was coming to the fore, eager to defend the interests of *Welsh* workers and conscious of the need to deal with government through the decentralized administration of the Welsh Office. Despite the official opposition of the British TUC, the TGWU and the South Wales NUM sponsored the launch of the Wales TUC, which held its first conference in February 1973. The British TUC soon came round, recognizing that previously:

it was argued that South Wales was linked economically with the south west of England and that North Wales had a closer affinity with West Lancashire, Cheshire and Merseyside than with the rest of Wales. However, recent events imply that this view has to be modified. The resurgence of interest in Wales nationhood and in Welsh culture which is reflected in the actions of the Government in treating Wales as a separate entity — particularly by the establishment of a Welsh Office and a Secretary of State for Wales — mean that the case for establishing an all-Wales trade union body is considerably strengthened. (Quoted Osmond, 1977, p. 122.)

Thereafter, the Wales TUC was to be a significant force in stimulating and maintaining support for devolution in Wales.

In Scotland, too, the industrial wing of the movement was active. Concern about rising unemployment led the Scottish TUC to organize a 'Scottish Assembly' in 1972. Representatives attended from local authorities, political parties, employers' associations, religious bodies, trade unions, trades councils, students' unions, the CBI, the Scottish Council (Development and Industry), and Scottish MPs. While discussion concentrated on the problems of the Scottish economy, a strong pro-devolution feeling was evident. A second assembly was held the following year but the Scottish Council of the Labour Party was unimpressed, dismissing the Assembly as merely a platform for the nationalists. The Council was not yet ready to shift its own position and was highly embarrassed at the connection being made between Scotland's economic problems and Home Rule, given its own continuing strategy of mobilizing Scottish opposition to Tory rule through Westminster.

However, at the UK level of the party, evidence of a change in thinking came from a speech given by Harold Wilson in 1973. Speaking at Labour's Local Government Conference in Newcastle, he indicated that devolution could be accommodated within the established ideological framework of the Party:

Instead of transferring functions from local to central government, or proceeding with one after another ad hoc, more or less appointive body covering wide areas of the country, we need, not only to halt this process, but to do two other things. First, to decentralise and democratise more and more work presently undertaken by central government either from Whitehall or through their own regional machinery and, second, to create democratic regional authorities accountable to the people they serve, to deal with those services for which local authorities are too small. (Newcastle, 10 February 1973.)

Within the party in England, there was widespread dissatisfaction at the reform of local government, which came into effect in 1974. This had been a partisan measure, overturning the recommendations of the Redcliffe–Maud Commission and its effect was to place many Labour urban areas under county councils which could normally be expected to be Conservative. At the same time, water services were taken out of the hands of local authorities and given to *ad hoc* regional water authorities. In a parallel reorganization of the Health Service, a three-tier system of regional, area and district authorities was set up to unify health administration. Both health and water authorities came under fire from Labour, especially Labour councillors, as undemocratic and unaccountable. One solution to all these problems which began to be canvassed was the establishment of regional councils, to take over the functions of water and health authorities and those county council functions which could not be transferred to the districts. As we show later, this proposal was to become bogged down in the battle of vested interests in the Labour movement but it did provide a further stimulus for thinking about constitutional change.

The publication of the Kilbrandon Report in October 1973 provoked a reaction in Parliament and the press which ranged from vague disinterest to outright derision. Mr Heath, a devolutionist since the Scottish Conservative Conference in Perth 1968, urged the Commons to give the report a 'proper consideration'; but the majority of his party were less than enthusiastic and the Labour opposition were relieved that the issue had resurfaced to embarrass the Conservatives.

All this was soon to change. Conflict between the Conservative government and the NUM precipitated a general election. A minority Labour government was returned and devolution, which one Labour government had sought to consign to political limbo in 1969, returned to confront another in 1974.

The Devolution Option

Devolution was now more intractable than it had been in the late 'sixties. In Scotland the SNP won 7 seats with 22 per cent of the Scottish vote and threatened a further 14 Labour seats. Labour's position in Scotland was far from secure but this was not altogether unexpected. The by-elections of 1973: Dundee-East in March, which Labour narrowly held, and Govan in November, which Labour lost, underlined the fact that the party could no longer take for granted its traditional Scottish strongholds. These results encouraged the Scottish Labour MPs to move towards support for a measure of devolution but the Scottish Executive remained a major obstacle. The Executive's policy document, *Scotland and the UK*, published the day before the Kilbrandon Report, had ruled out any 'new fangled Assembly' on the grounds that Scottish influence at Westminster would be reduced and that the economic unity of the United Kingdom would be threatened. Despite the ominous trends revealed in the February general election, the Executive remained intransigent, successfully preventing a card vote on the devolution issue at the party's Scottish Conference in March and formally opposing all devolution schemes as late as June.

The situation in Wales was significantly different. Plaid Cymru the nationalist party had won only two seats in Welsh-speaking Wales and had conspicuously failed to pose a serious threat to Labour's industrial strongholds in the South Wales valleys. There was another and crucial difference. The Labour Party's Welsh Executive was enthusiastically committed to an elected Welsh Council (or Assembly), a position consistent with the evidence given by the party to the Royal Commission on the Constitution in 1970 and grudgingly endorsed by the Welsh Labour MPs in 1973. However, the commitment of the latter was less than total and as a major election push by Plaid Cymru failed to materialize, their reservations to the policy in some cases hardened into outright opposition.

Thus the Scottish and Welsh organizations of the Labour Party were divided. Whereas the Scottish group of Labour MPs were impelled by pragmatic electoral considerations to embrace devolution, in Wales the same policy was promoted by an Executive in sympathy with the traditions of Welsh radicalism. However, in both parties there were elements deeply suspicious of the new policy, subscribing to the old belief in a unified working-class movement whose needs could only be met through a centralized system of social and economic planning.

The minority Labour government viewed the issue from a quite different standpoint. It could not afford the luxury of an ideological debate. The loss of either Scotland or Wales would effectively deny the Labour Party the opportunity of ever forming a government again. In such circumstances the development of a Scottish and Welsh strategy was too important to be left to the Scottish and Welsh wings of the party. Two responses were possible: pragmatic expedients for short-term advantage, or a more fundamental review of policies relating to devolution. In the event the party adopted both approaches.

It was not fully convinced as to the inexorable nature of the nationalist tide. After all, that had ebbed spectacularly in 1970 following the expedient of the 1969 Royal Commission which had enabled the party to avoid an immediate confrontation of this issue. To those for whom de-centralization was ideologically anathema, a similar 'holding operation' presented considerable attractions. Clearly something had to be done before the next general election which could not be long delayed, but the party might avoid delivering any hostages to fortune in hope that the SNP advance would again be reversed. The White Paper, *Devolution within the United Kingdom: some alternatives for discussion*, published in June 1974, reflected this view. With the government still playing for time, the White Paper called for further consultations and studiously avoided any clear commitment to devolution.

However, while the White Paper was being prepared, a series of private polls in Scotland revealed a continuing drift towards the SNP and convinced Downing Street that a more positive response was needed. Wilson's Newcastle speech in February 1973 had suggested a personal interest in regionalism and democratic-decentralization and his appointment of Lord Crowther-Hunt as constitutional adviser represented a serious attempt to confront the issue. Shortly after the election, Wilson gave a clear indication that the government had decided upon action. In the debate on the Queen's Speech, he declared: 'Of course we shall publish a White Paper *and* a Bill' [our emphasis]. Lest any doubt remain, the pledge was repeated the following week by Robert Sheldon, Minister of State at the Civil Service Department (Keating and Bleiman, 1979).

Furthermore, the party bureaucracy was charged with the task of developing an appropriate policy. The Home Affairs Committee of the NEC translated its Regional and Local Government sub-committee into a Devolution Working Group which collaborated with Ted Short, Leader of the House of Commons and the Cabinet minister with special responsibility for devolution. During June and July proposals were drafted granting legislative devolution to Scotland and executive devolution to Wales. They were pushed through a pre-occupied cabinet and a largely disinterested NEC and then forced upon a reluctant Scottish Executive which was obliged to call a special conference in August. That conference overwhelmingly approved the proposals and brought the Scottish party into line with the Welsh, which had recorded its support for the proposals a month earlier. In September the government was able to publish a second White Paper, *Democracy and Devolution: proposals for Scotland and Wales* which mirrored the party's new policy.

This exercise of devising a devolution policy has been seen as a purely pragmatic response to electoral pressure. But it was more than that. Territorial concerns which cross-cut Labour's traditional working-class constituency were permitted to exercise a decisive influence. The party's Scottish and Welsh organizations, usually confined to a subordinate administrative role within the party structure, were brought into the policy-making process and delegations from the Scottish and Welsh parties served on the NEC sub-committee and devolution working group. Furthermore, the process of policy legitimization was extended to include extraordinary Welsh and Scottish conferences specifically called to endorse the policy of devolution which was only later approved by Labour's Annual Conference.

These significant departures from the norm were adopted, together with the devolution policy itself, in the hope of reversing the nationalist tide. Had Labour won a resounding victory in the October election no doubt the policy would have been allowed to lapse as it had in the 1920s. However both the Scottish and Welsh nationalists increased their seats; the SNP raised their share of the poll in Scotland to 30 per cent and pushed the Conservatives into third place. Labour had managed to avoid the electoral catastrophe predicted by the polls and to that extent the party's new devolution policy could be judged a success. However, to the consternation of many within the party hierarchy, the Labour government's narrow majority and the increased salience of the nationalists in Parliament meant that the devolution pledge now had to be redeemed. The party was thus obliged to confront directly an issue it had avoided since Plaid Cymru's Carmarthen by-election victory in 1966. This raised the question of whether Labour could learn to live with a policy which was incongruent with its traditional ideology.

In Wales, Labour's manifesto in October 1974 attempted to accommodate the interests of the traditional centralist wing of the party with the aspirations of Welsh radicalism but only at the expense of highly ambiguous phrasing. Thus, while the Welsh Assembly would be in 'no way akin to a legislature' it would have 'an area of wide decision making'. The Welsh Executive's position at this critical time was weakened by the loss of devolutionists from the Welsh Labour Group, most notably James Griffiths, so that after October 1974 there was increasing opposition to the idea of an elected Welsh Assembly among Labour MPs. The sceptics doubted the wisdom of such a reform in the immediate aftermath of local government reorganization, they questioned the logic of undermining the authority and status of the Welsh Secretary of State and the Welsh Office by creating an alternative power centre, and they were also deeply suspicious of the role Welsh Assemblymen might play. Underlying these criticisms were the two major tenets of socialists orthodoxy; a commitment to maintaining the unity of the working-class movement and a belief in the primacy of central planning. To the critics neither was reconcilable with the new devolution policy.

In face of a similar reluctance by the Scottish Executive to embrace devolution, the national leadership had exerted considerable pressure, particularly on loyalist union leaders in Scotland. This was the period of the first 'social contract' and union leaders were generally prepared to support the government on a purely 'political' matter, given assurances that their economic interests would remain unaffected; hence the peculiar form of the devolution policy. The political structure of the state was to be changed but in a way which had a minimal impact on the 'real' economic world which the trade-union leaders inhabited. The activists and the ideologues in the party posed a more difficult problem.

There is a limit, in the Labour Party, to the extent that a leadership can dictate to its followers without provoking a serious backlash; the followers have, in some degree, to be won over. Thus, the rapid transformation in the posture of the Scottish Party suggests either that the old centralist stance was not a matter of deeply held ideology or that it had not seriously been infringed. There is some truth in both these. The issue was not one which divided the party on the usual Right–Left lines and therefore was not seen as part of the fight for the soul of the movement. As we have seen, the party possesses a decentralist tradition and was able very quickly to build an ideological justification, summoning the shade of Keir Hardie in aid. Thus a return to the Home Rule policy or the espousal of some form of regionalism or political decentralization, unlike some other consessions to public opinion, was always an available option.

There are serious doubts as to the extent to which the 1974 devolution policy may be regarded as a significant move away from centralization. The role of the national leadership in pushing the policy is a prima-facie indication that radical decentralization was not being contemplated. This interpretation is supported by the two White Papers published in 1974. One of the few unambiguous statements in the June White Paper was an outright rejection of federalism and in the September White Paper, the government emphasized that it was 'firmly convinced that the United Kingdom must remain one country and one economy and that constitutional change must be undertaken with the clear object of strengthening rather than weakening this unity'. Within Scotland, and particularly among Scottish MPs, support for the policy was secured only on the condition that the economic unity of the UK would be unimpaired and that Scotland would retain its Secretary of State and its full complement of seventy-one MPs. The unions' support was conditional on the assurance that economic centralization and national wage bargaining would be unaffected. Furthermore, the decision *not* to grant Wales legislative devolution, influenced by Plaid Cymru's inability to pose a serious threat, provided additional evidence that the party's commitment to a comprehensive policy of decentralization was hardly more than skin deep.

In fact, we can see the devolution proposals of the 1970s as an attempt to build a new 'dualist' strategy for territorial management. Those aspects of social and environmental policy already decentralized to the Scottish and Welsh Offices would be devolved to the assemblies; economic policy would remain with the centre. And, to confirm the party's determination to have its cake and eat it, the offices of Secretary of State for Scotland and for Wales would be retained.

The concessions made during the course of 1974 were the minimum which the party thought necessary to preserve the essential features of the centralized state and to ensure the survival of the Labour Party. To that extent the national leadership had grasped the decentralist nettle but neither it nor the party as a whole, had come to terms with the devolution policy. It was only with the publication of the White Paper *Our Changing Democracy: Devolution Scotland and Wales* in September 1975 that the party awoke to the need to reconcile devolution with Labour's traditional values and objectives. The ensuing battle in the party was between those in the majority for whom devolution was, despite its superficial electoral advantage, a somewhat distasteful necessity which appeared to be a concession to narrow nationalist aspirations; and others, mostly party activists in Scotland and Wales, who were genuine decentralizers as a matter of political principle.

In Wales the succession of government White Papers leading up to the Scotland and Wales Bill in November 1976 progressively clarified the devolution proposals but, in the process, removed the ambiguities that had partially cloaked the divisions within the party. Leo Abse, a long-term opponent of devolution, who had reluctantly accepted the policy in 1973, renewed his opposition and was joined by a group of newly-elected Labour back-benchers. The high proportion of Welsh Labour MPs in the government left the political initiative in the hands of the anti-devolution back-benchers who argued that too much had been conceded to the 'Welsh radical' wing of the party; that such concessions were unnecessary because Plaid Cymru had failed to match their nationalist counterparts in Scotland, and that Welsh public opinion seemed unenthusiastic for the proposals which should at least be tested by a referendum. Subsequently, the arguments were refined to include the charges that Wales had no community of interest and that a Welsh-speaking élite would dominate an Assembly. In the face of such criticisms the Welsh Executive produced a dual response, exploiting the 'loyalty factor' and seeking to link the policy more securely to the traditional economic, and centralist elements of Labour Party thinking. The first response was strongly supported by the Wales TUC and trade-union sponsored MPs were put under pressure. In its second response the party produced a more detailed exposition of the rationale behind its devolution proposals. The original local government content for an elected Welsh Assembly was updated and a new policy statement produced, proposing a single tier of all-purpose authorities under an elected Welsh Assembly. Numerous information sheets were published by the Welsh Executive detailing the scope and cost of the various nominated bodies in Wales and the extent of their non-accountability. The Welsh Office was subjected to a similar test with the intent of proving the need for a Welsh Assembly. Finally the Welsh Labour Conference in 1978 overwhelmingly approved a policy statement entitled 'Political and Industrial Democracy in Britain' which attempted to place the devolution proposals in the context of the House of Lords reform, workers' control and industrial democracy, apparently accommodating a policy of political decentralization within the broader ideological and traditional working-class ethos of the party.

In Scotland the issue on which battle was joined concerned the powers which the Scottish Assembly should exercise. With the pro-devolutionists retaining the initiative, the 'antis' sought to limit the powers of the Assembly: but the bulk of the party aimed for a reasonable balance which, while not prejudicing the party's basic principles, could be defended electorally. The party debate was influenced by the immense pressure under which Labour in Scotland suffered in the three or four years after 1974. It was this which determined the attitude of a great many of the activists in the constituencies, where support for devolution was weak. Continued nationalist successes at local elections and the 1976 breakaway of the Scottish Labour Party persuaded Labour activists in Scotland that the party was fighting for its life and that some form of devolution was its only salvation.

The major issue in the debate was whether the assembly should have significant economic powers. As the granting of such powers would strike at one of the fundamental elements of Labour's centralist beliefs, it was a key issue dividing the committed decentralizers from the rest. Support for the devolution of economic functions came from two sources; the group of devolutionist MPs around Jim Sillars, and the trade unions, who began to see the possible value of an assembly as a means of securing economic advantages for Scotland, although they were not prepared to push this to the point of endangering the economic unity of the UK.

The party's divisions came out into the open at the 1975 Conference. A composite resolution from the TGWU calling for economic and revenue-raising powers was opposed by the Executive and defeated on a card vote, with most of the constituency parties voting with the Executive. This was something of an embarrassment to devolutionists within the government, who were pushing for the devolution of the Scottish Development Agency. By the following year, with the government's second White Paper to consider and a string of local government by-election defeats behind them, both the Executive and the Conference were in a more devolutionary mood. The Executive, whose report was accepted by Conference, demanded that the SDA be devolved, that the Secretary of State's veto be removed, and that the Assembly be given revenue-raising powers. The mood of the party as this time was accurately summed up by Geoffrey Smith in *The Times* (4.3.76):

There remains the convinced anti-devolutionists. But among the rest there is a general movement to a compromise position where the majority can stand and fight. There is a widespread recognition that something more than the White Paper will be needed to satisfy Scottish opinion., In some cases, that recognition is enthusiastic. More often it is the reluctant acceptance of political necessity. But one also encounters a feeling that, while there must be more devolution than the Government have yet proposed, there must none the less be strict limits as to how far it would be safe to go without jeopardising the integrity of the United Kingdom.

The party divisions on the devolution issue most apparent to the general public were those within the Parliamentary Labour Party as it grappled with the task of pushing the devolution legislation through Parliament. The Scotland and Wales Bill published in November 1976 marked the first parliamentary attempt. There were indications even at this early stage, that the government was lacking in resolution. It failed to call the implied bluff of Leo Abse's private motion for a referendum; and it allowed a slow accretion of Labour back-bench support of the motion to build up to a point where it was obliged to concede the referendum demand as the price for winning the second reading. Despite that concession, or perhaps because of it, the government failed to carry its guillotine by 314 to 285 with 29 abstentions. This defeat reflected both the government's lack of will and the hostility to devolution amongst English Labour MPs from the North-East and London. It brought home at last to the party leadership the difficulties of integrating a decentralist policy within the conventional wisdom of the party's socialist ideology.

The reintroduction of the devolution legislation as separate Scotland and Wales Bills in November 1977 marked a new strategy and a new attitude. The government no longer sought to persuade its back-benchers of the virtues of devolution. Their support was now canvassed as a means of maintaining the government in office. The task was made easier because the government could now argue that the ultimate decision no longer rested with Parliament but with the Scottish and Welsh electorates. In such circumstances, basic legislative principles became negotiable. The government was prepared to tolerate a series of damaging amendments to both bills, and it acquiesced in the face of a series of Labour back-bench revolts largely instigated by Tam Dalyell and Leo Abse, who were both to exercise a crucial role in the referendum campaign.

The parliamentary party's growing distate for devolution was attributable to a variety of circumstances. No doubt Harold Wilson's retirement in 1976 was a factor; he had a personal sympathy for some form of regionalism and democratic decentralization whereas his successor Mr Callaghan had little if any. The economic crisis and the ideological problems associated with the IMF loan also diverted the party's attention. But the main reason was the party's heightened appreciation of the disquieting consequences of its devolution policy specifically with regard to the English regional dimension.

In *Labour's Programme 1973* the party had declared a general wish to bring about 'an effective devolution of decision making and functions from Whitehall' to the regions and nations of the United Kingdom but without specifying how. The devolution crisis, heralded by the advance of the nationalists in the February 1974 election, now obliged Labour's leadership to adopt a more positive stance in respect of the English regions.

There was already a groundswell of opinion within the party in England amenable to some form of regionalism. It stemmed from a dissatisfaction with the regional '*ad hoc*' health and water authorities set up by the Conservative government and a growing disillusionment with the newly-reformed local government system. The latter attitude was particularly prevalent within former county borough parties which, estranged by the two-tier district/county system, saw a division of functions between regions and districts, and doing away with the counties, as a possible solution. A move in this direction confronted obvious problems in determining English regional boundaries.

Nevertheless, some regional councils of Labour, most notably the North West Regional Council, took advantage of the devolution debate engendered by the nationalists' electoral success, to press for a system of directly-elected English regional councils.

In September 1975 the NEC produced a discussion document *Devolution and Regional Government in England* to stimulate debate within the regional councils of the party and, more specifically, for the consideration of the party's Local Government Conference in January 1976. Partly as a result of this process of consultation, the party in July 1976 endorsed a programme advocating:

About a dozen directly elected regional authorities responsible for planning and for infrastructure development . . . they should take over from the 'ad hoc' authorities for water and sewerage, health and economic planning, plus certain powers devolved from central government, some of them already decentralised in the various departments regional offices. (Labour Party, 1976.)

However, it was not intended simply to add the proposed regional authorities to the existing framework of local authorities. The party statement declared:

Our aim is to simplify the local government structure. There would therefore have to be a much more straight-forward local government system below the regional tier with multi-purpose authorities reflecting genuine local communities and responsible for housing, education social services and other major functions. (Labour Party, 1976.)

The attempt to integrate the regional proposals with a further reform of local government was made more explicit in the party's second consultative document *Regional Authorities and Local Government Reform* published in July 1977. Clearly there was a measure of enthusiasm for elected regional authorities with executive functions capable of taking over responsibility for the various *ad hoc* bodies operating at the regional level. Thus Peter Shore's cautious suggestion of 'organic change' was accepted and welcomed as an 'interim step to full reform of the system'.

However, the response by the regional party conferences to the consultative document was mixed. Although all saw the value of regional bodies playing a role in economic development, few were prepared to alienate powers from local government. Labour councillors had established vested interests in the reformed structure and were apprehensive of yet another radical and disruptive overhaul of the local government system. Health Service unions were also hostile to the proposed regional authorities, preferring to establish some form of industrial democracy within the Health Service, while the regional water authorities, which presented the most obvious case for 'democratic regionalism', were constrained by hydrologically-determined boundaries which conspicuously failed to fit the socio-economic regions envisaged by the consultative document.

Thus by the autumn of 1977 the Labour Party had come to realize that a comprehensive policy of democratic regionalism contained two serious handicaps. It had alienated a wide range of functional interests within the party and it threatened to generate territorial demands which a Labour Party would be unable to satisfy or control.

That danger was always implicit in the devolution policy and had been recognized from the outset. In *Our Changing Democracy* the government had declared that 'devolution must never be seen as conferring unfair advantage in Scotland or Wales'. Subsequently, the threat of inter-regional competition was constantly raised by critics and refuted by the government during the passage of the devolution legislation through Parliament. The precise nature of the problem, as Drucker and Brown (1980, p. 111) saw it, was that 'the government whips had to do enough to shake English MPs out of their deep boredom with devolution without rousing them to resistance'. These tactics were not entirely successful. Of the twenty-nine Labour abstainers to the guillotine motion which destroyed the first devolution bill, ten came from the North East, an area most apprehensive of the advantages which devolution could give to Scotland. The remainder were concerned with the effect which devolution would have upon the procedures of Parliament, the status of MPs and the machinery of economic planning. In short, they were motivated by a desire to preserve and maintain the central institutions of the state.

In face of this reassertion of British statism implicit in the opposition of Labour back-benchers and explicit in the case of the Conservatives (particularly the Union Flag group of MPs) the decentralist component with the Labour Party crumbled (Keating and Lindley, 1981). It did so because it was an imperfect coalition of interests. Within its ranks were traditional 'home rulers' including, perhaps surprisingly, Mr Foot; some real devolutionists, such as Lord Crowther-Hunt and perhaps Mr Wilson as well as a smattering of English MPs; some Welsh and Scottish MPs who supported the proposals because of the economic advantages which they expected would accrue to their communities; and, lastly, by far the largest group, those who saw the policy purely and simply as a means of keeping a Labour government in office sufficiently long for the scars of the economic crisis of 1976–7 to have healed. Within such an alliance there was little unanimity of purpose and few commonly-shared basic principles. The alliance proved incapable of effectively steering the devolution bills through Parliament; still less was it able to provide a platform from which to fight the referendums in Scotland and Wales.

By any criterion the result of the referendums was a humiliating rebuff to the Labour Party. In Scotland the party had come to accept devolution as a more or less desirable necessity but few realized it would have to be fought for. Labour's devolution campaign consequently lacked conviction. The 'No Campaign', regardless of the involvement of renegade Labour back-benchers in its ranks, exploited the government's declining popularity and the fears of more bureaucracy and higher taxation. Despite Labour's dominant position in Scotland, the devolutionists obtained victory by only the narrowest of margins and failed to surmount the 40 per cent threshold requirement. There was even less support for the government's proposals in Wales where the party was more deeply divided. A majority of the Welsh constituency Labour parties publicly opposed the devolution proposals and a group of back-benchers, headed by Leo Abse and Neil Kinnock, directed a powerful campaign raising issues similar to those in Scotland but to which was added the spectre of a Welsh-speaking élite taking power. However, in both referendum campaigns a trump card, played by the Labour anti-devolutionists, was the charge that devolution was synonymous with separatism and the break-up of the British State.

Rebuilding the strategy

After its 1979 general election defeat, the Labour Party's territorial strategy was in disarray. It had a commitment to devolution in Scotland; the decisive referendum rejection in Wales relieved it of obligations there. At the same time, it faced a continuing English backlash against any special favours for Scotland. This coincided with a growing concern about regional policy and the English regional question as a whole. By the late 1970s, the lack of economic growth and of mobile investment had effectively put an end to the old regional policy of diverting investment, based on a non-zero-sum strategy assumption of growth everywhere for everyone. Former boom areas such as the West Midlands and Inner London were feeling the beginning of de-industrialization. In the regions, Labour activists and councillors were beginning to look at the prospects for indigenous growth policies and local government intervention. In the party leadership, there was a recognition that the 1979 election had not been lost in Scotland or Wales and that a new strategy was needed.

In the English regions, local government reform was an unfinished item from the 1974-9 government. For a long time, Labour-controlled city councils in Conservative-held shire counties had been pressing for a restoration of major functions, including education and social services. Opposition was also strongly expressed to the non-elected health and water authorities. In 1976, the Labour Party had committed itself in principle to solving the problem by abolishing the counties, and dividing their functions between single-tier local authorities and regional councils. The latter would take over water, but control of health was disputed by the Health Service unions who were pushing for what they called 'industrial democracy'. By the time of the 1979 election, practical agreement had been reached only on proposals for 'organic change' whereby powers would gradually be transferred from the counties to larger cities. Only with the major functions safely in the hands of city councillors would the party's local government interests be prepared to countenance the creation of regions.

By the early 1980s, there was an increasing concern about the centralist implications of Labour's programme and, in particular, the Alternative Economic Strategy. This was partly the result of the rise of the 'new urban left' (Gyford, 1983), described by Boddy and Fudge (1984, p. 7) as an alliance of 'socialist councillors, party and community activists and radicalised members of local government professions, particularly social work, planning and, to a lesser extent, housing as well as the growing number of "political" appointments to strategy groups within the town halls'. Individuals previously outside the party began to come in from one-issue campaigns and community groups and local Labour parties and, in due course, council Labour groups, moved to the left.

Among the major policy initiatives launched, notably in Greater London, the West Midlands, and Sheffield, were local economic development policies. Both the Greater London Council and the West Midlands Metropolitan County Council set up enterprise boards while Sheffield set up an Employment Department with a similar purpose. Although the original concern was as much with the immediate crisis of unemployment as with transcending capitalism, gradually, the experience of 'building from the bottom' (Blunkett and Green, 1983) affected the ideological stance of those involved, producing a philosophy of decentralized economic and industrial policies. This could represent a major challenge to traditional Labour thinking, with its emphasis on nationalization and central economic control. Sheffield's ambitious aim is 'to gain more direct, democratic control over employment, and to impose a greater degree of social planning upon the structural and technological changes taking place in Sheffield' (quoted, Boddy, 1984, p. 166). While this may seem beyond the resources of a district council, they do add that there is an exemplary purpose, to ensure 'that a future socialist government has working examples available of socialist planning and how this can be implemented' (Boddy, 1984, p. 166). Critics have maintained that, for all the rhetoric of advancing socialism, local economic intervention merely supports the capitalist system by partially socializing the costs of production. Others have pointed to the inevitably marginal impact, given the limited financial resources of local government. The detailed policy objectives also tend to suffer from a lack of clarity or consistency, with the emphasis being put variously on the retention of existing industry, diversification, manufacturing industry, profitability, employment maximization, and opportunities for minorities and women. So it would be an exaggeration to claim that a coherent new philosophy of local economic intervention is emerging; the relationship of local initiatives to the central thrust of Labour's economic strategy remains vague. There is, however, a challenge to central economic remedies which could have major implications for the future.

The same has happened in relation to other policy areas where there has been a ferment of ideas which have put local political activity back at the centre of the stage and raised its status in the eyes of the Labour Left (Boddy and Fudge, 1984). Financial cutbacks putting local government in the first line of defence for many public services have had a similar radicalizing effect, while the poor prospects for Labour's return to national power in the early 1980s concentrated many minds on local affairs. Increasingly, local government has been used as a political platform for issues well outside its legal competence. Many local authorities have declared themselves 'nuclear-free zones'. In practical terms this may mean little, but symbolically it represents a defiance of the central state by those claiming to speak for local communities. There have been battles over control of the police, with local councils disputing central government's (and Chief Constables') definition of law and order. All this has served to repoliticize local government and to move the party away from the old technocratic-administrative traditions. The Conservatives' proposals to abolish the Greater London Council and the Metropolitan counties merely underlined this, showing that the government did see Labour councils as a political threat.

It was to restore some coherence to Labour's devolution and regional policies and reconcile them with the Alternative Economic Strategy that John Prescott, a Hull MP, was appointed by Michael Foot as spokesman on devolution and regional affairs. We must be clear about the status that this gave him in Labour Party policy making. As a spokesman, he could present party policy and could propose new ideas, but any proposals would have to make their way through the traditional route of the National Executive Committee and resolutions to party conference. There were other influences at work in those forums, pushing policy in different directions.

The NEC has rarely seen territorial politics as a priority, but has often been prepared to take a pragmatic line on such questions. In the early 1980s, it was beset by the continuing civil war between Right and Left and was subject to strong pressures from conflicting interests. The party in Scotland was by now firmly committed to the devolution policy, and in 1981 lodged a strong protest against the failure to include any mention of the policy in Labour's interim programme. This oversight — which it is almost certain is all it was — was soon put right after protests from the Scottish Executive; after further urging, the NEC issued a statement at the beginning of 1983 unequivocally backing a devolved assembly. The only proviso was that the details of tax powers would have to be considered in the context of reforms for the whole of the United Kingdom.

Within the Parliamentary Labour Party, on the other hand, there was still considerable opposition to devolution. In 1981 the Northern group of English Labour MPs expressed their opposition to any new scheme for Scotland. The Yorkshire group also expressed disquiet, but in a more positive form, claiming a measure of equal treatment for themselves. Local government interests in the party were divided and, while primarily interested in new powers for the cities, some councillors, particularly in the North of England, were by no means hostile to the idea of regional government. The influential local government subcommittee of the NEC, however, was determined to give priority to the cities rather than to any experiments in regionalism.

The trade unions' interest in territorial government was sporadic but, as part of its reconsideration of economic policy, in 1982 the TUC produced a document, *Regional Development and Planning*. This recognized the need for a regional dimension in planning, but proposed that this should be done through tripartite Regional Development Planning Authorities. Throughout the debate, both the TUC and individual unions continued to insist that the English regional dimension should be accommodated through corporatist institutions on which they would have direct representation, a contrast with their support for an elected assembly in Scotland.

Prescott (1982) assembled a working group of academics and other interested people to produce the document, *Alternative Regional Strategy: A Framework for Discussion*, before the autumn 1982 Labour Party Conference. This takes the commitment to Scottish devolution as so far beyond debate that Scotland is dealt with only in an appendix, where the Scottish Council's proposals are laid out. The bulk of the paper is about England and Wales. Given the decisive rejection of Welsh devolution at the 1979 referendum, it is recognized that proposals for Wales would have to be brought in via England. The document approaches the regional question from the perspective of economic and industrial policy, and works from there to institutions. National and regional economic planning are seen as vital parts of Labour's AES although the limited possibilities for diversionary regional policy in contemporary conditions are recognized.

The *Alternative Regional Strategy* proposes both a reform of the national machinery for regional planning and the establishment of new machinery at the regional level. There would be regional assemblies and regional planning boards for the regions of England and for Wales. Ultimately, the regional councils would be directly elected and could take over some of the work of regional offices of government departments; initially they would probably be nominated by industry, unions, and local authorities. The councils and boards would draw up economic, social, and physical plans and be able to comment on the financial plans of all agencies, including nationalized industries. At national level, there would be a minister for English local and regional development with responsibility for regional and local economic policy, including inner-city policy. A Regional Planning Council would bring together all ministers with responsibilities for industry, economic development, expenditure planning, and the nationalized industries, together with the Prime Minister and the chairmen of the regional assemblies. There would be a regional input into the annual public expenditure review system with the regions making bids on the basis of their assessment of the total impact of proposed spending levels by the public sector as a whole in their areas. These would be fed through the Regional Planning Council to a Minister for Expenditure Co-ordination. Public expenditure would be broken down regionally as well as sectorally, although the major decisions would continue to be taken at national level. Labour's proposed National Planning Council would also have some regional representation.

The powers and resources of the regional assemblies are not discussed in detail, but it is suggested that in due course they could take over health and water authorities and other appointed agencies. The integration of these bodies and the development of regional expenditure statistics would, it is recognized, take some years to achieve. Scotland would be linked into the system through the Regional and National Planning Councils, thus providing some degree of equality of treatment and, it was hoped, defusing the English backlash. Taxation and finance for regional assemblies were the subject of the working group's further discussions, overtaken by the election announcement.

Three points stand out in an assessment of the Prescott proposals. Firstly, they recognize that equality of treatment as between Scotland and the English regions need not mean institutional uniformity. Rather, the respective demands of each should be met in so far as they can be reconciled with Labour's overall strategy. In Scotland, this means going for a legislative assembly; in England it is more important to promise development agencies, redistribution of public expenditure, and a revived regional policy. Secondly, there is an attempt to avoid the 'dualist' trap, by establishing centre-periphery linking machinery. As it is considered neither possible nor desirable to devolve major economic powers, these would be retained by the centre, but the regions would be given more influence over them. Nor are the linking mechanisms seen in the consensual terms of the 1960s Regional Planning Councils and Boards. It is recognized that territorial bargaining and regional planning will be an intensely political activity. Thirdly, for this very reason the proposals would be extremely difficult to carry within the Labour Party or to implement in government. If the territorial bargaining and planning were to be truly political and the proposed assemblies were to be have weight, they would need to be directly elected and control substantial resources. Yet this would cut across the power of many established office-holders in the Labour movement.

In the course of 1982 and early 1983, Prescott travelled around the country to sell his proposals to regional conferences of the party and to local government and union interests. Meanwhile, the working group continued to meet, coming round to the view that any regional authorities would have to be directly elected and could replace the county councils as the tier between central government and the districts. This ran into opposition from both union and local government interests.

The union's preference for corporatist institutions, which had hampered moves in the 1960s and 1970s for directly-elected regional government, was carried into the TUC–Labour Party Liaison Committee, which was extremely influential in the elaboration of the 1983 party programme. At a series of special regional conferences to discuss economic and regional strategies, the TUC document on *Regional Development and Planning* and the joint TUC–Labour Party Statement, *Economic Planning and Industrial Democracy* were discussed alongside Prescott's Alternative Regional Strategy. Differing interpretations have emerged of the mood of these conferences. There was clearly a lot of support for reviving regional policy and tying it into economic planning, but there were also differences on the form of the planning machinery and the role of the trade unions and local government.

Local government interests, having moved away from the organic change proposals towards outright abolition of the county councils, now often favoured unitary authorities for England and Wales. By 1982 this was party policy, endorsed by annual conference, but the means of implementing it were extremely vague. While the regionalists in the party saw the chance of combining the abolition of counties with the establishment of regions, many local councillors were deeply opposed. It was argued that this would merely recreate all the problems of two-tier government and hand over large parts of England to virtually permanent Conservative rule. Whatever happened, there was an insistence that local authorities should maintain their direct links with Whitehall. This would clearly reduce the weight of the regions. Neither the NEC nor its local government committee, nor the party conference, nor the party's local government conference was able to give more than vague approval in principle to a regional tier of government, with regional development agencies and regional planning machinery, but without any specification of the form it might take.

In Scotland the assembly commitment, though bounced through rather hastily in 1974, has gradually become accepted and solidified in the Labour Party. In the aftermath of the 1974 election, the party appeared to be strengthening it, with Scottish Conference resolutions calling in a sweeping way for an assembly with real economic powers. Conference rhetoric, from both union and constituency delegates, however, failed to distinguish between the autonomy and access strands of Labour's Scottish strategy. The Scotland Act of 1978 combined autonomy in the devolved social and environmental sphere with privileged access to the centralized economic sphere. When demands for an assembly with economic teeth were put beside the unshakeable commitment to the economic and political unity of the United Kingdom (often by the same speakers), all that could emerge was another dualist scheme.

Such a scheme was produced in 1980 by a working party set up by Labour's Scottish Executive. Devolution supporters succeeded in getting a commitment in principle to tax-raising powers and control of the Scottish Development Agency, the Highlands and Island Development Board, and some of the functions of the Manpower Services Commission. However, economic and industrial policy generally would remain with a central government assumed to be promoting an interventionist economic strategy and a rigorous regional policy to the benefit of Scotland and other needy areas. These proposals were presented to the Scottish Conference in interim form in 1981 (Labour Party Scottish Council 1981), and in their final version in 1982.

In essence, this was a restatement of the 1974–9 strategy, an attempt to reconcile devolution with the party's continued centralist commitments, especially in economic matters. This refurbished dualist strategy would be crucially dependent on a Labour government at Westminster, and sufficient economic growth to permit a strongly diversionary regional policy. However, just as the mainstream of the Labour Party in Scotland had come to terms with the commitment into which it had been pushed in 1974, undercurrents were at work which could render the policy redundant as the old

Home Rule policy was made redundant in the 1930s. While the 1979 general election restored the normal two-party majority government system to the House of Commons, it did not mark a complete return to traditional voting habits. The major parties' share of the vote was higher than in 1974 but by post-war standards, at 81 per cent, was still low. Even more striking was the geographical imbalance. Swings to the winning Conservatives ranged from 6.4 per cent in Greater London to minus 0.1 per cent in Scotland where Labour gained a Conservative seat. The result was a complicated mosaic of territorial politics. Wales appeared to be moving towards a more evenly balanced multi-party system. In Scotland, Labour was more dominant than ever. Since then, while Labour's strength in Scotland has proved remarkably resilient, in the South it has fallen further.

In the past, periods of Conservative government at Westminster have not, at least since the 1920s, led Scottish Labour to contemplate going it alone because that might put at risk the bigger, if distant, prize of power at United Kingdom level. In the 1979 Parliament, dominated by Margaret Thatcher's Conservatives, sections of the party, especially on the Left, began talking seriously about the possibility of a Labour defeat in Britain but a Labour majority in Scotland. In that case, some were prepared to contemplate a policy going well beyond devolution, in the direction of separatism. The argument was strengthened by the declining possibilities for diversionary regional policies. Not only has access to the levers of power at the United Kingdom level been made more difficult, but such access is in any case less valued and no longer weighs so heavily as an argument against autonomy.

The emergence within the Scottish National Party of the '79 group', on the left wing of the SNP, created common ground between neo-nationalists in the Labour Party and 79-groupers. Both saw Scotland as ripe for socialism but held back by England, and with no hope for a national movement without a base in the working class. This differed profoundly from the Labour Party line both before and after the 1974 elections. For the Labour Party, nationalism has been something to be fought as inimical to socialism and working-class interest; or it is something which can be handled by devolution devices tacked on to, and marginal to, the main centralist economic strategy. The nationalist-left analysis harks back to Labour's early days when Home Rule was a major element in the party's philosophy.

There are countless problems with the nationalist-left analysis, at both theoretical and practical levels. Theoretically, there is the problem of reconciling an advanced Home Rule or separatist strategy with the Alternative Economic Strategy to which the Left is committed and which involves strengthened levers of control at the United Kingdom level. It could be resolved by going for a purely Scottish AES, but this would mean import controls for Scotland, customs posts at the border, and Scottish withdrawal from a Common Market of which the rest of the United Kingdom continued to be a member; in short, Scottish economic autarky. Few have gone so far as to recommend this. Nor has the neo-nationalist Left faced up to the philosophical contradictions between the AES, and Bennism generally, which Tom Nairn (1982) is undoubtedly right to see as a form of English nationalism, and Scottish nationalism. Certainly there are few English left-wingers who would be prepared to view Scottish nationalist demands as having anything whatever in common with their own demands for emancipation from the EEC and the multinationals.

At a practical level, the neo-nationalist strategy faces the problem of how to carry the trade unions, still firmly committed to the United Kingdom, and of how it could actually be implemented faced with a Conservative government. There has been vague talk of civil disobedience, boycotts, and Sinn Fein tactics, but little serious thought of how power could be usurped and exercised, at what cost, or who would back it.

There was a constant worry among Scots pro-devolutionists in the 1979–83 period that the issue would fade away or become a mere relic, like Labour's Home Rule policy in the 1930s and 1940s. A ginger group, Labour For a Scottish Assembly, was set up in 1981 under the chairmanship of George Foulkes, MP. Foulkes also convened a group of MPs and advisers to consider strategy. A proposal to put a strong devolution resolution to the 1981 National Conference , however, was dropped because of the possibility of a defeat which could have put the policy back decades; given the trade unions' position, such a defeat was in fact highly unlikely. Meanwhile, all sides were at least agreed that the United Kingdom strategy deserved one more try and that the issue could not be forced in advance of a general election.

The declaration of the 1983 general election found Labour's plans for Scotland intact, but its English territorial strategy in disarray, and a British territorial strategy, linking all the elements together, almost non-existent. The Labour manifesto was produced in record time because the gap between Left and Right was so large that verbal quibbling would have been a waste of time, and the Right was unwilling to be saddled with the blame for the looming defeat by trying to dilute Conference policy. The recently-produced policy document, *The New Hope for Britain*, became, unchanged, the election manifesto. On Scotland, it declared, that Labour would:

Establish a directly elected Scottish Assembly, with an executive drawn from members of the assembly. Provide the Assembly with legislative and executive powers over a wide range of domestic policy, including matters such as health, education and social welfare. Ensure a major role for the Assembly in assisting the regeneration of Scottish industry — including the preparation of a plan for Scotland — within the context of our overall national plan. As well as receiving grants from central government, the Scottish Assembly will have tax-raising powers, thus ensuring that the level of services provided can be determined in Scotland (Labour Party, 1983.)

As usual, a separate but very similar Scottish manifesto was published by the Scottish Council of the Labour Party albeit sloppily giving its name as the Scottish Labour Party — actually the name of a break-away left-nationalist group led by Jim Sillars in the 1970s. *The New Hope for Scotland* (1983) contains a paragraph on devolution identical to that in the British manifesto, with an extra few words to explain how the assembly proposed in the 1978 Scotland Act would have protected Scotland from 'many of the worse excesses of Tory rule'.

For local government in England and Wales, the Labour manifesto is appropriately vague:

We are examining how best to reform local government. We believe that services such as health, water and sewerage should become answerable to a much greater extent to elected members and we aim to end, if we can, the present confusing division of services between two tiers of authority. Unitary district authorities, in England and Wales, could be responsible for all of the functions in this area that they could sensibly undertake.

A separate section on the inner cities pledges to: 'Use regional development agencies to prepare sites, encourage municipal and co-operative enterprise and help improve transport and other facilities'. In the Scottish version, an otherwise identical paragraph substitutes the SDA for reference to regional development agencies. On the composition of the English regional development agencies, the manifesto simply states that Labour will:

Develop regional development plans with plans also being drawn up at local level by local authorities. Regional development agencies will be established, extending our present commitment to a Northern Development Agency to other English regions in need of them. These agencies will have similar powers and resources to those in Scotland and Wales. We will also consider using new regional job subsidies.

Labour's 1983 election defeat saw renewed moves to push the Scottish party towards a more aggressive Home Rule stance, with party leaders in Scotland trying to hold the line at the devolution within the United Kingdom approach, giving equal weight to access and autonomy. A group of MPs tried to commit the party to the 'no mandate' argument, denying the legitimacy of Conservative rule in Scotland. It was the old dilemma for Labour in Scotland but with a vital difference. In the past, Labour had chosen the United Kingdom strategy because it was advancing; now the party leadership holds to it in retreat.

For Labour, at the United Kingdom level, the dilemma is no less acute. While the electoral needs of the party now point more strongly than ever to the need to win more seats in the more prosperous parts of Southern England, the internal weight of interest in the party is against this. Labour is likely to emphasize the needs of its regional and urban bases. With power continuing to drift away from the Parliamentary Labour Party, it could develop a philosophy of local power. Such local powers would rest on fragile institutional support, especially with the Conservatives pledged to abolish the Greater London Council and metropolitan counties and setting their faces against a Scottish assembly. What is clear is that the British Labour Party cannot now return to its old strategy of territorial management, which has failed to achieve both local autonomy and central planning.

CHAPTER 6

Labour and the machinery of government

SINCE the early 1960s, Labour has come back intermittently to the question of the machinery and personnel of government, recasting its approach to the issue in accordance with its general aims and priorities. However, the party's attempts to come to grips with this revealed the same ambiguities and tensions which we have noted have historically marked its approach to the institution and power of the state. In particular, we detect a tension between two key sets of objectives in relation to the machinery of government, which we can characterize as *instrumental* and *intrinsic*. Instrumental objectives encompass the reforms needed to create a machine capable of implementing Labour's programme as it developed. Intrinsic concerns include Labour's desire to democratize the state, to make it more responsive, participative and open and to reform it as a social institution, widening opportunities for entrance and advancement and removing privileges. The two sets of objectives are by no means always compatible though this is often obscured by the habit of selling total packages of reform including elements of both and asserting that the one will necessarily support the other. To some extent, this is a manifestation of the old dilemma, between a centralist, directive, planned strategy and a decentralized, pluralist approach which has dogged Labour's attempts to come to terms with the territorial dimension of politics. It is often assumed that the experience of political participation and democratization will break down resistance to socialist ideas and educate the working class into a true perception of their unified class interest; but even among left-wing exponents of this view there remains an uneasy awareness of the possible conflicts in developing 'socialist alternatives and ways forward, while seeking active inputs and popular involvement from the grass roots' (Boddy and Fudge, 1984, p. 14). There is also an ambiguity in Labour's attitude towards professionalism in government. Labour needs experts and specialists to carry out its policies but to favour them carries the risk of encouraging both professional élitism and technocratic solutions to policy problems. This in turn can hinder Labour's intrinsic objectives with regard to the state, of making it more democratic and participative and less exclusive.

Labour has rarely given much thought to basic constitutional matters such as parliamentary sovereignty, cabinet government, or ministerial responsibility; as we have seen, these questions were largely closed off in the course of the party's historical evolution. Other machinery of government questions were swept aside in the urgency to carry through the 1945 programme and the fact that the existing state apparatus was used successfully to do that served further to downgrade the reform question. As the 1964 election approached, the issue came back on the agenda as the party absorbed the fashionable thinking about modernization and change but in a rather piecemeal fashion, focused often on secondary issues whose outcome was largely predetermined by Labour's prior acceptance of the basic government conventions. In the late 1970s, the debate re-opened, focusing on the machinery needed to carry out Labour's new, radical plans and the lessons of the Labour governments of 1964–70 and 1974–9. This time, basic issues of power were at last confronted but, like other policy issues, the debate was soon caught up in Labour's internal divisions and the issue of the machinery of government soon subordinated to that of 'party democracy'. The latter, we shall show, often involved little more than a 'chain of command' theory in which policy demands could flow from the party activist cadre to the leadership, who would in turn be obliged to toe the line by the prospect of party sanctions. Complex questions about making policy in government and then carrying it out in the face of the constraints and uncertainties inherent in contemporary conditions tended to be dismissed in favour of preparing a detailed programme in advance and assuming that implementation failures could only stem from treachery or bad faith, which could be eliminated by strengthening party discipline.

The issue was a vital one because of the fundamental shift in party strategy between 1964 and the late 1970s. The consensus strategy of 1964 aimed at national mobilization to increase economic growth and provide a surplus for progressive redistribution. The accent was on efficiency and modernization. Equality of opportunity could advance both while being socially progressive. It was an advanced liberal package with a strong commitment to an expanded Welfare State, well illustrated by Harold Wilson's campaign speeches (Wilson, 1964) in which the attacks are directed at the aristocracy, old-fashioned management, the 'old school tie' system and the socially-exclusive

Conservative leadership, rather than at the capitalist system, industrial management as a whole or the new (acceptable) managerial élites. The defeat of the government in 1970 heralded a steady move to the left, towards a non-consensual strategy of irreversibly 'shifting the balance of power and wealth'. In the event, the 1974–9 government largely pursued the old strategy and it was this which led to the serious rift in the party and the moves to strengthen party control over the leadership. The left-wing strategy, however, and notably the Alternative Economic Strategy adopted in the late 1970s, did entail a major increase in the role of the state. In turn, this should have entailed a major re-examination of the machinery of the state and the parliamentary system to establish its suitability for the pursuit of a non-consensual strategy of shifting power relationships. This was indeed begun in a small way but was distracted by the debate on 'party democracy'; the failure to come to grips with the problem is perhaps nowhere better illustrated by the fact that by 1977 the item chosen for highest priority in the reform of government, seen as 'the obstacle to socialism' was the abolition of the House of Lords. We will trace Labour's changing view on the machinery of government by examining policies on the reform of the Civil Service, the reform of the House of Commons and the reform or abolition of the House of Lords.

The Reform of the Civil Service

Labour's attitudes to the personnel of government have revolved round four sets of views encompassing both instrumental and intrinsic objectives. First of all, there is the view that the Civil Service is politically neutral and will work for any government provided that ministers have the skill and determination to make it do so. Harold Wilson was known to believe that if ministers could not make the Civil Service work for them it was their own fault (Crossman, 1977). Others, like William Rogers, have had 'the style and temperament that civil servants tend to find least unacceptable in a Minister' (Rogers, 1980, p. 10). Richard Crossman was less charitable about the role of senior civil servants, maintaining that they did withhold information from ministers and collude behind their backs (Crossman, 1977), but even he came to believe that a strong minister should be able to control his department. Of course, a belief in the essential neutrality and competence of the Civil Service may be combined with a desire for a wider social basis of recruitment, for instrinsic reasons.

Secondly, there is the 'managerialist' view that the Civil Service is politically neutral but old-fashioned, inefficient, lacking in innovative talent, and imbued with an anti-industrial culture. What is needed is a change in recruitment patterns to break the dominance of the public school gentleman-amateur and bring in people with relevant professional and managerial skills, together with a reform of management procedures on modern business lines. In so far as changed recruitment procedures favour a new meritocratic élite as against the privileged, but technically less competent, cadre who may have dominated the service in the past, such a reform can be presented as fulfilling both the instrumental and the intrinsic aims of party policy. Clearly, the Fulton Report falls into this category. The grammar-school meritocracy was to the fore in the Labour Party leadership from the 1950s and Fulton fitted perfectly their view of the conditions for national modernization.

Thirdly, there is the view that the Civil Service is biased politically to the Right. Brian Sedgemore and some of his Labour colleagues on the 1977 Expenditure Committee wrote that 'political bias may have played a part' in the frustration by civil servants of the then government's interventionist industrial policies and complained of Department of Trade civil servants 'totally out of sympathy with a positive trade policy' and 'hostile to any meaningful form of industrial democracy' and of Home Office 'reactionaries ruthlessly pursuing their own reactionary policies' (Sedgemore, 1980, p. 232). Such complaints are commonplace in Labour circles but rarely form part of a coherent critique of the state as an institution or even of the machinery of government as a whole. For such a critique, one has to look to Marxist analyses outside the Labour Party. Marxist observers tend to maintain that the Civil Service will support the capitalist economic order either because of the class background of those involved (Miliband, 1973) or because of the structural position of the state within the capitalist economic system (Poulantzas, 1969). Few Labour Party observers have advanced the latter proposition which, in its pure form, would render political action through the party futile, though some critics have come near it. For example, the Conference of Socialist Economists' London Working Group drew attention to 'the structural constraints on the way the state can intervene' as a concession to Left critiques of the Alternative Economic Strategy (CSE, 1980). Others have hinted that there may be something in the former, Sedgemore and his colleagues claiming that civil servants 'seek to govern the country according to their narrow, well-defined interests, tastes, education and background' and conceding that 'some would say they perceive (the public good) in the interest of their own class' (Sedgemore, 1980, p. 231). However, they do not *explicitly* accuse the Civil Service of right-wing bias caused by its social composition. Their task might have been easier if they had gone all the way with such an analysis, for then changing the pattern of recruitment would naturally follow as the means for making the service more socially representative *and* a better policy instrument.

Instead, most recent left-wing critics have adopted a fourth perspective, that top civil servants are biased in favour of maintaining the status quo. This is the main thrust of Sedgemore's critique (Sedgemore, 1980) and that of Tony Benn who writes of 'the process of civil service containment successfully practised against both Conservative and Labour governments over the last thirty years' (Benn, 1981, p. 52). He maintains, indeed, 'it would be a mistake to suppose — as some socialists have suggested — that the senior ranks of the Civil Service are active Conservatives posing as impartial administrators . . . The problem arises from the fact that the Civil Service sees itself as being above the party battle, with a political position of its own to defend against all-comers, including incoming governments armed with their philosophy and programme' (Benn, 1981, p. 50). According to this analysis, what is required is not merely a reform of recruitment procedures to bring in people with different preconceptions but also firmer political *control* of the Civil Service to swing the balance of power back to the politicians. As Sedgemore and his Labour colleagues on the Expenditure Committee's inquiry into the civil service put it, 'We regard the resolution of the struggle for power between the executive . . . and the bureaucracy . . . in favour of political power and authority and against bureaucratic power and authority as a central need of our age' (Sedgemore, 1980, p. 229). Such a view sees the Civil Service as representing, not a class in the Marxist sense, but an élite caste assiduously defending its own power and privileges and ensuring its own collective self-perpetuation by recruiting in its own image and likeness.

We have set out these four perspectives as though they were quite separate. In fact, any one observer of the Civil Service is likely to draw on more than one of them at a time and, indeed, part of our argument is that reform has too often been presented as a single, inter-related set of issues. The contrasts and contradictions between the approaches are worth stressing, reflecting as they do the confused state of Labour thought on the issue. We have already drawn attention to the possible contradictions between Labour's instrumental and instrinsic objectives. The debates have also revealed contradictions among the four points of view we have just summarized. For example, left-wingers have often criticized the Civil Service for its close links with private business, including the *pantouflage* of top civil servants into private jobs on retirement, claiming that this builds in a right-wing, private business-oriented bias. It is claimed at the same time that the importation of business personnel and techniques into the civil service itself creates an anti-socialists bias (Labour Party, RE:904/1977). Yet many of those subscribing to our second point of view and supporting the Fulton critique would wish to *increase* the role of business management in government and criticize the *isolation* of government from the world of business. Once again the ambiguity reflects a wider uncertainty about the role of the state and its composition, as well as its relation to business interests.

Let us now trace the development of Labour Party attitudes to the Civil Service to see how they have reflected these concerns over the last two decades or so. Concern with the Civil Service, essentially based on the second of our points of view, the managerialist critique, had been growing in opinion-forming circles through the late 1950s and early 1960s. Hugh Thomas's 1959 book, *The Establishment*, included a chapter by Thomas Balogh attacking the amateur tradition in the service. In 1963, Brian Chapman, in *British Government Observed*, compared British civil servants unfavourably with their French counterparts. In 1964, a Fabian pamphlet, *The Administrators*, accused the Civil Service of being isolated from industry, local government, and other fields of society and criticized the cult of the generalist. Its recommendations for reform bore resemblance to those later approved by the Fulton Committee which was not entirely fortuitous. The anonymous Fabian pamphleteers were to be very influential in the later debate. In the run-up to the 1964 general election, Harold Wilson took up the theme of Civil Service reform as part of his modernist appeal. Deadwood should be cut out of boardrooms and ministries alike, for Britain's future depended on 'the thrusting ability and even iconoclasm of millions of products of our grammar schools, comprehensive schools, secondary moderns and the rest' (Wilson, 1964). 'Socialism', he declared, 'means applying a sense of purpose to our national life . . . Purpose means technical skill . . . If you fly the

Atlantic in a jet, you want to be sure the pilot knows the job that he's been trained for' (Wilson, 1964). These ideas were widespread well beyond the Labour Party; indeed the Labour party should be seen as latching on to this thinking and incorporating it in its strategy and appeal rather than as originating it. It corresponded well to the needs of the consensus-based growth strategy of the time.

A more dynamic and efficient Civil Service could assist Labour's plans for growth and scientific advance, upon which its welfare pro-posals rested. At the same time, Labour's political fortunes could be helped by a successful appeal to the growing body of scientists, administrators, and professional people including the white-collar salariat produced by the Welfare State, described in the Transport House document, *Labour and the Sixties*, as in many cases 'politically isolated. They are not in with Labour yet they are disgusted with the Tory view that status-seeking and ladder-climbing are the most important human activities' (quoted, Butler and King, 1965, p. 73).

In 1966, in response partly to a critical report from the House of Commons Expenditure Committee, Wilson set up the Fulton Com-mittee, with a brief to 'examine the structure, recruitment and man-agement, including training, of the Home Civil Service and to make recommendations'. These were narrow terms of reference, precluding examination of the machinery of government as a whole, or the rela-tionship between ministers and civil servants. The report (Fulton, 1968), published in 1968 and said to be largely the work of Dr Norman Hunt (later Lord Crowther-Hunt) of Exeter College, Oxford, reflected closely the current criticisms. Six defects were identified:

— The tradition of the generalist administrator was obsolete;
— the system of classes and grades was inefficient;
— there were too few opportunities for specialists to rise to top administrative posts;
— there were too few skilled managers;
— there was not enough contact with the 'community';
— there was a lack of personnel management and planning.

As well as suggestions for remedying these defects, notably by reforming selection and promotion procedures, there were hints at improving the management performance of government through devices such as Management by Objectives and the 'hiving off' of functions to accountable units within government.

Despite its provocative opening sentences —

The Home Civil Service today is still fundamentally the product of the nineteenth-century philosophy of the Northcote–Trevelyan Report. The tasks it faces are those of the second half of the twentieth century —

Fulton was not a radical document. Such a radical approach would have required a wider examination of the role of government, the structure of the state, and the power of the various elements within it. Perhaps this would be unrealistic to expect from an official committee of inquiry; but what is striking is that the Labour Party itself did not attempt to present a more radical critique. Its evidence followed closely on fashionable thinking and the 1964 Fabian pamphlet, raising controversy only with its claim — denounced by Wilson (Crossman, 1977) — that civil servants withheld information from ministers. Fulton's ambiguities, indeed, reflected those of the Labour Party itself, for instance in its assumption that both efficiency and democracy could be enhanced by the same set of personnel changes, and in its ambivalence on the appropriateness of private business techniques in government and on the élitist implications of greater professionalism.

Ashford (1981, p. 72) has pointed out the Report's 'naive conviction that if different kinds of people, presumably more socially representative and more professional, were put in the upper ranks of the civil service, then the policy making process would be simultaneously more "democratic" and more efficient'. There was a fundamental ambiguity on the question of élitism. The existing Civil Service structure was criticized for being élitist as well as amateur but the recommendations, to encourage greater professionalism and, above all, the admiration shown for the French *École Nationale d'Administration* (ENA), implied élitism of a different sort. It is true that, in its own evidence, the Labour Party did deplore the narrow social basis of ENA recruits but the basic thrust of its message was a call for a more meritocratic élite. How this could be reconciled with a more egalitarian style was a question left unresolved. Similar questions can be raised about Fulton's enthusiasm for managerialism in government and the potential for applying private-sector business techniques. The assumption was that these techniques were in themselves neutral and could be harnessed to any political programme. In fact, they often reflected definite views about the way in which the British economy and Welfare State should be run. Most notably, they were set within the assumption of general consensus about the growth/efficiency strategy and the means to achieve it. Furthermore, the connection between new management techniques and the traditional constitutional principles, such as ministerial accountability and parliamentary control, were not spelt out. Indeed, changes in these constitutional principles or in relationships between ministers and civil servants were seen as beyond the Committee's terms of reference.

Predictably, Fulton was received rapturously by those who had long advocated the changes it recommended. Roger Opie in the *New Statesman* (28.6.68) declared that, within its regrettably narrow terms of reference the Committee had gone 'far to meet the criticisms of many Socialist critics'. He looked forward to 'howls of outrage' from civil servants. Thomas Balogh (*New Statesman*, 28.6.84) saw it as 'the beginning of a new, vigorous period of change'. Other comments were more cynical. Retired civil servants Lord Helsby (*Listener*, 18.7.68) and F. A. Bishop (*Spectator*, 18.7.68) saw little radical in the report, merely an endorsement of trends already under way. Eric Hobsbawn (*Spectator*, 18.7.68) dismissed it as a 'compendium of the commonplaces of the 1960s', full of fashionable 'pop theory'. Specifically, he claimed that the attack on the generalist tradition was not thought out and the report had shied away from the fundamental question of the social and political control of bureaucracy; the chapter on 'The Civil Service and the Community' mixed up several different problems — the relationships of administrators to Ministers and Parliament, to the press, to organized interests, to other top people and to ordinary citizens.

Its critics notwithstanding, Fulton was immediately endorsed by the government with only minor changes. This was hardly surprising in view of its origins, though Crossman (1977) suggests that the Cabinet gave Wilson 'an easy time' in view of his personal commitment. Much has been written about the non-implementation of the Report. Kellner and Crowther-Hunt (1980) claim it was sabotaged by the civil servants themselves. Self (1977) criticizes the Committee for misunderstanding the British political system, placing too much emphasis on the needs of 'management' and not enough on the political environment in which civil servants operate. We would agree and add that, had the Committee and the Government paid more attention to this, they might have realized that the question of Civil Service structure and management cannot be divorced from wider questions about the political system and the purposes of government. No doubt the Civil Service did drag its feet on the implementation of some of Fulton's recommendations, but the main reason for the lack of radical reform was the confusion of purpose on the part of both the Committee and the government. The lack of concern with the scope and purposes of government contrasts with the attitude of the post-1970 Conservative administration. As far as the Civil Service is concerned, there was a failure to distinguish the types of criticism which could be levelled against it and the remedies appropriate to each. Instead, it was assumed that the problems of élitism, efficiency, and power could all be solved together, largely through changes in recruitment patterns. Even this was not thoroughly followed through, the implementation of the recommendations being entrusted to the civil service itself, which continued to recruit in its own image and likeness.

For the Labour Party, the issue of Civil Service reform, never a central priority, died away in the late 1960s. It reappeared again in the mid-1970s as the party, seeking to explain the failures of 1964–70 noticed that the Labour government elected in 1974 was already being driven off course. In 1977, the Expenditure Committee of the House of Commons investigated the Civil Service, coming up with an analysis and recommendations very similar to those of Fulton. Of particular interest to our theme, though, was the 'alternative first chapter', in effect a minority report drafted by Brian Sedgemore and supported by the majority of the Labour members of the Committee (Expenditure Committee, 1977). This accused the Civil Service of wishing to govern the country according to its own views and warned of a trend towards a corporate state. The analysis was crude, with no attempt rigorously to define what civil servants' own interests were and, as we noted above, stopped short of accusing them of acting on behalf of external class interests. Nor was 'corporatism' adequately defined and explained. However, the chapter was significant as one of the first attempts in the Labour Party seriously to face up to the question of Civil Service *power*, the relationships between ministers and civil servants and the bureaucratic pre-requisites for radical political change.

Such a reconsideration was becoming urgent as the Labour Party moved towards the adoption of the left-wing Alternative Economic Strategy, endorsed by the National Executive Committee and Conference during the 1974–9 government and gaining rapid ascendancy after the fall of the government. In 1976, the NEC's Home Policy Committee re-established a Machinery of Government Study Group, commenting:

Hitherto these matters have often been seen as outside the range of party policy. Now British membership of the Common Market, the Devolution debate, the renewed obstruction of the House of Lords and certain other issues have moved governmental machinery and practice more into the centre of political discussion. (RE:515/March 1976.)

Matters to be examined were the Civil Service, open government, select committees, party democracy, the House of Lords, the honours system, and the Crown.

The deliberations on the Civil Service revealed the whole range of attitudes then prevalent in the Labour Party, from continued 'Fultonism' to left-wing attacks on the service for bias towards right-wing and business interests. As an example of the latter, a paper from the research department, prepared 'in collaboration with members of the Study Group', claimed that 'As the view of business has gained ground — that Britain's poor growth record is heavily due to the lack of entrepreneurial spirit within the government machine — ideology has become subordinated to consultancy exercises on managerial efficiency'. The remedy for this   — which could almost be read as an attack on the 1960s Labour Party leadership, Fulton and all — was to be found in greater ministerial control over the Civil Service, a quota for working-class recruits to the service and assistance in public appointments by 'one or more members of the Minister's personal *cabinet*, working in conjunction with a small unit in Transport House which should be exlusively concerned with advising on patronage' (RE:904/Jan. 1977). Not surprisingly, these latter items made little progress but the tone of the debate was none the less shifting markedly from the consensus stance of the 1960s to the requirements of a non-consensual political strategy. The view that civil servants would obstruct *any* radical government, of Right or Left, rapidly gained ground and the recommendations of the group, endorsed by the 1978 conference, were to:

— establish ministerial private offices, or *cabinets* to strengthen political control;
— give ministers the right to choose their own top officials;
— give junior ministers more responsibility;
— introduce new selection procedures for the Civil Service;
— create a unified structure, with more opportunities for specialists.

Again, there is here a mixture of unfulfilled Fultonism, and the confusion of reform of personnel with political control. However, what generally distinguishes this from the earlier approach is that they confront the issue of *power* directly and place this at the centre of discussion.

The weakness of the new approach, and the reason it makes only a limited contribution to resolving the question of Labour's relations with the state, is that it tends to reduce the *whole question* to one of power. The decisions to seek greater ministerial control over civil servants and, as we see below, greater parliamentary control over both, were closely related to the moves to establish greater *party* control over ministers and MPs. The assumption was that such control, reaching back to the Labour activists in the constituencies and unions, would keep the leadership on the straight and narrow. As Hindess (1983) points out, this in turn rests upon an assumption that such a power structure would automatically produce socialist policies because of the essential socialism of the rank and file. Hindess goes on to remark that the significance of democratizing the Labour Party is 'not so much to transform the conditions in which policy questions are debated . . . but rather to strengthen support for existing Labour Party policy against the leadership'. Geekie and Keating (1983) similarly see the 'party democracy' issue less in terms of democratizing procedures than as a means of shifting power from one ideological faction to another and, indeed, from one élite to another.

The exclusive focus on power relationships and the related obsession with the belief that the Labour governments of the 1960s and 1970s had been led to betray their principles by the evil men of the Civil Service and business served to distract attention from the complex problems of managing the state machine, of carrying out a left-wing programme, and of coping with the often unforeseeable obstacles which such a programme was bound to encounter. Specifying the programme in detail in advance or giving the final power to bodies who do not have the responsibility for carrying out the decisions are no solutions to the problem. Indeed, it can be argued that, in constructing a chain-of-command from the activists cadre into the heart of the state machine and expecting one end of the string to move when the other is pulled, the Labour Left have fallen into one of the basic errors of the classical management school. The party is still a long way from a considered theory of state power and the possibilities and constraints on political change. It is also far from a considered position on the politicization of the state machine and on the relationship of its plans for radical change to the continuing system of partisan alternation in power, a point to which we return in our conclusion.

House of Commons Reform

The issue of the organization and function of the House of Commons, including the role of the back-bench MP and the relationship of the Commons to the executive, illustrates particularly well Labour's ambivalent approach to the machinery of the state. On the one hand, there is the support for a strong executive, able to carry through the party's proposals for change untrammelled by constitutional obstacles; on the other is the radical-liberal tradition of suspicion of executive power, and support for popular democracy and control over leaders. Neither tradition was coherently developed and articulated before the 1960s, both being compatible with a reverence for the institution of Parliament and an insistence on its utrammelled sovereignty. There was no Labour philosophy about the organization of Parliament and though, in the 1930s, some worries had been voiced about the capacity of the parliamentary machine to cope with a radical Labour programme, no proposals for dealing with the problem had been worked out. In the event, the fact that the Attlee government's programme *was* put through — albeit with some difficulty, pushed the issue altogether beyond the range of Labour's thinking (Crick, 1970b).

In the run-up to the 1964 election, parliamentary reform was another issue — like that of Civil Service reform — which came onto Labour's agenda from the outside. In 1963, Bernard Crick published *The Reform of Parliament* and the study of Parliament Group, set up in 1964 and comprising academics and officers of the House, began to advocate reforms, notably the establishment of specialized select committees to scrutinize the work of the executive. In 1963 and 1964, Wilson had dropped hints that parliamentary reform might feature in the programme of a Labour government, though details tended to be unclear and confused (Crick, 1970b). After the election there was increased support for reform among the new intake of Labour members, some of whom formed the Labour Reform Group as a consciously partisan Lobby for reform. The response of the parliamentary party was to set up a working party 'packed with senior members with no record of reforming interest and [including] none of the new Group's activists' (Barker, 1970). Nevertheless the 1966 manifesto did include a promise of parliamentary reform and the movement gained powerful impetus from the large intake of new MPs, often younger, university-educated, and not content with the traditional passive and often deferential role of the back-bencker. There was a view that change was in the offing, that attitudes were being fundamentally reappraised. We shall follow the fortunes of the movement by examining two innovations, select committees and the 'ombudsman' or Parliamentary Commissioner for Administration.

In 1965, the Select Committee on Procedure had recommended the establishment of a series of specialized sub-committees of the Estimates Committee and this was done in the two following sessions. The major development, however, came with the appointment of Richard Crossman as Leader of the House in 1966. Although the *Diaries* show that parliamentary reform was not a central interest of Crossman's, he was certainly prepared to undertake more radical experiments than his predecessor (Crossman, 1976). Specialized select committees were set up with increased powers during the rest of the Parliament and many observers were convinced that a quiet revolution was under way.

Bernard Crick described the change in Labour Party thinking in graphic terms:

Some sort of fusion has been taking place of two strains of Labour Party thinking, which are now both, if taken separately, all but completely abandoned: the 'populist' democratic school, in which popular participation and/or workers' control would solve everything — the Bevanite chapel; and the élitist Fabian–Webbite–Hampstead–Highgate–Bloomsbury, or for short 'public administration' school, in which proper institutional forms and administrative rules would confer all the blessings that are to be had on the ignorant rest of us — Beatrice *oblige*. (Crick, 1970b, p. 211.)

This reflected a widespread view that the old debates about executive *versus* back-bench power were becoming redundant, in that parliamentary reform could serve to improve policy-making and thus serve the interests of both front- and back-benches (Morris, 1970). This sort of thinking closely parallels contemporary thinking about Civil Service reform which, as we have seen, largely side-stepped the issue of power by stressing common goals of efficiency and modernization.

The rejoicing, however, was premature for the evidence strongly points to the view that the government was interested in parliamentary reform primarily as a means of expediting its own business (Crick, 1970b). Select committees were, in some degree, a quid pro quo for streamlining the legislative process and, as Johnson commented, 'nowhere was the lack of definition, and uncertainty, greater than in respect of select committee developments' (Johnson, 1970,

p. 242). Among back-benchers, the active supporters of the select committee idea were still a minority, albeit a vocal and articulate one, and there was some back-bench opposition. The problem was that at the time most supporters of select committees, especially in the study of Parliament Group and the Procedure Committee, saw them as suitable principally for consensus matters (Morris, 1970). Some went further and saw them as a means of *promoting* political consensus across party lines. Many reformers held that the effectiveness of committees would be enormously strengthened if they could reach bi-partisan agreement, either replacing the Government/Opposition division with a Government/Back-bench one, or even blurring all divisions altogether. In an adversarial political system such as that of Britain, this was always unlikely and, in any case, the suggestion aroused deep opposition within the Labour Party. Michael Foot, for example, was unyielding in his opposition:

Anybody with any experience of committees upstairs knows that the cosier the atmosphere the less the clash between the parties. I am in favour of the clash between the parties and the debates between the parties being in the open, because the public has a right to hear them (Morris, 1970).

So select committees were opposed as a threat to adversary politics on the floor of the House. This was a common view on the Labour Left, as on the Conservative Right. From other back-benchers there was apathy as the new committees appeared politically irrelevant.

In the event, the reforms were carried through in a most conservative fashion, avoiding any challenge to the traditional tenets of the constitution, such as ministerial responsibility, Civil Service anonymity, secrecy, or the interpretation of parliamentary sovereignty which allows it to be used as a cover for executive dominance. The Agriculture Committee was wound up after two sessions amid a great deal of acrimony. The government insisted that the intention all along was that committees would be temporary, to allow MPs to move onto new areas of inquiry; the committee itself protested and insisted that committees would need a measure of permanence to do their job (Wiseman, 1970). Generally, by 1970, a good deal of disillusionment had set in amongst the supporters of the experiment. No clear idea had emerged of what the committees were for or what their relationship to the executive should be. Under a Labour government, should they be seen as a means of permitting opposition to the government, including dissent from Labour back-benchers? This could be justified on a liberal, pluralist interpretation of Labour's traditions. Should they be used as a means whereby Labour could mobilize support for its programme, confident that factual enquiry could only strengthen its case? Few argued this. Were they, then, to be used to achieve bipartisan political consensus or find solutions beyond the range of ideology? On the loyalist Right of the party was a fear of the former and on the Left a fear of the latter. So the tradition of executive dominance, which Labour had taken over with the rest of the constitution, was to be largely undisturbed. Above all, from our point of view, there had been a failure to integrate them into Labour's strategy for change or into a coherent view of the institutions of government.

The establishment of the 'ombudsman' or Parliamentary Commissioner for Administration (PCA), shows the same ambivalence about state power and its control. Support for an ombudsman had been growing in informed circles in the early 1960s. In 1962, the organization Justice recommended the appointment of a PCA and the case was pursued by Geoffrey Marshall, of The Queen's College, Oxford, among others. In 1964 Labour adopted the idea, despite some opposition, for example from Douglas Houghton, who regarded it as unnecessary in the British parliamentary system, Houghton argued that, instead of promising a PCA, Labour should pledge that, in government, it would avoid maladministration! (R:774/May 1964).

In office, Labour did indeed create a PCA but in the most constitutionally conservative manner possible. He was to be approachable only through MPs, so as to preserve the MP's role as mediator with the administration. His decisions were to be advisory, so as to preserve the doctrine of ministerial responsibility. He was even forbidden, in the pursuit of the same principle, to name civil servants, though this proved impossible to sustain in practice (Marshall, 1970).

Even in this weakened form, the PCA encountered opposition from ministers (Crossman, 1976) and was only grudgingly accepted. With Labour so tied to a parliamentary tradition stressing executive dominance and discretion, suggestions for the creation of a system of administrative law which clarified the rights of the citizens *vis-à-vis* the state authorities and specified the role and responsibilities of civil servants, and limited ministerial discretion did not, even in opposition, reach the agenda.

After 1970, though a considerable number of developments in Commons procedure did take place, Labour's concern with the issue died away. It came back in the late 1970s in a different form, more closely tied in this time to the party's programme and priorities. As with Civil Service reform, one of the key factors was a reaction against the 'betrayal' of the governments of 1964–70 and 1974–9 and the need to strengthen mechanisms of control. Back-bench power was in any case boosted by the increasing number of rebellions by both Left and Right over the years, culminating in major defeats during 1976–9 on incomes policy and devolution. Traditionally, the Left had espoused the cause of strong executive government, with support for the strengthening of Parliament and curbs on the executive coming from the centre and the less authoritarian sections of the Right. Now support for parliamentary reform began to come from a Left searching for mechanisms to keep Labour governments on the straight and narrow and to strengthen the political side of government against the bureaucratic.

In the late 1970s, the Machinery of Government Study Group gave its attention to the matter and by 1978 the NEC was able to issue a statement linking the reform of Parliament directly to the new left-wing programme. Powerful investigative committees would be set up to scrutinize departments. Bills would be dealt with, not by standing committees but by new legislative committees which would have powers to call ministers, civil servants and outside experts to give evidence. The justification was a far cry from the old calls for cross-party consensus and impartial investigation:

Since we see no future in consensus government by all-party committees, these departmental committees would, in addition to the necessary secretariat, be staffed and advised by specialists and on party poltical lines. Effectively, the establishment of such committees would disperse power in Parliament and out of it to the political parties, and to those individuals and groups who support political parties (NEC, 1978).

This, like the parallel development of policy on the Civil Service, takes us to the heart of Labour's new attitude to state power. It is neither Parliament nor the back-bench MP which is to be strengthened here, but the *political parties*. Although the movement for parliamentary reform has its supporters right across the political spectrum, there is a world of difference between wanting to increase the capacity of the back-bench MP to make sound judgements on the basis of better information — the policy of the old reform school — and a view of the MP as a transmission belt from the party to the government machine. Judge (1983) has pointed to the contradictions of Tony

Benn's ideas on this, noting that Benn seeks both a strong socialist government bound to a radical manifesto — rejecting proportional representation because it would leave such a government beholden to changing coalitions in the House — *and* a strengthened House of Commons. As Judge (1983, p. 194) comments, 'only if Benn assumes a consensus for socialism within the House and within the electorate generally does his vision of collective parliamentary control over a future socialist government make sense'. Labour's new policy, taken with the contemporary moves towards greater party control over MPs, sidestepped the whole problem through its 'chain of command' theory in which the party activists would stand in for the working class.

Sedgemore (1980), seeking a way out of the dilemma succeeds only in impaling himself more firmly upon it. Conceding that both Right and Left may support similar parliamentary reforms, he insists that their reasons are very different. The Left support the development of select committees as a means of 'strengthening the spine of weak Cabinets, and in the process strengthening Cabinet government by making it more responsible to the democratic process' (Sedgemore, 1980, p. 180). There is no suggestion here of reform contributing to a more pluralistic political system, of helping to develop policy in a workable form, or of altering the policies of a genuine left-wing government. Once again, the underlying assumption is that Labour's programme exists and is knowable and practicable; the only problem is holding the leadership to it.

The proposals drew a sharp response from the parliamentary leadership which saw them as making the work of a Labour government unnecessarily difficult. The TUC–Labour Party Liaison Committee was unanimously hostile; they would make it impossible for a Labour government to get legislation through in the first or second session of a new Parliament (RE:1697/June 1978). This, of course, was not the objective of the proposals which were intended to keep a Labour government to the programme; but the critics were undoubtedly right to see the implications of limiting the prerogative of the executive and that such limitations could not be expected to work in one direction only. Strengthened parliamentary control over the executive could not constitutionally be limited to left-wing control over right-wing governments. Between the lines, one also reads a shared concern by trade-union and parliamentary leaders that 'corporatist' summit-level deals could be upset by a more assertive back-bench cadre.

Labour's thinking on parliamentary reform has advanced since the 1960s. There is a greater awareness of the issue of power and the political nature of the question. The conflict between pluralist democracy and 'strong' executive government, however, remains unresolved. We have noted attempts to square the circle and the tenuous assumptions on which they rest.

Perhaps the most significant clue to Labour's thinking has been the absence of a debate on proportional representation. A myriad of proposals have been put forward for the reform of Parliament in the name of democracy and accountability, yet the grossly distorting effect which the present electoral system has on the composition of Parliament itself is ignored. In a mirror-reflection of the mandate theory so popular in the contemporary Conservative Party, it is assumed on the Labour Left that a majority of seats, albeit based on the thinnest plurality of votes, will provide democratic legitimation for change and mobilize the 'working class' to overcome obstacles in its way. Yet, if the theory were correct and a majority of the population were — or could be persuaded to be — committed to socialism, then socialists would have nothing to fear from PR, which would inevitably produce a socialist majority in Parliament. It is the implicit admission that a fundamentalist programme will command at best a plurality of support which underlies the insistence on the present electoral system. Yet the programme continues to be wrapped up in the rhetoric of mass democracy and participation.

The House of Lords

For the Labour Party, the existence of a hereditary House of Lords is anathema, unacceptable to all shades of party opinion, indefensible on grounds of efficiency or democracy. The only policy at all consistent with Labour's general beliefs and philosophy is total abolition of the hereditary principle and this was indeed party policy up to the 1930s (Morgan, 1975). However, like other constitutional concerns inherited from Labour's radical forebears, this then gave way to more immediate items of social and economic policy. After 1945, the Attlee government's experience seemed to show that the Lords were by and large prepared to play the democratic game and, respecting the government's electoral mandate, were of only limited nuisance value. However, they also demonstrated a considerable capacity for nuisance towards the end of a Parliament on matters such as the nationalization of iron and steel, and their very existence gave the Conservatives scope for ingenious constitutional inventions which, given the permanent Tory majority in the upper House, were effectively binding only on Labour — for example, the argument that the Lords were entitled to obstruct legislation in the last two years of a Parliament. So the issue of Lords reform stayed on the agenda, by no means resolved by the 1949 Parliament Act further limiting their delaying powers.

This left the party with a dilemma. Having chosen to play the parliamentary game Labour could only proceed to reform the House of Lords by all-party consent. Yet gaining the consent of the Conservatives would probably mean concessions towards the Tories' inbuilt majority, leaving the cards, to some degree, still stacked against them. On the other hand, unilateral action would raise practical problems. Abolition or reform could probably be put through in time under the provisions of the 1949 Parliament Act itself but at the cost of massive disruption and delay to the rest of the party's programme.

There was a further problem: if the Lords were to be abolished or drastically reformed, what should be put in their place? Does the party believe in bicameralism in principle? A House of Lords reformed in its composition would enjoy greater legitimacy than a largely hereditary house and could represent an even greater obstacle to radical change. Indeed, as the whole principle underlying bicameralism is to place constraints on the action of the majority in the first chamber, *any* second chamber was seen by some people as unacceptable. So it might be preferable either to move to outright abolition or deliberately to preserve its undemocratic basis and allow it effectively to wither away.

The 1964 manifesto was non-commital: 'Certainly we shall not permit effective action to be frustrated by the hereditary and non-elective Conservative majority in the House of Lords'. This was not put to the test. The government's wafer-thin majority in the Commons meant that, in any case, controversial issues like iron and steel nationalization had to be postponed. The 1966 manifesto was slightly more specific, promising legislation, 'to safeguard measures approved by the House of Commons from frustration by delay or defeat in the House of Lords'. After the election, the government chose the path of bipartisan agreement and launched an Inter-Party Conference in 1967, immediately raising suspicions about the genuineness of its radical intentions not only on the back-benches but among some Cabinet members too, though it seems that the option of unilateral action was kept open all along.

In the event, the government ended up with the worst of all worlds. Agreement was largely reached with the Conservatives on a complex scheme covering both the composition and powers of a reformed house when the Conservative majority in the Lords rejected the 1968 Rhodesia Sanctions Order. The talks were broken off amid speculation that the government would now introduce a short bill for abolition. 132 Labour back-benchers voted for a 10-Minute Rule bill, sponsored by Willie Hamilton, to abolish the Lords; but the government drew back from such a drastic step. Instead, it decided to legislate on the basis of the proposals agreed at the Inter-Party talks, but as a unilateral measure, so losing the support both of the Conservatives and of a large proportion of their own back-benchers. The bill, when it duly appeared in the 1968–9 session, became the object of a famous filibustering campaign on the floor of the House of Commons where, as a constitutional measure, it had to take all its stages. With the abolitionist Left and the anti-reformist Right united in unholy alliance, the measure became so bogged down that it was eventually abandoned, ostensibly to make way for a bill on industrial relations implementing the proposals of the White Paper, 'In Place of Strife'.

After this, the issue lay dormant for a number of years, resurfacing in the mid-1970s as a result of clashes between the 1974–9 government and the Lords. Among a series of measures affected between 1975 and 1977 were the Aircraft and Shipbuilding Industries Bill, the Rent (Agriculture) Bill, the Education Bill, the Dockwork Regulation Bill, and the Health Services Bill (RE:1231/June 1977) though it must be remembered that the reason why the Lords were able to flex their muscles at this time was the government's lack of majority in the Commons to overturn Lords defeats. These irritants continued with a renewed interest on the Left in the Lords question and a focus on the upper house as a potential obstacle to a radical Labour government. As early as 1976, the NEC's Home Policy Committee decided that, in view of the large number of conference resolutions on the subject, reform of the House of Lords should be the first priority of the Machinery of Government Study Group. By mid-1977, the Group reported that, as all schemes for the reform of the Lords had their drawbacks, the best policy was to go for simple abolition. This was accepted by the 1977 party conference.

There was a great deal of disquiet about this in various quarters. Ministers warned about the dangers of moving too hastily on what might not prove a popular policy and Labour peers continued to bring forward alternatives involving reforms in structure and powers. The 1979 draft manifesto prepared by the NEC promised abolition, with the creation of new peers if necessary to put the legislation through. Callaghan's veto on this was one of the items which most infuriated the Left and fuelled demands for full NEC control of the manifesto. Thereafter, abolition of the Lords came to feature more and more prominently on the Left's agenda for consitutional change and by the time the 1983 manifesto came to be drawn up, the message was clear and a firm pledge on abolition was included.

So the party had at last made up its official mind and now had the clearest possible policy; but a series of important issues remained unresolved. First of all, it is still not clear just how abolition is to be carried through, over the opposition of the Lords themselves, though there has been no shortage of suggestions. More importantly, there has been little thought of what, if anything, should take the place of the Lords. By opting for simple abolition, the party committed itself to unicameralism but the positive justification for this was never made explicit. Once again, the party has failed to make clear whether it believes in powerful, centralized government or a pluralist dispersal of power. It is true, of course, that the existing House of Lords acts as a brake on Labour governments but hardly at all on Conservative governments. That does not obviate the need to consider whether there should be institutional constraints on *all* governments. Labour's view on this has usually been that, as Conservative governments are committed to the status quo and Labour governments to change, any such constraint will constitute a partisan bias. However, faced in the 1980s with a radical right-wing government engaged in dismantling the post-war welfare settlement, it is Labour which is on the side of the status quo and on the defensive. The Lords have come to Labour's help over local government issues in 1983 and 1984 and, while this hardly constitutes a reason for retaining them in their present form, it does indicate the usefulness of some form of guarantee for dispersed power.

Conclusion

We began this chapter by drawing attention to the tensions between Labour's *insrumental* and *intrinsic* objectives with regard to the machinery of government. We have traced the way in which the party has tried to come to grips with these in the transition from the consensus politics of the early 1960s to the polarization of the 1980s and seen how, even on an apparently straightforward issue like the House of Lords, the party has had difficulty formulating coherent and workable policies. As the party has committed itself to more radical policies, the issue of the machine to carry them out has become more difficult. An administrative machine that will switch easily from radical 'Thatcherism' to radical 'Bennism' would be difficult enough to construct. With both Labour and Conservatives now seeking 'irreversible' policy shifts the task becomes well-nigh impossible. The question of the power of the state and the restraints on power in the state is posed starkly. Yet answers are still wanting.

There is the further problem of the nature of Labour's policy programme itself and the way it is to be implemented. On the one hand, there is the understandable desire to remove non-democratic obstacles to the programme, a concern based both on efficiency and democratic considerations. On the other hand, there is the desire, rooted in Labour's traditions of liberal democracy, to introduce more democratic and participative mechanisms into the state. Yet the effect of these must be to permit obstructions or diversion of Labour's programme itself. The dilemma has only been resolved, as we have seen, by some dubious assumptions about the nature of the programme and its support, with the assumption that increasing 'party democracy', parliamentary control over ministers and ministerial control over civil servants will necessarily serve the cause of carrying it out. Then the interests of 'working people' will receive their expression in public policy. If this were based upon a coherent definition of who the 'working people' are, it would at least be comprehensible. Combined with a vagueness about the interests the party is there to promote and an unwillingness to explore these, it becomes a recipe for rule by the party faithful. So the whole scheme is open to objections, both as an example of democratic practice and as a means of coming to grips with the practical problems of making and carrying out policy in government.

CHAPTER 7

Labour and British sovereignty

LABOUR's rapid integration into the British political process contributed to the party's relatively uncritical acceptance of existing constitutional norms. Its membership of wartime coalition governments dedicated to preserving the state and its institutions from the threat of external force was an additional factor as was the party's success in electing Labour governments whose actions and positive state interventionist policies enhanced the state's authority (Luard, 1979, p. 40). But the party rarely found it necessary to address itself to determining the source of sovereignty within the British state. It was encouraged in this attitude by the fact that the most pressing political issues — social welfare and economic re-distribution — coincided with Labour's primary concerns and did not raise the issue of British sovereignty. In creating a socialist society the Labour Party was able to regard sovereignty, the ultimate basis of political power, as simply there to be used. However, in the 1960s the Northern Ireland question and British membership of the EEC appeared on the political agenda. Both fell outside Labour's traditional framework of socio-economic policies and each obliged Labour to confront the issue of British sovereignty.

The nature of sovereignty in the British state, its source, and its location, has been examined and explained elsewhere. However, there are three aspects of the concept which are particularly pertinent to our analysis of the Labour Party's relationship with the state. First, there is the ambiguity of the concept which in the context of the British political tradition has confused parliamentary sovereignty with popular sovereignty. Secondly, parliamentary sovereignty has become a most potent engine for the concentration and centralization of political authority in the executive. Finally, the concept of sovereignty raises fundamental and largely unanswered questions about its relationship to the nation and how the nation is constituted. These three aspects have posed difficulties for all actors within the political process but particularly so for a Labour Party traditionally committed to exercising and extending the authority of the state.

The concept of sovereignty as some supreme power unrestrained by law, is one which was readily accepted by English legal and constitutional theorists because it seemed to fit the facts of English political institutions (Jennings, 1959, p. 149). In Parliament, England possessed a supreme legislative body which since the glorious revolutions of 1688 had dominated thinking on the source of political authority. Despite the fact that the principle of parliamentary sovereignty had never been established in Scotland, the new British Parliament established in 1707 after the abolition of both Scottish and English parliaments was soon deemed to have all the attributes of the latter.* So was created such a powerful monolithic political tradition that by the nineteenth century John Austin (1954, p. 230) could declare:

Adopting the language of most of the writers who have treated of the British Constitution, I commonly suppose that the present parliament, or the parliament for the time being, is possessed of the sovereignty.

Dicey took issue with Austin's definition which he described 'as merely legal conception' and argued that it was possible to distinguish between legal sovereignty and political sovereignty. By the former he meant the Queen in Parliament while in the latter category he placed what he referred to variously as the electorate, the people, and the citizens (Dicey, 1919). In this particular respect his views were not totally dissimilar to Austin's who regarded as a constitutional fact the delegation of authority from the people to their representatives who then held that authority in trust.

Despite these nineteenth-century considerations, no constitutional theory of popular sovereignty has been constructed. The extraordinary continuity of the British political experience and the lack of a serious challenge to the idea of parliamentary government consolidated the supremacy of Parliament and frustrated the emergence and development of an alternative source of political authority (Johnson, 1977, p. 30). Indeed, as we have shown, the innate conservatism of English radical movements in seeking access for disfranchised interests into the parliamentary process and the later absorption of radical pressures from Scotland and Wales both recognized and, by implication, legitimized Parliament's supremacy. Consequently, the establishment of

---

* There is some dispute on this matter. In *McCormick* v. *Lord Advocate* 1953 the court declared that 'the principle of the unlimited sovereignty of Parliament is a distinctively English principle which has no counterpart in Scottish Constitutional law' (quoted, Hood Philips, 1957, pp. 52–3).

the democratic principle by successive Representation of the People Acts during the late-nineteenth and early-twentieth centuries failed to undermine parliamentary sovereignty but, in a curious and rather paradoxical fashion, identified it with political democracy.

It has become part of the current constitutional conventional wisdom that sovereign power ultimately emanates from the people of the United Kingdom. The Labour Party would certainly endorse this view and accept it as the political fact which explains and justifies Labour's adoption of an electoral strategy in the pursuit of political power. However, the fact is one to which the constitution itself is blind (Marshall and Moodie, 1967, p. 15). Although one may talk of the electors exercising their political will to determine the complexion of the government and its policies, 'the judges know nothing about any will of the people except in so far as that will is expressed by an Act of Parliament' (Dicey, 1919, p. 73). The argument that the will of Parliament was synonymous with the will of the people was difficult to sustain in the nineteenth century when Dicey was writing, but the progressive extension of the franchise made it more credible in the twentieth. It has never, however been wholly convincing. The persistence of the House of Lords is an obvious anomaly but the deficiencies of the electoral system and the inadequate representative character of the House of Commons are more serious limitations. Nevertheless, they were limitations which British governments, Labour no less than Conservative, were willing to overlook. The Labour government in 1945 did not doubt that the will of the people had been clearly expressed in favour of socialism despite the fact that only 48.3 per cent had voted Labour. Similarly, in February 1974 Labour was no less certain that the British people had determined the fall of the Heath government than were the Conservatives that socialist controls had been decisively rejectd by the people in 1951. In both instances the message delivered by the people was rather different from that expressed by the Commons.

The dubious assumption that parliamentary sovereignty is in some way equivalent to popular sovereignty is maintained, however, because of the practical benefits it bestows on governments. The fact that governments in Britain are not separate from but 'the Crown's agent in Parliament' (Johnson, 1977, p. 82) has significant implications. The greater the authority assumed by Parliament the more considerable are the powers available to government; the tendency is accentuated by a disciplined party system and the dubious doctrine of

the electoral mandate. Thus governments with heavy legislative programmes directed to an extension of state intervention are likely to
endorse this particular interpretation of sovereignty. In the case of the
Labour Party, it enabled the construction of a battery of weapons for
the establishment of socialism and accelerated the drift towards
centralization in party attitudes.

Historically, sovereignty, both as a legal and as a political concept,
has been closely identified with the secular nation-state and with the
attempt to create an alternative basis for the state's authority in its
conflict with an international Church. Where the boundary of the
state coincided with that of the nation, there was an obvious impetus
for sovereignty to assume a national character and, given radical
reform or political revolution, this could provide the basis for the
evolution of popular sovereignty. This development failed to take
place in Britain because of a general obscurity in constitutional doctrine as to what constituted the nation. Cromwell's Instrument of
Government in 1653 declared that legislative power resided in the
person of the Lord Protector and 'the people' without specifying
whether these included presbyterian Scots or catholic Irish. The early
English Parliament was identified with the English and, after 1536,
the Welsh nations but that Parliament extinguished itself in the 1707
Act of Union with Scotland and transferred its sovereignty to the new
Parliament of Great Britain, a constitutional transformation repeated
in 1800 with the Act of Union with Ireland. Throughout those constitutional vicissitudes and the changing boundaries of the state, the
concept of parliamentary sovereignty survived intact and unfettered,
virtually disregarding the plurality of nations subject to its authority.

It is a remarkable paradox that for all the antiquity of the constitution, the British state as presently constituted dates back no further
than 1922 and the Irish Free State Agreement Act, which gave
dominion status to the Irish Free State and set up a subordinate
legislature in Northern Ireland. In this sense the territorial identity of
the present United Kingdom lacks a political tradition with a lon-
gevity to match that of France or the United States. Nor does it possess
a revolutionary tradition which in France and the United States provided the basis for their popular sovereignty. There is a distinct lack of
a sense of nation associated with the 'British' state. Despite a profound and extended imperial experience there is no discernible
'British' nation other than in a strictly legal and limited sense, a
deficiency acknowledged in the terms of reference granted to the

Royal Commission on the Constitution in 1969 which were: 'to examine the present function of the central legislature and government in relation to the several countries, nations and regions of the United Kingdom'.

Labour may be criticized for accepting the traditional concept of sovereignty so problematic for a party intent on expanding the role of the state and for its ambivalence towards British patriotism and the multinational character of the British state. However, in the absence of an alternative or of competing political traditions of the state, the party had little option. Furthermore, accepting parliamentary sovereignty not only presented certain instrumental advantages for the implementation of socialist policies but also helped buttress the authority of the parliamentary wing of the party. For much of its history the party was able to avoid the consequences of its tacit acceptance of the anomalies inherent in the concept of British sovereignty. Labour's particular misfortune during the 1960s and 1970s was to be confronted by a coincidence of two separate issues which both raised the issue of sovereignty from opposite perspectives. To appreciate the challenge this posed to the Labour party we need to examine the historical antecedents of Labour's policy on Northern Ireland and the development of the debate on British membership of the European Community.

The Northern Ireland Question

Labour's policy towards Northern Ireland has been not so much inadequate as non-existent. During the inter-war years the party maintained its historic attachment to Irish Home Rule (and reunification) but it was never part of the broader anti-imperial posture that embraced Home Rule for India and the other colonial possessions. Ireland was too close for comfort. It intruded into British domestic politics and embarrassed the Labour party, its working-class constituency, its trade-union connection, and its perception of the British state.

After the First World War a significant proportion of Labour's working-class vote was made up of first, second, and third generation Irish immigrants, but for every three or four who supported Irish Home Rule and, after 1922, the unification of Ireland, one was a unionist. British trade unions were also compromised. They organized in Northern Ireland, many of their members paid the political levy and were thus affiliate members of the British working-class movement. However, the 1922 settlement which gave virtual independence to the Irish Free State while leaving the Northern Ireland segment within the United Kingdom state, proved the most acute embarrassment to the Labour Party. It was one thing to advocate a policy of Home Rule for Ireland and to associate it with 'Home Rule all round'. These policies implied restructuring but, in the final analysis, maintaining the unity of the Kingdom. However, once Southern Ireland was independent and perceptibly outside the United Kingdom, to enthusiastically endorse its new constitutional status and to call for that status to embrace Northern Ireland had obvious implications for the remaining Celtic peripheral nations. If Home Rule was totally inadequate for Ireland why should it be deemed appropriate for Scotland? In these circumstances Labour found it prudent to allow its Home Rule policies to lapse and simply ignored the anomalous position of Northern Ireland. Some Labour MPs with Irish connections attempted to raise the issue from time to time but the party as a whole was inclined to let sleeping dogs lie. As Labour embarked on its grand strategy of winning control of the levers of power in the British state, it was disinclined to countenance policies which could threaten the viability of the political and constitutional mechanism which it confidently expected could be used to create a socialist Britain. Northern Ireland thus remained a low priority issue until events in the late 1960s restored it to the centre of the political agenda.

Labour's non-policy on Northern Ireland has been characterized as another example of the 'great betrayal' inflicted on the party by the parliamentary leadership. While it is undoubtedly true that successive Labour governments found it politically expedient to disregard the constitutional and moral issues raised by Northern Ireland, they were only able to do so because the party as a whole, its activists, trade unions, and rank-and-file members, were prepared to ignore a question which only muddied the waters of the socio-economic policy priorities the party had set itself. Some individuals enthusiastically endorsed Irish nationalism and re-unification and there was always a significant Irish lobby within the party, but Labour as a whole was never enthusiastically committed. To understand this attitude we need to examine the origins and the development of Labour's relationship to Irish nationalism and of Labour's perception of the two Irelands created by the 1922 Act.

The Labour Party never developed a distinctively Labour or

socialist policy on Ireland. It was part of a clutch of policies inherited from the Liberals which reflected the sectional interests of the Liberal Party (Pelling, 1968, p. 30). Labour, however, had different sectional interests. Even before the turn of the century it was clear that the interests of the Labour movements in Britain and Ireland did not coincide. If the British Labour movement was concerned with Ireland, it was more likely to be with controlling the competition of cheap Irish labour on British labour markets than with Home Rule (Hechter, 1975, p. 284). The creation of a separate Irish TUC in 1894 reflected the view of Irish trade-unionists that the economic interest of a largely agricultural community with a weak industrial base could not be fully comprehended by a British trade-union movement in which the economic interests of mining and manufacturing were dominant (Clarkson, 1925, p. 187).

There were also profound differences of attitudes and strategies between the respective political wings of the British and Irish Labour movements. The Fabians who provided the intellectual leadership of the British Labour movement believed Irish nationalism had little to do with socialism and that it actually did a disservice by undermining class solidarity with national loyalties. The Fabians also presumed the capacity of the British state for socialist reform and advocated a constitutionalist approach at both parliamentary and municipal levels. These views were diametrically opposed by James Connolly whose socialism was syndicalist, revolutionary, and nationalist. He rejected Fabian municipalization dismissing it as a device to frustrate the Irish working class from developing a revolutionary tendency and asserted the Irish nation's right to be separate and independent (Levenson, 1973, p. 68). He was contemptuous of the policy of Home Rule advocated by the Irish Nationalist Party and criticized Labour leaders in their support of both:

. . . as far as the Socialists of Great British are concerned, they always seem to me to exhibit towards the Irish working-class democracy of the Labour movement the same inability to understand their position and to share in their aspirations as the organized British nation, as a whole, has shown to the struggling Irish nation it has long held in subjection. No one, and least of all the present writer, would deny the sympathy of the leaders of the British Labour movement towards the Labour and Socialist movements of Ireland, but sympathy not based on understanding is often more harmful than a direct antagonism (quoted, Levenson, 1973, p. 56).

The criticism, though harsh, appears in retrospect to be justified.

Labour leaders were beguiled by the Irish Nationalist Party whose parliamentary tactics and organization the Labour Representation Committee strove to emulate after its creation in 1899. The Nationalist party's policy of Home Rule while maintaining the unity of the Imperial Parliament unimpaired, also commended itself to Labour. Although, as Connolly admitted, the Labour movement sympathized with the aspirations of the Irish nationalist and socialist movements, its commitment was always less than total. In the early years of the century Labour leaders were bored with the whole business and unwilling to adopt an official position (Bell, 1982, p. 16). The situation was so fluid that in 1905 MacDonald was able to act as an agent in a North Belfast by-election for William Walker, a Labour candidate and protestant-unionist opposed to Home Rule. He subsequently justified his action on the grounds that Labour had not made an official pronouncement in favour of Irish Home Rule (Bell, 1982, p. 18). In fact, Irish Home Rule was not adopted as official party policy until 1913. Even then it was regarded as a marginal political issue — something to be 'carried and put out of the way' (Bell, 1982, p. 24) — which had diverted the Labour Party from its primary objective of social and economic reform.

Labour's parliamentary leadership was more than content that the Liberal government should pass the Home Rule bill and so remove the Irish question from British politics, because agitation surrounding this issue had become an embarrassment to Labour. The Irish Labour movement, under the leadership of Larkins and Connolly, was more revolutionary and pro-Irish sentiments were strong amongst rank-and-file trade-unionists in Britain. Some Labour Party members were sceptical of the constitutionalist approach adopted by the parliamentary leadership and the Dublin lock-out of September 1913 opened up the prospect of a workers' revolution sweeping through Ireland and Britain. For Labour leaders the Irish question had to be resolved because it threatened the coherence of the British labour movement, the constitutionalist approach advocated by the Fabians, and the parliamentary strategy preferred by the trade-union movement. But the parliamentary party had no wish to be closely identified with a policy which while falling far short of the aspiration of the Irish Labour movement also antagonized Orange working-class elements in Liverpool, Glasgow, and Belfast. Thus, to quote MacDonald, Labour took 'the position of a detached party listening to what is said, and noticing what is said helping, as we have done during the last two years in every possible way, Home Rule to be inscribed on the Statute book of this realm' (Hansard vol. 19, col. 939, 1914).

The approach described by MacDonald was deficient on two counts. It presumed that an Act of Parliament would settle the business and that Irish aspirations would be satisfied by the qualified degree of independence envisaged by the Home Rule legislation. Both were clearly invalidated by the 1916 Easter Rising but the party's instinct was to deplore the armed uprising 'with a rare strength, unanimity and without equivocation' (Bell, 1982, p. 33). The party's subsequent actions and policy statements reinforce the impression that Labour, failing to appreciate the dynamic and revolutionary force of nationalism in Ireland, continued to regard it as a British constitutional problem. Thus in its 1918 conference, the party specifically rejected an amendment which would have transformed the Home Rule resolution into one supporting complete independence. Despite a deteriorating security situation in Ireland Labour's policy remained resolutely in support of the type of Home Rule envisaged by the 1914 Act. The party continued to talk of 'Home Rule all round' to include Scotland and Wales, with the obvious intent of securing a settlement in a British-wide context. As late as 1919 Labour remained opposed to the establishment of an Irish republic and to any settlement which led to the separation of Ireland from the United Kingdom.

After the 1918 general election Labour emerged as the official opposition. The damaging split in the Liberal Party held a realistic promise of parliamentary power and appeared to vindicate Labour's parliamentary strategy. In these circumstances the continuing conflict in Ireland was dangerously divisive for a Labour party which already felt obliged to balance public opinion and electoral considerations against the interests of affiliated trade unions and party activists. In December 1920 Labour's Commission of Inquiry published its report detailing and condemning instances of outrages by Sinn Fein and reprisals by British military and para-military forces. It formed the basis of an extensive public campaign; but as well as seeking to activate public opinion Labour also felt constrained by it. The party's insistence that Irish self-determination should be limited by British military and naval requirements was partly a response to 'public superstition and prejudice' (quoted, Bell, 1982, p. 64). The Parliamentary Labour Party totally opposed any initiative by the Council of Action to resolve the crisis in Ireland because 'public opinion was not prepared for a settlement of the Irish troubles by means of strikes' (Bell, 1982, p. 64).

Evidently, the Labour Party was progressively assuming the mantle, the rhetoric and the attitude of a British national party.

However, Labour could not ignore its working-class constituency, its greatest strength and the point at which it was most vulnerable. In certain key areas Irish workers constituted a significant element in local divisional Labour parties. They were encouraged by the Irish Labour Party to organize into groups, and to pressurize their local party organizations to declare unambiguous support for Irish self-determination. The Independent Labour Party declared in favour of an Irish Republic in April 1920 and the same year Labour's annual conference amended an NEC resolution restricting Irish sovereignty to 'exclusively Irish affairs' and endorsed unconditional support for Irish self-determination.

This was a serious reverse for Labour's leadership but it was unwilling to concede defeat and remained adamant that Irish self-determination should not be allowed to endanger the security of the British state. The Fabians were still opposed to separatism (Shaw, 1914) while the trade-union movement with strong organizational links and a substantial membership in Ireland, particularly in the Belfast area, were prepared to go no further than 'Dominion Home Rule' (Clarkson, 1925, p. 421). The Labour movement as a whole was thus unable to speak with a single authoritative voice. In this situation the attitude of the trade unions was crucial. The majority of organized workers in Ireland were still affiliated to British unions. Railway workers and dockers in Dublin presumed relations between themselves and British trade-unionists were so close that they could depend on their support (Clarkson, 1925, p. 180). However, when sympathy strikes were formally requested, British trade-union leaders prevaricated in the belief expressed by J. H. Thomas that 'not five per cent of the men would strike in England on the issue'. According to Boyce (1972, p. 71) 'British working class opinion was simply not much concerned about the fate of Irish workers or the struggle for Irish independence'.

Given this background almost any settlement of the Irish question would have been welcomed by Labour. Such was the case. The Articles of Agreement offended many of the issues of principle which the Labour Party had put down as markers for its support. Labour conceded on its requirement that any settlement should satisfy the majority of the Irish people as it conceded on partition. On two issues it was uncompromising: its opposition to republican form of government

for Ireland and the limitation of Irish sovereignty to meet the requirements of British naval defence. Both were reflected in the final settlement, but they related to the British state, the preferences of its general
public, and the perceived needs of its territorial defence. In welcoming
the Articles of Agreement Clynes described them 'as a triumph of
national patriotism, a victory for national spirit' (Hansard, vol. 149,
cols. 18–9, 1921) confirmation, if such were needed, that during the
course of the Irish Troubles Labour had fully acquired the role of a
British national party.

After 1921, Labour's concern for Ireland and Irish problems rapidly
and perceptibly declined. The party expressed sympathy for the Irish
Free State from time to time but was conspicuously mute on Northern
Ireland. Irish matters were no longer debated in the annual Conference
and partition evoked only a negligible interest. In practice, however,
the party's apathy led to a gradual acceptance of the constitutional
status quo and the new territorial boundaries of the United Kingdom.

When Labour formed its first majority government in 1945 with a
clear national mandate it fully accepted Northern Ireland as an integral part of the United Kingdom. The war had done much to incul-
cate a sense of British patriotism amongst the general public to which
the Labour government was particularly sensitive. In a Cabinet
memorandum, Morrison, the Home Secretary with responsibility for
Northern Ireland, noted that the impact on British public opinion of
Eire's neutrality during the war, the great loyalty of Ulster to the
Crown and the value of Northern Ireland ports and airfields (Bell,
1982, p. 75). Thus, once again British public opinion and the security
of the British state loomed large in Labour's deliberations.

Eire's decision in 1948 to secede from the Commonwealth also
appeared to raise the spectre of British security. Faced with the prospect that a completely foreign country would share a frontier with the
United Kingdom, the Labour government's instinctive reaction was
to consolidate partition. In 1948 Attlee introduced and enunciated the
right of Northern Ireland to veto any alteration to the border. The
following year during the debate on the Ireland Bill, Herbert
Morrison repeated the pledge which became clause 1(1)B of the 1949
Ireland Act. But Morrison went much further, and reiterated that
Northern Ireland was part of the United Kingdom and to allay any
remaining doubts he announced:

Quite frankly, This Government is not going to seek to take the initiative for
the purpose of losing a part of the United Kingdom . . . it is no part of the

business of this Government — and it is not going to do it — to take the initiative to diminish the territory of the United Kingdom (Hansard, vol. 46, col. 1957–9, 11 May 1949).

Since the early 1950s the Northern Ireland question has at different times confounded or dismayed but always perplexed the Labour Party. The party found itself trapped between its historic commitment to Irish independence and its obligations as a major party of the British state. The two were not perfectly compatible; the commitment belonged to Labour's age of innocence while the obligation required full account to be taken of the majority opinion in Northern Ireland. Confronted with this genuine dilemma Labour's natural instinct was acquiescent support for the status quo, a *de facto* unionist position, and a general reluctance to consider the issue. The existence of a devolved government in Stormont further encouraged Labour politicians to disregard the Province and the political and moral questions that it raised. In Attlee's government the minister with responsibility for Northern Ireland, Chuter Ede, was so keen to distance himself from the Province that he regarded the Northern Ireland Parliament as virtually sovereign and mistakenly declared he had no right of intervention (Hansard, vol. 438, col. 1556, 13 June 1947). Some twenty years later and shortly before the outbreak of the 'new' Troubles the Labour Cabinet under Wilson was still uncertain of its powers. According to Crossman (1977, p. 187), the precise nature of the financial and constitutional relationship between Northern Ireland and the British government was 'a very large expensive secret'.

The instinct not to get involved was very strong in the Wilson government. After 1964 the government was under growing pressure from a Labour back-bench group, the Campaign for Democracy in Ulster, which criticized Stormont's record on civil rights and made increasingly strident demands for intervention. Wilson met O'Neill, the Northern Ireland Prime Minister, in August 1966 to discuss his progress in attacking the problems of discrimination and human rights, but agreed not to press him further and allowed him a period of consolidation although, on Wilson's own admission 'time, the most precious commodity in the explosive Northern Ireland situation, was inevitably being lost' (Wilson, 1971, p. 350). Later, Callaghan opposed Wilson's suggestion of a British government minister resident in Northern Ireland because he felt it would increase the chances of greater involvement (Callaghan, 1973, p. 66); even after the troops had been sent in, the government's main preoccupation was to ensure that Britain did not get more embroiled in Northern Ireland than was absolutely necessary (Callaghan, 1973, p. 71).

Labour's disinterest in, and obvious attempts to distance itself from, Northern Ireland indicated that the party did not regard the Province as fully part of the state. The Labour Party had not organized in Northern Ireland since 1921 because it presumed that a united Irish state should possess a single labour movement. Thereafter, despite the consolidation of partition and the retention of Northern Ireland within the constitutional framework and territorial boundaries of the United Kingdom, the Labour Party persisted in excluding members of the working class in Northern Ireland. The semi-autonomous status of Northern Ireland was reflected in the Northern Ireland Labour Party created to fill the void left by Labour's unwillingness to organize in the Province. Yet, throughout its chequered history, the Northern Ireland Labour Party perceived the interests of British and Northern Irish working classes as identical and regarded Northern Ireland as an integral part of the United Kingdom. As late as 1964 it unashamedly declared that 'the vital question for Ulster men and women is — What part will Northern Ireland play in these [Labour] plans for a more prosperous Britain?' (NILP 1964, p. 2.) Such sentiments, presuming an identity of interests between all members of the working class were regularly voiced a decade later when Labour confronted the threats of Scottish and Welsh nationalism. Then Kinnock had explained his opposition to devolution by declaring himself a 'democratic socialist, a representative of the working class' (Hansard, vol. 903, cols. 291–2, 12 January 1976). But the sentiments were never expressed about the Northern Irish members of the working class although they belonged to British trade unions and paid taxes and received benefits voted by the Westminster Parliament.

Whatever confusions the Labour Party entertained about the Northern Irish working class and what role, if any, it should play in Labour Party counsels, Labour governments consistently asserted and exercised.British sovereignty in the Province. During the 1940s a Labour government confirmed and consolidated partition and recognized and legitimized the unionist veto. In 1969, following riots in Belfast and Derry, it sent in British troops and reaffirmed the consitutional status of the Province; in the words of the Downing Street Declaration:

The United Kingdom Government reaffirm that nothing which has happened in recent weeks in Northern Ireland derogates from the clear pledges made by successive United Kingdom Governments that Northern Ireland should not cease to be a part of the United Kingdom without the consent of the people of Northern Ireland or from the provision in Section I of the Ireland Act, 1949, that in no event will Northern Ireland or any part thereof cease to be part of the United Kingdom without the consent of the Parliament of Northern Ireland. The border is not an issue. (Quoted, Hepburn, 1980, p. 197.)

Furthermore it was made clear that Labour governments would continue to treat Northern Ireland as part of the United Kingdom, 'as long as Britain is satisfied that the majority of the population accepts the final sovereignty of the Westminster Parliament' (Callaghan, 1973, p. 186).

When Labour lost office in 1970s its policy towards Nothern Ireland was confused. Lacking any members from Northern Ireland it was uninformed of shifts in grass roots opinion. The most knowledgable and vocal contributors to the policy process were concerned back-benchers many of whom were second or third generation Irish immigrants with a strong emotional attachment to a united Ireland. The party, therefore, was regularly reminded of its historical commitment to a united independent Ireland. However, successive Labour governments had acquired another commitment: to Northern Ireland and specifically to the majority opinion in that province. Additionally, there were Northern Ireland trade-unionists. Although the working class in Northern Ireland were denied Labour Party membership, they were unionized and their desire to remain within the United Kingdom was recognized if not fully endorsed by the trade-union leadership. Given this background one can appreciate Wilson's anguished incomprehension when confronted by the 1974 Ulster Workers Strike which brought down the power-sharing executive and effectively halted the constitutional process which could have resulted in an all-Ireland framework. Wilson's words are particularly revealing of the paradox implicit in Labour's position:

British taxpayers have seen the taxes they have poured out, almost without regard to cost — going into Northern Ireland. They see property destroyed by evil violence and are asked to pick up the bill for rebuilding it. Yet the people who benefit from all this now viciously defy Westminster, purporting to act as though they were an elected government; people who spend their lives sponging on Westminster and British democracy and then systematically assault democratic methods. Who do these people think they are? (Quoted, Hepburn, 1980, p. 211.)

Wilson clearly regarded the Ulster workers as quite distinct from the British working class. It is inconceivable that a Labour prime minister would have used such language of British workers on strike. No matter what the provocation, a form of words would have been found either blaming a minority or condemning an unrepresentative leadership. Furthermore, Wilson's reference to taxpayers' money pouring 'out' of Britain and 'into' Northern Ireland implied Northern Ireland's separateness and discounted the fact that the population in Northern Ireland were UK citizens paying UK taxes. The most vitriolic comments, however, were reserved for the Ulster workers' disregard of Parliament, 'for purporting to act' as a government and for 'sponging off' Westminster. The answer to Wilson's rhetorical question was obvious; these poeple were subject to the sovereignty of the Westminster Parliament which represented the will of the people, the British taxpayers. They should obey the laws made by that Parliament. Thus although Wilson regarded the 'Ulster worker' strikers as outside the British political community, he still presumed them to be subject to its sovereignty. The fact that they regularly and spectacularly re-affirmed their Britishness with anthem, flag, pipe, and drum only served to embarrass further a Labour Party suspicious of such populist patriotic expressions which on mainland Britain had partisan connotations.

The absence of clear policy objectives on Northern Ireland reflected Labour's confused view of the United Kingdom state and resulted in dramatic shifts in policy. In 1971 the PLP gave its tacit approval to internment. Two months later Wilson made a frantic thirty-six-hour visit to the Province and returned with a fifteen-point plan involving a constitutional commission with representatives from Britain, the Irish Republic, and Northern Ireland to agree a constitution for a united Ireland. Within twelve months the policy initiative had disappeared into the sands as the Party Conference emphasized the need to secure the agreement of the unionist majority. However, in the interim Wilson and Merlyn Rees, Labour's spokesman on Northern Ireland, had met secretly with the Provisional IRA. Two years later a newly-elected Labour government introduced and passed through the House of Commons, without a hint of revolt from the Labour Left, the draconian Prevention of Terrorism Act, evidence of its intent not only to adopt a strong security line in Northern Ireland but to allay the fears of the British electorate following the Birmingham pub bombing. The military truce with the IRA which began in February 1975 was matched by the strong security line adopted by Roy Mason in September 1976 and largely sustained until Labour's defeat in May 1979.

Although the policy — or policies — gave the impression of a government verring erratically from one position to another, a degree of consistency did emerge. The continued violence in Northern Ireland against the forces of law and order hardened opinion in the party. With the United Kingdom, including mainland Britain, under threat from terrorist activities, now was the time for all good men in the party to come to the aid of the state. Pro-unionist sentiments were expressed at several levels within the party and talk of Irish unity was condemned in some Labour circles as tantamount to sabotage of the government's security policy (Bell, pp. 125–31). Eventually this resulted in a pact with the Ulster Unionists; Northern Ireland was given six extra parliamentary seats in return for keeping Labour in office. In fact the strategy failed. The defection of the Scottish Nationalists and the alienation of the Northern Irish non-unionist MPs was sufficient to bring the government down. Labour was defeated because it was unable fully to comprehend or to accommodate the disparate national communities within the United Kingdom.

A Labour Party in opposition and relieved of the responsibilities for the day-to-day government of the United Kingdom, is more able to follow its inclinations. However its policy on Northern Ireland although significantly changed is no more convincing. The 1981 policy statement, on which was based Labour's 1983 manifesto, was intended to provide a 'clear credible and socialist policy' but it fell somewhat short of these goals. The unionist veto was rejected but majority consent was endorsed as the only basis for unity; Irish unity was endorsed as a policy commitment but as a long-term objective attainable only by peaceful means and while power-sharing arrangements were developed in Northern Ireland. The ambiguities concerning the role and authority of the state in Northern Ireland remained. Indeed the question of whether Northern Ireland, pending its eventual unification with the Irish Republic, was an integral part of the British state with all the associated rights and responsibilities, was not even raised.

The issue now confronts the Labour Party more directly and more urgently than at any time since 1921. We identify three distinct views within the party: ideological, trade-unionist and instrumentalist. The party must seek to accommodate each one in formulating its policy.

The ideological view has two dimensions, nationalist and Marxist, which tend to overlap in a confused fashion. The former expressed mainly, but not exclusively, by members of Irish extraction, is the product of an emotional commitment to a united Ireland. This determines all policy perspectives. Others ideologically committed to Irish unity perceive the problem as a post-imperial legacy in which British colonialism has frustrated the natural course of the Irish national liberation movement. According to this view, partition was a crime against the Irish people (Benn, 1980). Thus the concept of a united Ireland is not so much the policy objective as its mainspring; the veto of the unionist minority in Ireland must be repudiated because it is an artificial minority operating in an illegitimate statelet; the British presence is a prop for sectarianism. Lacking moral legitimacy in the Province, the British Parliament should legislate the termination of Her Majesty's jurisdiction in Northern Ireland (Benn, 1983). The viewpoint, organized and articulated by the Labour Committee on Ireland, is shared by only a minority in the party but its significance exceeds its numerical strength, largely because the whole issue of Northern Ireland has been incorporated into the general left-wing critique of the Labour Party's parliamentary leadership during the sixties and seventies (Bell, 1982, p. 139). At its most extreme the ideological viewpoint incorporates an element of wish-fulfilment. Thus some on the party's left-wing support Sinn Fein, and identify its 'programme of social and economic reforms as akin to that of the British Labour Party' (Livingstone, 1983). As yet, however, the left-wing's ideological analysis is more relevant to divisions in the Labour Party than to unity in Ireland.

The view associated with the trade unions reflects their differing experience of Northern Ireland since partition. While committed to Irish unity as an objective, they are sensitive to the sectarian divide, a factor either ignored or dismissed as an aspect of socio-economic deprivation by the ideologists. According to this view working-class unity in Northern Ireland is a pre-requisite to any form of Irish unity. Alex Kitson warned the 1983 Labour Conference:

There is no way forward in Northern Ireland unless you can with the agreement of ordinary working people. Because if you don't get that consent, because if you try to impose a solution on people then you have a recipe for disaster. (Labour Party, 1983, p. 257.)

There are suggestions that the trade unions should take the initiative in creating a political organization to represent the interests of the

Labour movement in the Province. The view finds favour with some trade-unionists in Britain and is shared by the Labour Party's Northern Ireland Liaison Committee and its chairman Alex Kitson. The diagnosis is also shared by the Campaign for Labour Representation in Northern Ireland which argues that non-sectarian politics will only evolve if there is a working-class political party. Although the campaign has attracted the support of some left-wingers, notably Frank Allaun, the chances of the Labour Party actually involving itself in Northern Ireland's politics are slight. An alternative trade-union-based party, while more probable, is still far removed from practical politics.

The instrumentalist view recognizes British responsibility for, and sovereignty in, Northern Ireland and argues for carefully negotiated interim arrangements to ensure that both communities are safeguarded. Advocates of this viewpoint start from the fact that existing policies are manifestly not working and that the embrace of bipartisanship has been unduly restrictive of the kind of initiatives needed to break the stalemate. Accordingly, the withdrawal of British troops to barracks is a necessary pre-requisite to establish the right climate for a political initiative. Linked to social and economic reforms and safeguards for the Protestant population this would lead to a timetable for British withdrawal and the peaceful reunification of Ireland. In the final analysis however a unionist veto would not be allowed to frustrate the British government's political initiative and the wishes and requirements of the British population would prevail whether or not the Northern Ireland majority agreed (Bell, 1982, p. 140).

The presence of such groups competing against each other in the policy-making process creates considerable problems for the Labour Party but its difficulties in dealing with Northern Ireland are more profound than merely balancing intra-party factions. As we have seen there is a considerable degree of ambivalence in Labour's attitude towards Northern Ireland. The Labour Party's predicament in evolving a policy for Northern Ireland derives from an obscured view of the state which, when in government, the party is called upon to administer, and of the nature of Parliament's sovereignty in Northern Ireland. Labour's ambivalence on this issue and, as we will see, on British membership of the EEC, reveals the party's historical unwillingness to confront constitutional issues and its susceptibility to intra-party pressures when they operate outside the traditional frame of reference by which Labour usually evaluates its policy options.

Membership of the European Community

Whether or not Britain should become or remain a member of the EEC is an issue which has plagued the Labour Party since 1961 when Britain's first application to join was made. The issue has displayed an infinite capacity to confound the attempts of successive Labour leaders to frame a policy capable of commanding the support of all sections within the party. Indeed, the leadership itself has been divided. Roy Jenkins resigned from the deputy leadership in 1972 because of Labour's weakening commitment to the EEC and its decision to hold a referendum on the issue. George Thomson and Harold Lever left the Shadow Cabinet at the same time for similar reasons. In 1975 the constitutional convention of collective responsibility was not so much broken as torn asunder by Wilson's decision to permit Cabinet members 'who [did] not feel able to accept and support the Government's recommendation [to] be free to support and speak in favour of a different conclusion in the referendum campaign' (Hansard, vol. 884, cols. 1745–50). In the event seven members took advantage of this dispensation.Wilson, the consummate party manager, admitted: 'In all my thirteen years as Leader of the Party I had no more difficult task than keeping the Party together on this issue' (Wilson, 1979, p. 51).

From the ideological perspective, British membership of the European Community does not obviously transgress any socialist principles. European socialist parties and even Euro-communists, have accepted that Community membership is compatible with their socialist beliefs. Why then has it posed such an intractible problem for the Labour Party? A review of Labour's position, whether in government or in opposition, suggest that the party's main concern has been with the 'terms' of British membership. Gaitskell in 1961–2, Wilson in 1974, Callaghan in 1979, and Foot in 1983, all argued that the terms currently available were inadequate and that a Labour government would negotiate a better deal. The most frequently-repeated criticisms concerned budgetary arrangements and the Common Agricultural Policy. Leaving aside the fact that the revisions Labour was intent on negotiating would have fundamentally transformed the EEC, it is possible to infer that Labour's opposition was less one of principle than of percentage points. Quite clearly this was not the case. The internecine character of the intra-party debate, the emotion it generated, and the personal animosities it aroused, suggest that Labour's opposition to British membership was more profound.

We would argue that the question of membership of the European Community proved intractible to Labour because it threatened the autonomy of the British state and the sovereignty of the Westminster Parliament, two concepts and two institutions to which the Labour Party has been committed emotionally and strategically since its inception. It was this central and basic concern which underpinned Labour's suspicion of, and opposition to, the European Community. The party's opposition was expressed in three distinct but linked arguments: instrumental, patriotic, and constitutional. According to the instrumental argument British membership of the Community would frustrate the application of those policies necessary for the creation of a socialist society in Britain. Labour governments should not have their legislative initiatives frustrated or inhibited by a supranational body unaware of the particular needs and interests of the British working class. The patriotic argument has, over the years, been subjected to amendment. At the start of the Common Market debate in the 1960s it presumed Britain's status as a world power. However, as Britain's military capacity declined and her special relationship with the United States became less important, the argument changed. Britain was regarded as possessing some kind of moral authority which she could exercise through the Commonwealth and in the context of Third World countries. According to the patriotic argument this distinctive role would be denied her within the European Community. The constitutional argument concerned parliamentary sovereignty. It was, of course, implicit in the instrumentalist critique and in the belief that Labour governments should be free to legislate as they deemed fit. It was also integral to the patriotic argument because the maintenance and assertion of British sovereignty in the international sphere were obviously dependent upon the preservation of parliamentary sovereignty. As we have shown, there is a considerable degree of confusion in constitutional and political thought about the distinction between parliamentary and popular sovereignty so that the two are sometimes regarded as synonymous. This particular confusion surfaced repeatedly during the Common Market debate and culminated with the development of a referendum, the ultimate and direct expression of the people's will, in an effort to secure the sovereignty of Parliament.

These arguments have very little to do with socialism but are deep rooted in the native English (and later British) radical traditions.

Small wonder therefore that the advocates of these views were described as 'Little Englanders'. Because the arguments lacked an ideological focus, support 'for them did not coincide with the ideological fault lines within the party. Whereas left-wing critics of the Common Market would naturally emphasize the instrumental arguments, and right-wing opponents would be more evident in advocating the constitutionalist criticism, there was no clear left–right demarcation. However, the issue touched the Labour Party's tap roots, its role in and relationship with the British state, and as such, it acted as a solvent. Historically, Labour has adopted a constitutionalist approach, and adhered to the institutions, procedures, and norms of the British state. That was now called into question by British membership of a supra-national body of which many in the party were deeply suspicious. Links between different groups in the party were also weakened by the fundamental differences over the political arena in which the Labour Party most appropriately or most effectively would operate. The breakaway of the SDP cannot be divorced from the issue, and with its departure the debate assumed a greater ideological and potentially disruptive configuration. As in so many other issues which impinge on the nature and form of the British state, we have to take account not only of Labour's ideological inheritance but also of the policy precedents established by earlier Labour governments.

The 1945–51 Attlee government now occupies an honoured position in Labour's pantheon; its policy initiatives and the statements of its leaders competing with the 1918 constitution as a fount and legitimizer of Labour Party policies. The precedents established in the field of British relations with Europe are highly significant. On three successive issues relating to the Organization for European Co-operation in 1948, the Committee of Ministers of the Council of Europe in 1949, and the European Coal and Steel Community in 1950, the Labour government declined to grant any autonomous decision-making powers to a supra-national body. At the time powerful arguments existed to justify this attitude. The special relationship with the United States was, so soon after the shared experience of the Second World War, real and close. The new Commonwealth which Labour was creating from the old Empire provided an exciting new dimension for British interests. But most important, the countries of Western Europe were dominated by right-wing parties. The Labour Party with a secure majority in the House of Commons was not prepared to surrender important fields of national policy 'to a supra-national

European representative authority, since such an authority would have a permanently anti-Socialist majority' (quoted, Kitzinger, 1968, p. 69). Thus the three themes we have identified, maintaining the autonomy of the British Parliament, preserving Britain's world role, and regarding European supra-national organizations as endemically or potentially anti-socialist, were established. With some variation they have been a persistent element in Labour Party thinking on the EEC.

In 1961 the Labour Party was by no means hostile to the idea of closer association with the EEC. The trade unions, impressed by the economic advance and rising wages of the member states of the EEC, took a pragmatic view. Provided satisfactory safeguards could be obtained for British workers the trade unions were unlikely to provide die-hard opponents of British entry. The political wing of the movement was more divided. The revisionist Right identified with the Campaign for Democratic Socialism were, by and large, convinced Europeans and they were joined by those electoral pragmatists in the parliamentary party who were able to point to public opinion which, despite a significant 'don't know' element, divided 2 : 1 in favour of Britain joining the Common Market (King, 1977, p. 20). The party's left wing encompassing the Tribune Group, Victory for Socialism, and CND were almost entirely critical. They regarded the EEC as deficient on two counts: it was a capitalist organization which would frustrate the emergence of socialism; and it was an imperialist force in world politics, the political extension of NATO.

Despite the obvious correlations, the issue of British membership did not degenerate along the left–right divide. Gaitskell, exercising an almost Attlee-like subtlety in party management, identified the issue as one which could heal many of the old party wounds (Robbins, 1979, p. 32) and what eventually emerged was a policy of 'conditional entry' which proved capable of winning the endorsement, if not the enthusiastic support, of all elements within the party. Five essential conditions for entry were established. Realistically they were little more than an interim settlement but they possess a singular utility for our analysis, enabling us to trace the subsequent intra-party debate on British membership of the EEC. We can summarize the conditions as follows:

— Binding safeguards for the Commonwealth
— Guarantees safeguarding the EFTA countries
— Freedom for Britain to conduct her own foreign policy
— Retention of Britain's right to plan her own economy
— Guarantees to safeguard the position of British agriculture

The conditions relating to the Commonwealth, safeguarding the trade and interests of Britain's Commonwealth partners, revealed a curious paradox in Labour perceptions. The modern Commonwealth was largely a creation of the Attlee government and the party's commitment to it was consistent with Labour's tradition of anti-imperialism; but the party's determination to secure the interests of Commonwealth food producers was not entirely altruistic. There was an element of national self-interest. The Commonwealth helped preserve a belief, not entirely confined to the ranks of the Labour Party, that Britain still had a world role. Thus loyalty to the Commonwealth connection was not only regarded as incompatible with membership of the European Community, it also appeared to facilitate an independent foreign policy. Furthermore, there was an undoubted chauvinistic element inherent in Labour's desire the preserve the Commonwealth ties. This is most vividly expressed in an article in *The Railway Review* in 1962:

They, the nations of the Commonwealth speak our tongue, practice our laws, honour our Queen and worship our God. Reach out to them across the four corners of the world . . . Therein lies the continued greatness of the people of these small islands. (Quoted, Robbins, 1979, p. 25n.)

Potentially the Commonwealth connection argument could have proved extremely effective. It elicited support across the political spectrum and arguably was the Conservative party's weakest point; but whatever the emotional ties of the Commonwealth, it was not a viable basis for British economic or foreign policy. By 1967, when a Labour government headed by Harold Wilson was preparing Britain's second application, the EEC had developed into a powerful economic block and had established a variety of commercial links with the EFTA countries. In contrast, the Commonwealth had proved disillusioning. Britain's trade with the Commonwealth countries had declined as had Britain's position in the world. At home a succession of economic crises promised continued economic stagnation. As Britain's traditional industries declined, a general belief emerged that Britain's future lay in developing high technology and that this could only be competitive with the United States if Britain collaborated with Europe and took advantage of what Tony Benn (1979, p. 94) himself described as the 'inexorable logic of scale'. Thus, by 1967 those major international economic and political concerns relating to EFTA and the Commonwealth, which initially had underpinned Labour's doubts on

British membership, had been largely invalidated by changes in the international and commercial environment.

The three remaining conditions, however, related to British sovereignty and were not so amenable to changes in the international environment. Indeed, adverse developments could, and did, heighten the sense of national consciousness. As the debate evolved it became clear that the overwhelming majority in the Labour movement remained wedded to the idea of British national sovereignty (Newman, 1983, p. 218). In fact the sovereignty argument had been present from the outset. A Fabian pamphlet published early 1962 argued that the Treaty of Rome would abrogate the sovereignty of Parliament which had been 'hard-won in centuries of struggle against arbitrary rule from Magna Carta to the Act of Settlement' (Pickles, 1962). Gaitskells's speech to the 1962 Labour Conference touched a similar vein with his reference to 'an end of a thousand years of history'. It was evident in Labour's 1964 manifesto which claimed that the Labour Party would 'rekindle an authentic patriotic faith in our future'. However, experience of government and a succession of economic and international crises produced a radical reassessment within the parliamentary leadership. In 1967 Labour's Chancellor of the Exchequer, addressing the House of Commons, but evidently directing his comments at Labour back-benchers, indicated the new direction the leadership were intent on taking:

I have been struck by the effect of the international forums in the world today on the politics of individual countries, an effect which is much more than I had assumed before I took office . . . The argument about sovereignty is rapidly becoming outdated. (Quoted, Kitzinger, 1968, p. 4.)

Britain's second application to join the European Community made in 1967 threatened to divide the party seriously. There was an almost even balance between pro- and anti- Common Market ministers in Wilson's Cabinet and some one hundred Labour back-benchers were deeply suspicious of any move into Europe. However, by dint of some astute manoeuvring, Wilson was able to defuse the crisis. There was confusion amongst Cabinet ministers as to the level of commitment to Europe made by the Cabinet (Robbins, 1979, p. 64) and the more extreme anti-Common Market criticisms were muted by the claim that Gaitskell's five conditions, in modified form, would still constitute the basis for entry. Fortunately for Labour, de Gaulle's veto removed the matter from the political agenda.

Wilson's achievement during the course of Britain's second application was to disguise the fundamental differences within the party and to promote the view that the issue was essentially one of terms for entry. As we have argued, this had never been the case, but whatever doubts remained were removed during the early 1970s and Britain's third and successful application . The translation of the issue from hypothetical realms to practical politics consolidated Labour opposition to British membership of the Community. Two lines of criticism emerged, constitutional and instrumental, which tended to reflect different ideological positions within the party. However, both were different aspects of a common theme: the preservation of the autonomy of the British state.

The constitutional argument against entry was implicit in the 1960s debates and underpinned the conditions that Britain should be free to determine its own foreign and domestic economic policies. It was explicitly raised by Douglas Jay in a series of articles in *The Guardian* in 1967 when he referred to the 'daunting snag' of the EEC Commission's powers to legislate for the internal affairs of member countries which would severely limit the sovereignty of the British Parliament. This, however, was but one section of an analysis overwhelmingly concerned with the economic consequences (Kitzinger, 1968, pp. 140–50). By 1970, the political situation had changed. A Conservative government had been elected to power and the prospects of entry were more realistic and immediate. The emphasis of Jay's criticisms also changed. Now the focus was constitutional. To sign the Treaty of Rome 'would be a more drastic change in our constitution and the basic rights of the British people than any since power was given to the modern electorate in 1832' (quoted, King, 1977, p. 57). The theme was sustained by Peter Shore. Speaking to the 1972 annual conference he informed conference that he had not entered 'socialistic politics . . . to connive in the dismantling of the power of the British people as represented in their parliament and their government' (quoted, King, 1977, p. 38).

Both Jay and Shore were on Labour's right wing but the constitutional argument proved equally plausible to the left wing of the party and found its most articulate spokesman in Tony Benn. During the referendum campaign Benn presented three arguments for ending British membership of the EEC; the first and most substantial was the loss of political self-determination. In Benn's (1979, p. 95) view:

Continued membership of the Community would therefore mean the end of Britain as a completely self-governing nation and of our democratically elected Parliament as the supreme law-making body of the United Kingdom.

The demand for a referendum was closely identified with the constitutional argument about the loss of sovereignty. It was raised by Jay in 1970 and taken up by Benn. King (1977, p. 55) has argued that the two issues were logically separate; the question of the referendum raising issues in the field of democratic theory and the question of EEC membership raising issues of foreign and economic policy. However, for those constitutionalist critics in the Labour Party the two questions were cognate. Despite the rhetoric, EEC membership was at root not about economics, butter prices, and New Zealand lamb, but about sovereignty of the British Parliament and of the British people. Thus we would argue that the demand for a referendum was not the product of political expediency, although the party leadership doubtless regarded it as an escape route from a perilous political predicament, but stemmed from the conviction that 'only the British people had the moral authority to decide whether to retain their full power of democratic self-government or approve its surrender' (Benn, 1979, p. 99).

The referendum however raised fundamental questions about the British constitution; the extent to which it was based on the concept of parliamentary sovereignty and the degree to which that was compatible with popular sovereignty. Those like Benn who advocated the referendum were in no doubt that British parliamentary democracy in Britain was based not upon the sovereignty of Parliament but upon the sovereignty of 'the people who . . . lend their sovereign powers to Parliament' (Benn, 1979, p. 95). Others in the Labour Party adhered to the more traditional view that Parliament was supreme. Thus, when in March 1972 Labour's Shadow Cabinet and NEC opted for a referendum, Roy Jenkins the deputy leader resigned, expressing his opposition to a referendum which would frustrate liberal reforms and change the balance of the parliamentary system (*The Times*, 11.4.72). The resignations (as we noted earlier Jenkins was followed by others from the Shadow Cabinet) were characterized in the press as a serious split in the party on the issue of EEC membership. In fact it was more deep-seated and reflected a fundamental divide in the Labour Party as to the ultimate location of sovereignty within the British state. Far from resolving these differences, the 1975 referendum and those on devolution in 1979 served only to accentuate and exacerbate divisions on this constitutional issue. The question of re-selection of MPs which raised the issue of popular versus parliamentary sovereignty in a slightly different guise, suggests that the party in the 1980s had still not resovled this dilemma.

The instrumental argument found numerous advocates on the left wing of the party. It claimed that EEC membership would frustrate the implementation of socialist policies in Britain either because the member states of the EEC were anti-socialist or because of the rules of the Treaty of Rome and the powers of the Commission. As social-democratic parties won power in member states the former reason declined in importance but the belief persisted that socialism in Britain was only attainable through the procedures and decisions of the Westminster Parliament.

The instrumentalist case was presented in its most articulate form by Neil Kinnock in an article entitled 'Socialism and Sovereignty' published by *Tribune* (2.5.75) on the eve of the referendum. He argued that socialist policies involving state intervention in the field of regional development and job creation would be impeded by Community rules. Benn raised the topic in a campaign speech, painting a picture of mass unemployment and increasing migration as a consequence of British membership as successive British governments would be unable to provide jobs (Goodhart, 1976, p. 159). The instrumental case was also linked with British working-class solidarity. Despite Labour's socialist ideology the concept of an international working class was not widely comprehended or accepted. Thus a sovereign British Parliament could be regarded as an expression of a sovereign British working class which was the custodian of the efforts of previous generations of the working class to build 'the Labour vote in Britain to change our society'. In the opinion of the ASTMS: 'we should use that power here — and now' (quoted, Robbins, 1979, p. 113).

It was a most persuasive argument and one to which the trade unions rallied. The complex network of consultative arrangements and institutions which they had evolved within the framework of the British state were clearly called into question if Britain remained in the European Community. With trade-union support the instrumental critique, linked to the implementation of socialist policies, progressively emerged as the new consensus within the Labour Party. It appeared to meet all Labour's concerns; the interests of its working-class constituency; the socialist aspirations of its activists; and the possibility of attracting electoral support. The consensus position was formally established in the special policy conference in November 1981 when British withdrawal from the Community and the restoration of British sovereignty were justified as the means whereby Labour's alternative economic strategy would be implemented. As the party document put it: 'the restoration of full sovereignty to the British Parliament will mean that we will be free to pursue our socialist alternative without being restricted by the strait-jacket of the EEC' (Labour Party, 1981).

The party's differences on British membership of the EEC were deep and profound. The various sides to the debate increasingly regarded the issue as a matter of principle and one which would not readily respond to the party's traditional resolution procedures. Wilson had recognized the danger as early as 1971 when he had warned the party against tearing itself apart on Europe and urged it to recognize that 'what divides us is an important policy issue, not an article of faith' (Labour Party, 1971, p. 359). However for many in the party it was an article of faith. The means whereby British socialists had determined to build a socialist Britain — a sovereign Parliament representing a sovereign people — although an ambiguous constitutional concept, was not to be lightly discarded.

Thus, we would argue, it is highly doubtful that Labour's defeat in the 1983 general election and the party's grudging acceptance of the reality of British membership of the Community marked a fundamental and irreversible shift. The official party line was no longer withdrawal but re-negotiation. Nevertheless, the problem of what a Labour government would do if re-negotiations failed remained unanswered. If Labour's anti-Common Market stance had been the product of a judicious assessment of the opportunities and limitations which continued membership of the EEC presented for the implementation of socialist policies, then some compromise formula might have been devised. But the debate had attracted the investment of an enormous amount of emotional capital. What was said in the debate 'was often true and important, but often it amounted to no more than a thin surface covering of a much deeper well of emotion' (King, 1977, p. 36). The emotion derived from a deep commitment to the British state typically expressed by Peter Shore when he asserted that British membership of the Community had resulted in 'a rape of the British people and of their rights and constitution' (Labour Party, 1980), or Tony Benn's (1979) view that Britain was a century ahead of continental Europe in democratic experience.

There is little doubt that the bitter nature of the intra-party debate hardened positions and exaggerated arguments as, what initially appeared to be a foreign policy issue, became a debate about the meaning of socialism and the manner of its attainment; a variant on the theme of socialism in one country. For the revisionist wing of the Labour Party, many of whose leaders left to found the SDP, sovereignty was an abstract principle of dubious validity in the modern world and one which they were willing to concede. For Labour's left wing, the trade unions and the party activists, to concede sovereignty was to sacrifice the dream shared by successive generations of political radicals: 'the dream of building a socialist Jerusalem in England's green and pleasant land' (King, 1977, p. 37). The defence of British sovereignty by the anti-marketeers thus encompassed three considerations: national autonomy, the party's ideological rationale, and its radical inheritance. It is a measure of the intergrative force of the history of the British parliamentary state that wide sections of the party were able to sustain this intellectual position and so frustrate the development of an agreed and coherent Labour policy for Europe.

Conclusion

Our examination of Labour's treatment of the Northern Ireland question and British membership of the European Community illustrates the party's difficulties in framing policies which relate to the issue of British sovereignty. On both questions Labour was obliged to take account of the force of British patriotism and the susceptibility of the working class to its appeal. In the case of Northern Ireland the Labour Party attempted to limit the impact of chauvinist sentiments while in its anti-EEC campaign it sought to exploit them. Despite the Labour Party's radical inheritance and internationalist ideology, successive Labour governments slipped into a defensive posture protecting the constitutional framework of the British state. We have shown how Labour's defence of British sovereignty on the Common Market issue was partly instrumental and derived from the statism inherent in the party's economic and social policies. The opposition of Labour's left wing can be explained in these terms; but it is difficult to discover a similar rationale for its perplexed manoeuvrings on Northern Ireland.

There, despite the party's early commitment to an independent and united Ireland, Labour governments have followed policies defending the intrinsic qualities of British sovereignty based on tradition and continuity; in effect, they have adopted implicitly unionist positions. On occasions (Morrison in 1949 and Wilson in 1969) they have quite explicitly expressed their determination to preserve the territorial integrity of the United Kingdom. There were far fewer inhibitions on the Common Market issue. As we have seen, a wide range of party spokesmen from both wings of the party were willing to express the most nationalistic and even jingoistic sentiments in order to preserve British sovereignty, both parliamentary and popular. Playing the 'British state' card was not, therefore, the exclusive preserve of either wing of the party. But, to sustain the metaphor, the card did not always win the game. Indeed its identification with constitutional procedures and nationalistic sentiments frustrated agreement. The party's left wing is increasingly contemptuous of the consitutionalism advocated and practised by the right and the spirit of nationalism once aroused is not easily placated. But most important, the British state with its historical traditions divided the party along lines which cross-cut the ideological divide and further complicated the party's policy-making process. On the twin questions of Northern Ireland and the European Community there was an attempt to develop the intra-party debate along ideological lines, to force the issues into the party's traditional policy frame. Such attempts however, increased the difficulties of creating the consensus necessary for issues which lay so close to the nature of the British state.

Conclusions

But the outcome . . . will depend on whether contemporary democracy can be preserved and made into an effective instrument of social transformation. (John Strachey, Contemporary Capitalism, 1956.)

AT various points in this book we have emphasized Labour's uncritical inheritance of a British pre-democratic state form (Nairn, 1981; Jenkins and Minnerup, 1984) onto which democratic practices were grafted over several generations. The lack of either a revolutionary tradition or a democratic foundation for the British state frustrated the development of a general set of principles by which the Labour Party could assess the institutions and practices of the state. The party's approach to the inter-connected issues of the state and political power has consequently tended to be piecemeal and guided by pragmatic consideratons. The policies it developed in relation to the state, its role, institutions, territorial integrity, and the nature and location of its sovereign power, were frequently marked by inconsistencies and incoherence.

The inconsistencies have been exhibited in a variety of policy areas as we have shown in the preceding chapters. Labour's Fabian inheritance commits it to the objectives of equality and efficiency through the agency of the centralized state. For many in the party, equality has come to mean centralization. Yet Labour persists in expressing support for a measure of economic decentralization implicit in its support for workers co-operatives and its demand that local authorities be granted the power of general competence. The party has also been responsive to the centrifugal pull of the Celtic periphery which has played such a significant part in its electoral success and which has evoked an intermittent attachment to Home Rule and, latterly to devolution. But Labour's enthusiasm for devolution has always been less than whole-hearted. It has tended to regard devolution as a means of preserving the unity of the state which sometimes leads the party to adopt confusing policy positions; for example, advocating a Scottish legislative assembly with taxation powers able to plan for Scotland but within the context of a highly centralized alternative economic

strategy (Labour Party, 1983). Also in the context of the territorial
state, Labour has vigorously opposed the demands of Welsh and Scots
separatists in the name of the wider interests of class but then itself
deployed precisely the same argument of territorial self-interest to
attack the European Community. Between Labour claims that North
Sea oil is a British natural resource and SNP claims that it is
'Scotland's oil' there is no difference in principle. The party is firmly
identified with central economic planning and to a form of state collectivism epitomized by the nationalized industries; but there is an
element of confusion in whether nationalization should primarily
reflect the needs of central planning or transform the economic and
political balance of British society. The party has espoused the cause of
industrial democracy but has shown itself incapable of establishing the
appropriate relationship between the national interest and consumer
and worker interests, either in nationalized industries or in the private
sector. The machinery of government has evoked similar contradictory responses from different sections of the party. Many Labour
activists are suspicious that the institutions and personnel of the
British state's administrative and judicial structures are antipathetic
to Labour's policy objectives, while others, with experience of government, are persuaded that the state is essentially neutral and that
Labour's pre-eminent task is to capture the commanding heights'
control of Parliament. But the distinction between Parliament's role
in supporting strong government and its role as a brake on the executive is confused. Finally, Labour's deep roots in the British radical
tradition render it sensitive to British patriotic appeals. Whatever the
disclaimers of the left-wing opponents of the Common Market, there
is no doubt that the anti-EEC campaign touched a vein of xenophobia
within the Labour movement or that this was the basis of much of
Labour's popular appeal. While large sections of the party regard the
British state as the natural vehicle for the advancement of British
working-class interests, British patriotism is a political emotion which
Labour has been reluctant to embrace; partly because of ideological
considerations but also because of the realization that the Conservatives, with their relatively uncomplicated perception of the state,
would always outbid them.

Labour's difficulties have been compounded by the conflicting
pressures which the party has had to accommodate. The trade-union
affiliates have made contradictory demands. On the one hand they
have become increasingly suspicious of state intervention in industrial

relations and the threat which that poses to their traditional rights. The 'In Place of Strife' proposals in the late 1960s set dangerous precedents which, to some extent, were followed by the Conservative government's trade-union legislation of the early 1980s. The trade unions again look to a future Labour government to restore their autonomous position within the framework of the industrial state. However, the considerable and apparently irreversible growth of state intervention in the economy has also fueled trade-union demands for a corporatist involvement in government along the lines of a continuing Social Contract similar to that of the mid-1970s with the Callaghan government. The ideological element within the party has been frustrated because a sustained period of Labour government between 1964 and 1979 failed to effect the hoped-for social and economic transformation of society. Criticisms of the Wilson and Callaghan governments have been linked to a revived 'mandate' doctrine and extended to embrace the institutions of the state. The House of Lords, the judicial system, and the Prime Ministerial powers of patronage, even Parliament, its prerogatives, procedures and precedents have increasingly been called into question (Benn, 1980).

The electoral pragmatists on the parliamentary wing of the party traditionally have been able to accommodate the party's disparate interests and to unite them behind an electoral strategy which implicitly accepted the constitutional norms and institutions of the state. However, the strategy's acceptability was dependent upon success measured in terms of winning control of Parliament and upon the state's ability to deliver the economic goods. By the 1980s neither expectation appeared well-founded. Labour's traditional socio-economic constituency, the manual working class, was in decline with a corresponding growth of employment in the service sectors which possessed different traditions and patterns of trade-union membership (Parry, 1980). The change was reflected in Labour's electoral support. In 1951, 40.3 per cent of the electorate voted Labour; only 20.6 per cent of the electorate did so in 1983. Furthermore with Labour's vote concentrated in the traditional industrial regions of the north of England, central Scotland, and south Wales, Labour's claim to be a national party was increasingly open to question. The task of accommodation was made more difficult by the changing nature of party membership. A general decline from a peak in 1952 of 1,014,525 to rather less than 300,000 in 1983 (Hayter, 1977; *Labour Weekly*, 4.5.84) was associated with the emergence of left-wing activists and the resurgence of ideology which sharpened the conflict with a parliamentary leadership intent on recapturing the middle ground of British politics. Thus the party consensus which had largely accepted and operated through the institutions of the state was subjected to additional strains.

The intra-party conflict was not solely responsible for eroding consensus. Parliamentary sovereignty was infringed by the 'consultative' referendums in 1975 and 1979, Cabinet collective responsibility was broken during the EEC referendum, as was the convention that governments should resign following a defeat in the Finance Bill. The two-party system was under attack by the nationalists in the 1970s and The Alliance in the 1980s. Thus many of the constitutional and procedural certainties which underpinned the British state were undergoing change with Labour unable to frame a coherent response.

The Falkland's War raised additional and uncomfortable questions about Labour, the state, and British patriotism. The issue posed no problems for either the 'little Englanders' or the 'British nationalists' within the Labour Party. The former, steeped in the radical tradition of opposition to imperialism were intractably hostile to what they regarded as an imperialist adventure; the latter were determined to teach Argentina a lesson. It was Labour's centre which was embarrassed. It could not decide whether the issue was one of self-determination (which would have alarming implications in places like Hong Kong), sovereignty, the imposition of fascist rule, or the use of force in international disputes. The strong internationalist wing of the party argued against any unilateral response by Britain, while the party's small but respected pacifist element decried the use of any force to resolve the crisis. Given these contrasting and conflicting forces the party oscillated between jingoism and pacifism before coming to lean on the prop of a United Nations initiative, the only policy option capable of preventing a deep and bitter divide within the party.

Preoccupied with the need to keep its diverse elements together, the party was unable to establish a coherent view as to what the Falkland's issue was about. By contrast the Conservative Party knew exactly what was at stake. As the crisis deepened it became clear that the government did not see the issue as that of enforcing UN Resolution 502, although the Foreign Secretary made soothing noises in this direction. Nor, despite some confused statements, was it about self-determination. The Falklands were a responsibility, if not a part, of the British state. The issue put simply was about British property and British sovereignty.

While the Labour party dithered, the wave of chauvinism and imperial nostalgia benefited, inevitably, the Conservatives, the party of Empire and Great Britain. Of course, the nationalism of a Tony Benn, derived from the 'little Englander' tradition of radical opposition to imperialism and looking back for its inspiration to the Levellers and the Diggers (Benn, 1979) is a quite different phenomenon. Yet by definition, 'little Englandism' cannot accommodate the non-English periphery which has its own traditions of radical dissent. Labour must tap the democratic and liberal traditions of these nationalisms more effectively if it is to avoid being hoist again on the imperial petard. It is still a long way from doing this.

During the late 1970s, and into the 1980s Labour activists became increasingly sceptical of the party's involvement in, and tacit acceptance of, the parliamentary institutions of the British state. The advance of the so-called 'Outside Left', creating a new electoral college for leadership elections and approving mandatory re-selection of Labour MPs has been chronicled elsewhere (Kogan and Kogan, 1982). It clearly represented a fundamental shift in the distribution of power within the Labour Party; but, most significantly, it undermined much of the traditional authority of the parliamentary party, removing its exclusive right to elect the party leader and subjecting ordinary Labour MPs to increased pressures from their local constituency parties. The identification of the 'Outside Left' with Labour local government politicians and their disposition to question the right of Conservative ministers to intervene in local affairs, was also symptomatic of a reluctance to accept the ultimate authority of Parliament. However, the case which attracted most notoriety was that involving Labour's candidate for the Bermondsey by-election. In an article published in *London Labour Briefing* (May, 1981) Peter Tatchell complained that the Labour Party was 'stuck in the rut of obsessive legalism and parliamentarianism' and argued for 'more dramatic and daring forms of protest'. He concluded: 'We might even be surprised by the extent to which a more direct challenge to the legitimacy of government actually inspires popular support'. These sentiments, initially earning the rebuke of the 'traditional parliamentarian', Michael Foot, nevertheless reflected the new attitudes within the party.

The changing perceptions of Labour activists were paralleled by a new mood in the Conservative Party. Under Mrs Thatcher's leadership the party's traditional role of defending the institutions and customs of the state, has been significantly — if temporarily — modified. For Conservative critics, the state possesses 'socialist excrescences' which must be removed to safeguard the health of the body politic. Thus trade-union corporatist pretensions have been demolished and the roll-back of state involvement in the economy has begun with the programme of privatizing nationalized industries. Tory populism, with its deep reach into the working class, has been able to argue its case in terms of the 'national interest and individual freedoms'; but its task was made easier by the unpopularity of nationalization among the general public. Labour's unimaginative approach to the question of social control, based on the construction of large bureaucracies is now widely seen as less responsive to consumer demands than capitalist enterprises. Much of the popular criticism of nationalized industry may be unfair; they are not as inefficient as often portrayed and have in many cases been based on industries which private enterprise had failed to operate profitably. The fact remains, however, that they are widely seen as an alien 'them' rather than part of 'us'. The crude attacks on public services from Mrs Thatcher's Conservative party have struck a responsive chord but the recipes for mass nationalization of the 1970s and 1980s showed next to no recognition of this, or way of overcoming it.

We have detailed Labour's ambivalence towards the state. Paradoxically, political circumstances now oblige the Labour Party to defend the state. The attacks come from two opposing quarters: from the Conservatives committed to dismantling its socialist extensions and from Labour activists who have little time for its traditional élitist institutions. Labour governments have always presumed that these institutions could be captured and used to promote economic and industrial development and thus effect social change, a form of incremental socialism. By the late 1970s, with a working class locked into a declining industrial system and the Labour movement looking no more than a nostalgic myth (Keating and Geekie, 1984), this belief was no longer tenable. Labour's historical role, as a national party synthesizing the interests and demands of the working class with other radical concerns in a coherent national programme, is thus put at risk. Partisan self-interest, therefore, requires Labour to define a legitimacy for the British state compatible with the interests of an expanded socio-economic constituency, no longer identifiable with the 'working class' or the 'Labour movement'.

The only legitimate foundation for the state which ought to be acceptable to Labour is democratic consent, and indeed the party has long proclaimed its commitment to democratization of the state apparatus. Yet in practice Labour governments have done little, taking democracy for granted and presuming that Labour governments automatically lead to a strengthening of democracy. The priority given to social reform rather than democratic advance, mistakenly supposed that the two were quite separate entities and led some critics in the party to conclude that 'socialist ideas on democracy are now confused and outdated' (Radice, 1968, p. 5). Public ownership has given power not to the people but to another set of managers. The drive for equality has led to centralization. Parliamentary sovereignty, for Labour governments no less than Conservative, has become the basis not so much for holding governments accountable, as for facilitating the flow of government business; the more dire the economic straits the more justified the centralized and bureaucratic approach. The inability to *implement* a bureaucratic solution and the intractability of Britain's economic crises of the 1960s and 1970s led Labour governments back repeatedly into quasi-corporatist deals with unions and employers. There were some real achievements but we would regard a mere strengthening of such corporatist arrangements in the future as a means of solidifying and institutionalizing the very problems they were designed to overcome, rather than as a means of transcending the inertia of British industrial society and pursuing innovatory approaches.

However, Labour's commitment and ability to democratize the British state apparatus must be suspect so long as its own constitution and practice pays it so little attention and so long as its claim to be a national party rests on such insecure foundations. The reforms to the party's constitution in recent years have undoubtedly shifted power from the parliamentary leadership and made MPs more responsive to party activists. Yet these reforms owed less to a desire for democratization than to a wish to produce substantively different policies, as the strident left-wing opposition to universal suffrage within the party — notably the proposal to allow all party members to participate in the selection of parliamentary candidates — shows. Indeed, the result of the changes of the 1970s and 1980s was that, with the selection of candidates reserved for the small cadre of activists in constituency General Committees, Labour MPs continued effectively to be chosen by the most restricted franchise in the democratic world.

It is revealing that the argument urged most forcefully against universal suffrage in the party is that it would 'disenfranchise' affiliated members, those whose unions are affiliated to the party but who are not individual members. In fact, the affiliated member is a myth. Unions affiliate for numbers of votes at the party conference (which may be more or less than their membership), not for named individual union members, so there is no means by which the 'affiliated members' can be identified. What is being defended is in fact a system of corporate representation for institutions, not the democratic rights of different types of party member. Given that such blatantly undemocratic practices are tolerated in the party itself, it is hardly surprising that, in government, Labour has looked for corporatist solutions.

The party's relationship with the trade-union movement must also be called into question. It is part of Labour mythology that the Labour Party, to use Ernest Bevin's graphic phrase, 'grew out of the bowels of the trade unions'; but the links between the industrial and political wings of the Labour movement were forged in quite different times. Then Labour was a sectional interest seeking redress from the governments of the day and creating a 'representation committee' to present its case in the House of Commons. Once Labour emerged as a national party of government with responsibility for the state and all its functions, the traditional relationship was no longer appropriate. In the modern age the democratic state must stand for political purpose rather than acting as a mere ringmaster. This does not mean that the state can do everything itself; but it must have its own view on policy questions and the means for implementing it. Labour governments cannot do this effectively as long as they remain tied to the trade unions; nor can the unions perform their proper role in bargaining over wages and conditions — within the framework of law, guarantees of their rights and public policy — as long as they are expected to act as policemen for government, disciplining the members they are there to protect. Labour's relationship with private industry, too, needs to be rescued from the corporate trap. The weakness and backwardness of British capitalism means that the state must assume a major responsibility for modernization and change. A vital requirement of this is a radical overhaul of the machinery and personnel of government to combat the traditional anti-industrial culture and bring into being a new breed of public entrepreneurs.

If the state is really to represent a wider political identity, it must be grounded more firmly in democratic legitimacy. The only legitimate basis for a democratic state is a fair and democratic electoral system. The British 'first past the post' elections fall far short of these requirements and governments returned on a reducing minority of the popular votes, are less able to claim and to exercise the authority of the state. The Labour party's initial enthusiasm for proportional representation was conveniently forgotten as the party benefited from the idiosyncrasies of the electoral system. However, the party's electoral strongholds, traditionally the basis of its electoral success, are now its greatest weakness. Located in declining industrial areas, they are unrepresentative of modern British society and help to insulate the party from the reality of its popular decline. Furthermore, as we have noted, the territorial distribution of the Labour vote now raises serious doubts about its credibility as a 'national' party. The present system encourages party activists to concentrate their efforts on winning power within the party, in the expectation that eventually the electoral pendulum will remove a discredited Conservative administration and install a Labour government. Given the fractured party system the analysis is suspect; but so long as it is accepted moves towards democratization will be impeded together with Labour's efforts to reconstruct a nation-wide constituency.

The debate on the role of the British state and Labour's place within it, has been renewed during the 1980s. The traditions of the co-operative movement have been rediscovered, large-scale nationalization of basic utilities is out of favour (Mitchell, 1983, pp. 114–17), pluralism in economic and industrial spheres attracts support from wider sections of the party (Heffer, 1980) and the Home Rule tradition has resurfaced (Labour Party, 1983). However, a clear consensus still eludes the Labour Party on the role the state should play in terms of economic planning, administering nationalized industries, and the relationship with the trade unions. Nor has Labour learned how to tap the democratic and liberal traditions of the various nationalisms in the United Kingdom. The task, largely avoided when Labour was in the ascendant, is still far from accomplished.

References

Allen, V. L. (1960): *Trade Unions and the Government* (London: Longman).

Ashford, D. (1981): *Policy and Politics in Britain: The Limits of Consensus* (Oxford: Blackwell).

Attlee, C. R. (1937): *The Labour Party in Perspective* (London: Gollancz).

Austin, J. (1954): *The Province of Jurisprudence Determined* (London: Weidenfeld and Nicolson).

Barker, A. (1970): 'Parliament and Patience', in B. Crick (ed.), *The Reform of Parliament* (London: Weidenfeld and Nicolson).

Barker, R. (1978): *Political Ideas in Modern Britain* (London: Methuen).

Bealey, F. and Pelling, H. (1958): *Labour and Politics 1900–1906* (London: Macmillan).

Beckerman, W. (ed.) (1972): *The Labour Government's Economic Record* (London: Duckworth).

Beer, S. H. (1965): *Modern British Politics* (London: Faber and Faber).

Bell, G. (1982): *A Troublesome Business: the Labour Party and the Irish Question* (London: Pluto Press).

Bell, S. (1980): 'How to Abolish the Lords', *Fabian Tract 476* (London: Fabian Society).

Benn, T. (1979): *Arguments for Socialism* (London: Jonathan Cape).

Benn, T. (1980): 'Manifestos and Mandarins', in Royal Institute of Public Administration, *Policy and Practice: The Experience of Government* (London: RIPA).

Benn, T. (1981): *Arguments for Democracy* (London: Jonathan Cape).

Benn, T. (1983): 'Agenda', *Guardian*, 18 July.

Bevan, A. (1952): *In Place of Fear* (London: Heinemann).

Blake, R. (1970): *The Conservative Party from Peel to Churchill* (London: Eyre & Spotiswoode).

Blunkett, D. and Green, G. (1983): 'Building from the Bottom: The Sheffield Experience', *Fabian Tract 491* (London: Fabian Society).

Boddy, M. (1984): 'Local Economic and Employment Strategies', in M. Boddy and C. Fudge (eds.), *Local Socialism* (London: Macmillan).

Boddy, M. and Fudge, C. (1984): 'Labour Councils and New Left Alternatives', in M. Boddy and C. Fudge (eds), *Local Socialism* (London: Macmillan).

Bornstein, S. Held, D. and Krieger, J. (eds.), (1984): *The State in Capitalist Europe. A Casebook* (London: Allen and Urwin).

Boyce, D. G. (1972): *Englishmen and Irish Troubles* (London: Jonathan Cape).

Brand, C. F. (1965): *The British Labour Party* (Stanford University Press).

Brittan, S. (1971): *Steering the Economy: The Role of the Treasury*, revised edn. (Harmondsworth: Penguin).

Budd, A. (1978): *The Politics of Economic Planning* (Glasgow: Fontana).

Bullock, A. (1960): *The Life and Times of Ernest Bevin* (London: Heinemann).

Butler, D. E. (1963): *The Electoral System in Britain since 1918* (Oxford: Clarendon Press).

Butler, D. E. and King, A. (1965): *The British General Election of 1964* (London: Macmillan).

Butterfield, H. (1944): *The Englishman and his History* (London: Harrap).

Callaghan, J. (1973): *A House Divided* (Glasgow: Collins).

Cawson, A. (1978): 'Pluralism, Corporatism and the Role of the State', *Government and Opposition*, 13.

Christie, C. (1984): 'The British Left and the Falklands War', *Political Quarterly*, 55,3.

Clarkson, J. D. (1925): *Labour and Nationalism in Ireland* (New York: Columbia University Press).

Coates, D. (1975): *The Labour Party and the Struggle for Socialism* (Cambridge University Press).

Coates, D. (1980): *Labour in Power? A Study of the Labour Government, 1974–79* (London: Longman).

Cole, G. D. H. (1972): *Self government in industry* (London: Hutchinson).

Cole, G. D. H. (1921): *Guild Socialism Restated* (London: Parson).

Cole, G. D. H. (1935): *The Simple Case for Socialism* (London: Gollancz).

Cole, G. D. H. and Postgate, R. (1946): *The Common People*, 1746–1946 (London: Methuen).

Cook, C. and Taylor, I. (1980): *The Labour Party* (London: Longman).

Cowling, M. (1971): *The Impact of Labour* (Cambridge University Press).

Cox, A. (1981): 'Corporatism as Reductionism: The Limits of the Corporatist Thesis', *Government and Opposition*, 16,1.

Crick, B. (1970a): 'Whither Parliamentary Reform?', in A. H. Hanson and B. Crick (eds.) *The Commons in Transition* (Glasgow: Fontana).

Crick, B. (1970b): *The Reform of Parliament*, revised edition (London: Weidenfeld and Nicolson).

Crosland, C. A. R. (1956): *The Future of Socialism* (London: Jonathan Cape).

Crossman, R. H. S. (1975): *The Diaries of a Cabinet Minister*, vol. 1 (London: Jonathan Cape).

Crossman, R. H. S. (1976): *The Diaries of a Cabinet Minister*, vol. 2 (London: Jonathan Cape).

Crossman, R. H. S. (1977): *The Diaries of a Cabinet Minister*, vol. 3 (London: Jonathan Cape).

Crouch, C. (1982): *Trade Unions: The Logic of Collective Action* (Glasgow: Fontana).

CSE (1980): Conference of Socialist Economists, London Working Group, *The Alternative Economic Strategy* (London: CSE).

Dahl, R. (1947): 'Worker Control of Industry and the British Labour Party', *American Political Science Review*, XLI.

Dahl, R. (1961): *Who Governs?* (New Haven: Yale University Press).

Davis, W. (1968): *Three Years' Hard Labour* (London: Andre Deutsch).

Dearlove, J. (1979): *The Reorganisation of British Local Government* (Cambridge University Press).

Dicey, A. V. (1939): *Introduction to the Study of the Law of the Constitution* (London: Macmillan).

Dobrée, B. (1937): *English Revolts* (London: Herbert Joseph).

Donovan (1968): Royal Commission on Trade Unions and Employers' Associations. Chairman: The Rt. Hon. Lord Donovan, *Report*, Cmnd. 3623 (London: HMSO).

Donoughue, B. and Jones, G. (1973): *Herbert Morrison: Portrait of a Politician* (London: Weidenfeld and Nicolson).

Drucker, H. M. (1979): *Doctrine and Ethos in the Labour Party* (London: George Allen and Unwin).

Drucker, H. M. and Brown, G. (1980): *The Politics of Nationalism and Devolution* (London: Longman).

Dyson, K. (1980): *The State Tradition in Western Europe* (Oxford: Martin Robertson).

Expenditure Committee (1977): *Eleventh Report of the Expenditure Committee, 1976-77* (London: HMSO).

Fabian Society (1962): *Fabian Essays*, 6th edn. (London: Allen and Unwin).

Fenley, A. 'Labour and the Trade Unions', in Cook C. and Taylor I. (1980): *The Labour Party* (London: Longman)

Feuer, L. S. (ed.) (1959), *Marx and Engels. Basic Writings on Politics and Philosophy* (Glasgow: Fontana).

Fulton (1968): Committee on the Civil Service. Chairman, Lord Fulton, *Report*, Cmnd. 3638 (London: HMSO).

Galbraith, J. K. (1967): *The New Industrial State* (Harmondsworth: Penguin).

Gamble, A. (1981): *Britain in Decline* (London: Macmillan).

Garrett, J. (1972): *The Management of Government* (Harmondsworth: Penguin).

Geekie, J. and Keating, M. (1983): 'The Labour Party and the Rise of Activist Democracy (Glasgow Fabian Society).

Goodhart, P. (1976): *Full Hearted Consent* (London: Davis-Poynter).

Graham, A. (1972): 'Industrial Policy' in W. Beckerman (ed.), *The Labour Government's Economic Record* (London: Duckworth).

Griffiths, J. (1969): *Pages from Memory* (London: Dent).

Griffiths, J. (1978): *James Griffiths and his Times* (Cardiff: Labour Party Wales).

Gyford, J. (1983): 'The New Urban Left: a Local Road to Socialism?', *New Society*, 64, 1066.

Ham C. and Hill, M. (1984): *The Policy Process in the Modern Capitalist State* (Brighton: Wheatsheaf).

Hill, C. (1958): *Puritanism and Revolution* (London: Secker and Warburg).

Harris, K. (1982): *Attlee* (London: Weidenfeld and Nicolson).

Hechter, M. (1975): *Internal Colonialism: The Celtic Fringe in British National Development, 1536–1966* (London: Routledge and Kegan Paul).

Hepburn, F. C. (1980): *The Conflict of Nationality in Modern Ireland* (London: Arnold).

Hindess, B. (1983): *Parliamentary Democracy and Socialist Politics* (London: Routledge and Kegan Paul).

Hobsbawm, E. (1948): *Labour's Turning Point: Extracts from Contemporary Sources* (London: Lawrence and Wishart).

Holland, S. (1975): *The Socialist Challenge* (London: Quartet).

Hood-Philips, O. (1957): *Constitutional Law* (London: Sweet and Maxwell).

Howell, D. (1976): *British Social Democracy* (London: Croom Helm).

Jenkins, B. and Minnerup, G. (1984): *Citizens and Comrades: Socialism in a World of Nation States* (London: Pluto).

Jenkins, P. (1970): *The Battle of Downing Street* (London: Charles Knight).

Jennings, W. I. (1959): *The Law and the Constitution* (London University Press).

Johnson, N. (1970): 'Select Committees as Tools of Parliamentary Reform', in A. H. Hanson and B. Crick (eds.), *The Commons in Transition* (Glasgow: Fontana).

Johnson, N. (1977): *In Search of the Constitution* (London: Methuen).

Johnson, R. W. (1981): *The Long March of the French Left* (London: Macmillan).

Judge, D. (1983): 'Considerations on Reform', in D. Judge (ed.), *The Politics of Parliamentary Reform* (London: Heinemann).

Keating, M. and Bleiman, D. (1979): *Labour and Scottish Nationalism* (London: Macmillan).

Keating, M. and Geekie, J. (1984): 'The Decline of the Labour Movement', *Bulletin of the Society for Cooperative Studies*, Autumn.

Keating, M. and Lindley, P. (1981): 'Devolution: The Scotland and Wales Bills', *Public Administration Bulletin*, 37.

Keith-Lucas, B. and Richards, P. G. (1978): *A History of Local Government in the Twentieth Century* (London: George Allen and Unwin).

Kellner, P. and Crowther-Hunt, N. (1980): *The Civil Servants: An Inquiry into Britain's Ruling Class* (London: Macdonald Futura).

King, A. (1977): *Britain Says Yes: the 1975 Referendum on the Common Market* (Washington: American Enterprise Institute).

Kitzinger, U. (1968): *The Second Try: Labour and the EEC* (Harmondsworth: Penguin).

Labour Party (1918): *Report on the Eighteenth Annual Conference of the Labour Party* (London: Labour Party).

Labour Party (1928): *Labour and the Nation* (London: Labour Party).

Labour Party (1934): *For Socialism and Peace* (London: Labour Party).

Labour Party (1963): *Signposts for the Sixties* (London: Labour Party).

Labour Party (1973): *Labour's Programme, 1973* (London: Labour Party).

Labour Party (1976): *Labour's Programme, 1976* (London: Labour Party).

Labour Party (1981a): *A Socialist Foreign Policy* (London: Labour Party).

Labour Party (1981b): *Northern Ireland* (London: Labour Party).

Labour Party (1983a): *The New Hope for Britain: Labour's Manifesto, 1983* (London: Labour Party).

Labour Party (1983b): *Annual Conference Report* (London: Labour Party).

Laski, H. (1925): *A Grammar of Politics* (London: Allen and Unwin).

Liason Committee (1978): TUC–Labour Party Liason Committee, *Into the Eighties: An Agreement* (London: Labour Party).

Lichtheim, G. (1969): *The Origins of Socialism* (London: Weidenfeld and Nicolson).

Leruez, J. (1975): *Economic Planning and Politics in Britain* (Oxford: Martin Robertson).

Levenson, S. (1973): *James Connolly* (London: Martin, Brian and O'Keefe).

Leys, C. (1983): *Politics in Britain* (London: Heinemann).

Lindbolm, C. E. (1959): 'The Science of Muddling Through', *Public Administraton Review*, 24.

Lindbolm, C. (1977): *Politics and Markets: The World's Political-Economic Systems* (New York: Basic Books).

Lindley, P. (1982): 'The Framework of Regional Planning, 1964–80', in B. Hogwood and M. Keating (eds.), *Regional Government in England* (Oxford: Clarendon Press).

Livingstone, K. (1983): Agenda, *Guardian*, 7 March.

Luard, E. (1979): *Socialism Without the State* (London: Macmillan).

Lyman, R. W. (1957): *The First Labour Government, 1924* (London: Chapman and Hall).

MacCormick, J. (1955): *Flag in the Wind* (London: Gollancz).

Macdonald, D. F. (1976): *The State and the Trade Unions*, 2nd edn. (London: Macmillan).

MacDonald, J. R. (1921): *Parliament and Democracy* (London: Social Studies).

MacDonald, J. R. (1905): *Socialism and Society* (London: Social Studies).

Mackenzie, R. T. (1964): *British Political Parties* (London: Heinemann).

Mackintosh, J. P. (1971): 'Will Britain lose sovereignty by joining the Common Market?', *Europe Left*, 2 (1).

Marquand, D. (1977): *Ramsay MacDonald* (London: Jonathan Cape).

Marshall, G. (1970): 'Parliament and the Ombudsman', in A. H. Hanson and B. Crick (eds.), *The Commons in Transition* (Glasgow: Fontana).

Marshall, G. and Moodie, G. (1967): *Some Problems of the Constitution* (London: Hutchinson).

Middlemas, K. (1979): *Politics in Industrial Society: The experience of the British system since 1911* (London: André Deutsch).

Miliband, R. (1972): *Parliamentary Socialism*, 2nd edn. (London: Merlin).

Miliband, R. (1973): *The State in Capitalist Society* (London: Quartet).

Miliband, R. (1977): *Marxism and Politics* (Oxford University Press).

Moore, R. (1978): *The Emergence of the Labour Party, 1880–1924* (London: Hodder and Stoughton).

Morgan, J. (1975): *The House of Lords and the Labour Government, 1964–70* (Oxford: Clarendon Press).

Morgan, K. (1981): *Rebirth of a Nation: Wales, 1880–1980* (Oxford: Clarendon Press).

Morris, A. (ed.) (1970): *The Growth of Parliamentary Scrutiny by Committee* (Oxford: Pergamon).

Morrison, H. (1964): *Government and Parliament* (Oxford University Press).

Mowat, C. L. (1966): *Britain between the Wars* (London: Methuen).

Muller, W. D. (1977): *The Kept Men* (Brighton: Harvester).

Nairn, T. (1981): *The Break Up of Britain,* 2nd edn. (London: Verso).

NEC (1978): Labour Party National Executive Committee, Statement, 'Reform of the House of Commons', April 1978).

Newman, M. (1981): *Socialism and European Unity* (London: Junction).

NILP (1964): *Signposts to the New Ulster* (Belfast: NILP).

Offe, C. (1984): *Contradictions of the Welfare State* (ed. John Keane) (London: Hutchinson).

Osmond, J. (1977): *Creative Conflict: The Politics of Welsh Devolution* (London: Routledge and Kegan Paul).

Panitch, L. (1980): *Social Democracy and Industrial Militancy* (Cambridge University Press).

Pelling, H. (1954): *The Challenge of Socialism* (Glasgow: A. and C. Black).

Pelling (1968): *A Short History of the Labour Party* (London: Macmillan).

Pickles, W. (1962): 'Not with Europe: the political case for staying out', *Fabian Tract 336* (London: Fabian Society).

Poirier, P. (1958): *The Advent of the Labour Party* (London: Allen and Unwin).

Posner, M. (1972): 'Policy towards nationalised industries', in W. Beckerman (ed.), *The Labour Government's Economic Record* (London: Duckworth).

Poulantzas, N. (1969): 'The Problem of the Capitalist State', *New Left Review,* 58.

Prescott, J. (1982): *Alternative Regional Strategy* (London: Parliamentary Spokesman's Group).

Reid, F. (1960): 'Keir Hardie's Conversion to Socialism', in A. Briggs and J. Saville (eds.), *Essays in Labour History,* vol. 2 (London: Macmillan).

Robbins, L. J. (1979): *The Reluctant Party: Labour and the EEC, 1961–75* (Ormskirk: C. W. and A. Hesketh).

Roberts, D. 'Labour in Office' in Cook C. and Taylor I. (1980): *The Labour Party* (London: Longman).

Rogers, W. (1980): 'Westminster and Whitehall: Adapting to Change', in Royal Institute of Public Administration, *Policy and Practice: The Experience of Government* (London: RIPA).

Rose, P. (1981): *The Backbencher's Dilemma* (London: Muller).

Ross, J. (1979): 'Local Government in Scotland', mimeo (University of Strathclyde).

Sabine, G. H. (1963): *A History of Political Thought* (London: Harrap).

Sedgemore, B. (1980): *The Secret Constitution* (London: Hodder and Stoughton).

Shanks, M. (1972): *Planning and Politics: The British Experience, 1960–76* (London: George Allen and Unwin).

Shaw, G. B. (1904): *The Common Sense of Municipal Trading* (London: Constable).

Shaw, G. B. (1914): *Irish Nationalism and Labour Internationalism* (London: Labour Party).

Skidelsky, R. (1967): *Politicians and the Slump* (London: Macmillan).

Stewart, M. (1968): *Frank Cousins: A Study* (London: Hutchinson).

Strachey, J. (1936): *The Theory and Practice of Socialism* (London: Gollancz).

Tawney, R. H. (1921): *The Acquisitive Society* (London: G. Bell).

Tawney, R. H. (1935): *Equality* (London: Gollancz).

Taylor, R. (1982): 'The trade union "problem" since 1960', in B. Pimlott and C. Cook (eds.), *Trade Unions in British Politics* (London: Longman).

Thomas, J. H. (1920): *When Labour Rules* (London: Collins).

Thompson, E. P. (1968): *The Making of the English Working Class* (London: Longman).

Trevelyan, C. M. (1922): *British History in the Nineteenth Century* (Harmondsworth: Penguin).

Webb, S. (1920): 'Introduction' to 1920 edn. of *Fabian Essays*, reprinted in 6th edn. (London: George Allen and Unwin, 1962).

Webb, B. and Webb, S. (1920): *A Constitution for a Socialist Commonwealth of Great Britain* (London: Longman).

Wilks, S. (1981): 'Planning Agreements: The Making of a Paper Tiger', *Public Administration*, 59.

Wilson, H. (1964): *The New Britain: Selected Speeches* (Harmondsworth: Penguin).

Wilson, H. (1974): *The Labour Government, 1964–70* (Harmondsworth: Penguin).

Wilson, H. (1979): *Final Term: The Labour Government 1974–76* (London: Weidenfeld and Nicolson and Michael Joseph).

Winch, D. (1972): *Economics and Policy: A Historical Survey* (Glasgow: Fontana).

Winkler, J. T. (1976): 'Corporatism', *Archives Européenes de Sociologie*, 17.

Wiseman, H. V. (1970): 'The New Specialised Committees', in A. H. Hanson and B. Crick (eds.), *The Commons in Transition* (Glasgow: Fontana).

Wright, A. (1983): *British Socialism: Socialist Thought from the 1880s to the 1960s* (London: Longman).

Young, S. (1974) with A. V. Lowe: *Intervention in the Mixed Economy* (London: Croom Helm).

Labour Party Records

Papers beginning RD and RE are Labour Party working papers in the archives at Labour Party headquarters.

Index

Abse, Leo 125, 128
Allaun, Frank 180
Alternative Economic Strategy 89,
    95–103, 129, 142–3
Alternative Regional Strategy 132–5
Anglo-Saxon Constitution 15, 18
anti-imperial tradition 22
Asquith, Herbert 37, 43
Attlee, Clement R. 54, 60, 152, 158, 173,
    183, 185
Austin, John 164

Baldwin, Stanley 44, 48
Balfour, Arthur 23
Balogh, Thomas 148
Barker, Sir Ernest 1, 11, 66
Barnes, George 37
Baxter, John 18
Beer, S. H. 66
Benn, Tony 91, 92, 144, 179, 185, 187,
    188–90, 197
Bentham, Jeremy 21
Bermondsey by-election 197
Bevan, Aneurin 45, 48, 65, 106
    and Welsh politics 65, 106
Beveridge, Lord 66
Bevin, Ernest 48, 51, 63, 200
Bishop, F. A. 148
Blackstone, Sir William 11
Blake, Lord 23
Bland, Herbert 30
Blatchford, Robert 7
Bracton, Henry de 13–14
British patriotism 191–2
British state 11, 166, 182–3, 192, 193
Brittan, Samuel 86
Broadhurst, Henry 28
Brown, George 73, 85, 87, 108
bureaucratic élite 5, 22
Burke, Edmund 11

Callaghan, James 100, 125, 174, 176,
    181, 186, 195

Campaign for Democratic Socialism 184
capitalism 68
Castle, Barbara 76
Cawson, A. 4
CBI 92
Celtic periphery 12, 22, 33, 64–5, 193
central economic planning 59, 67, 84–5,
    87–8, 95–7, 109
Chadwick, Edwin 21
Chamberlain, Joseph 23
Chapman, Brian 145
Chartists 19–20
Chrysler 93–4
Civil Service
    and Labour Party 145
    and political bias 143–4
    and reform 98, 142–51
    and status quo 144
Clay Cross 106
Clydeside MPs 49
Clynes, J. R. 48, 173
Cobbett, William 18–20
Coke, Sir Thomas 14, 15
Cole, G. D. H. 42, 51
collective responsibility 181
Commission on the Constitution 110, 167
Common Agricultural Policy 181
Common Market
    see EEC
Commonwealth 182–3, 185
Conference of Socialist Economists (1980)
    95
Connolly, J. 169–70
Conservatism and the state 6–7, 66, 194,
    198
    and planning 82, 85
Constitutional radicalism 18
Corporatism 96–7
    and Labour governments 71–2, 149,
        157, 199–200
    and the state 3–4
    and trade unions 134
Council of Action 45, 171

Cousins, Frank 74
Crick, Bernard 152–3
Cromwell, Oliver 166
Cromwell, Thomas 12, 13
Crosland, Anthony 77, 84, 86
Crossman, Richard 40, 75, 105, 110, 142, 148, 153, 174
Crowther-Hunt Lord 118, 127, 146, 148

Dalyell, Tam 125
Davis, John 75
Dearlove, J. 105
Department of Economic Affairs 73, 85, 87
Devolution 115, 150, 188
  and Labour Party, 131, 193
  and referendum 128
  and trade unions 121
Dicey, A. V. 164
Diggers 16, 197
Disraeli, Benjamin 23
Donovan Commission 75–8

Easter Rising 171
Economic Advisory Council 51
Economic Planning Councils 108
Ede, Chuter 174
EEC
  conditions for entry 184–5, 186–7
  membership of 113, 150, 181–91, 194
EFTA 186
Electoral System 43, 158, 165, 195, 201
English Common Law 14, 15, 17
English nation 25
English radical tradition 13–14, 182, 194

Fabians
  and civil service 147
  and EEC 186
  and Ireland 169, 172
  and nationalization 62
  and planning 67, 83
  and state socialism 27, 30–1, 42, 193
Factory Act (1833) 20
Falklands War 7, 196–7
Field, John 21
Foot, Michael 127, 131, 154, 181
Foulkes, George 137
French Civil Service 147
French Communist Party 36
French planning system 87
Fulton Committee/Report 143, 146–8

Gaitskell, Hugh 84, 181, 184, 186

Galbraith, J. K. 86
General Strike 36, 48
Great Reform Bill (1832) 20
Grierson, M. 88–9
Griffiths, James 106, 111, 120
guild socialism 42

Hamilton, William 160
Hardie, Keir 27, 32, 34, 36, 46, 121
Heald, Dand 68
Heath, Edward 68, 116
Heffer, Eric 75, 91, 92, 201
Helsby, Lord 148
Henderson, Arthur 37, 51
Hobhouse, J. C. 24
Hobsbawn, E. 148
Hobson, C. K. 24
Holland, Stuart 89–90, 96–101
Home Rule 27, 34, 57, 104, 114, 116, 121, 139, 193
Houghton, Douglas 155
House of Lords 32, 165, 195
  and local government 161
  and reform of 54–5, 65, 77, 158–61
Hyndman, H. M. 32, 33, 36

IMF Loan 125
'In Place of Strife' 76, 160, 195
Independent Labour Party 32, 49–51, 172
Industrial Relations Act 79, 114
Industrial Reorganisation Corporation 88–9
Instrument of Government, (1653) 166
Irish Free State Agreement Act 166
Irish Labour Movement 169–72
Irish Nationalism 35, 43, 168, 170
Irish TUC, 170

Jacobins 13
Jay, Douglas 187
Jenkins, Roy 75, 181, 185
Jones, Jack 80
Judge, David 156–7

Kearton, Lord 88–9
Kellner, Peter 148
Keynes, J. M. 47, 51, 66, 71, 83
Kilbrandon Report 116
Kinnock, Neil 128, 175, 189
Kitson, Alex 179–80

Labour Commission of Enquiry (1920) 171
Labour Committee on Ireland 179

Labour governments
    (1923-4) 47-8
    (1929-31) 50-3
    (1945-51) 60-3
Labour Party
    annual conference 40
    and anti-state tradition 56-7
    and constitutionalism 46, 51-2, 65, 180
    and ideology 44
    and incomes policy 72-83
    and machinery of government study
        group 149-50, 156, 160
    and membership 195
    and parliamentarianism 35, 39
    and parliamentary leadership 54, 100
    and participation 140
    and party constitution 39-41, 199
    and revisionists 84
    and trade unions 44, 200
    and unionist sentiments 174, 178, 192
    and World War I 36
Lansbury, George 52, 64
Larkin, James 170
Laski, H. 57, 84
Levellers 15-16
Lever, Harold 93, 181
Liberals and Ireland 169
Lichtheim, G. 20
Little Englandism 7, 183, 197
Livingstone, Ken 179
Lloyd-George, David 37, 43, 45, 46
Local government 31, 63-4, 104-6, 116,
    129-31, 138
Lockwood, Sir Joseph 89

MacDonald, Ramsay 28, 31, 36, 38,
    43-4, 46, 49, 50-1, 53-6, 170-1
Machiavelli, N. 10
Macmillan, Harold 68
Mandate doctrine 166, 195
Marshall, Geoffrey 155
Marx, Karl 5, 32-3
Marxism
    and critique of Labour 67-70
    and the state 5-6, 32-3, 57-8
Mason, Roy 178
Maxton, James 49, 51
Maxwell, Robert 88
Middlemas, Keith 67
Miliband, Ralph 5, 6
Mitchell, Austin 201
mixed economy 67
Montaigne 14

Montfort Simon de 12
More, Sir Thomas 13
Morris, William 13, 19
Morrison, Herbert 56, 60, 62, 65, 173-4,
    192
Moseley Memorandum 51
Municipal Socialism 169

Nairn, Tom 99
National Board for Prices & Incomes 73-4
National Economic Development Council
    73
National Enterprise Board 90-3
National Plan 85-6
Nationalism 136-7
    British 99
    English 137
    Scottish 107
    Welsh 107
Nationalization 59, 62, 83-4, 90-1, 95,
    101-2, 194
natural rights 10, 16
new urban left 129-31
Norman Yoke 15-18
North Sea oil 90, 112, 194
Northcote-Trevellyan reforms 22
Northern Ireland 167-8, 173-80
    and Westminster sovereignty 175-7
Northern Ireland Act, (1949) 173-4
Northern Ireland Labour Party 175

Ombudsman 155
O'Neill, Lord 174
Opie, Roger 148
Ostler, Richard 21
Outside Left Movement 197
Owen, Robert 19

Paine, Thomas 18
Parliament
    and procedure 156
    and reform 152-8
    and sovereignty 8, 11, 163-7, 186-90,
        196, 199
Parliament Act, (1949) 159
Plaid Cymru 110, 117, 120-1
Planning Agreements 93
'Poplarism' 64, 106
Popular sovereignty 163-5
Poulantzas, N. 6
Prescott, John 131-4
Provisional IRA 177
public ownership 31, 50

radical tradition
  and rural utopia 18–19

Redcliffe-Maud Commission 105–6
Rees, Merlyn 177
Referendum 128, 181, 188–9, 196
Regionalism 106
  and England 125–7, 138–9
  and Harold Wilson 116, 118
  and planning 108–9
Ricardian socialists 13
Rogers, William 142
Ross, William 114

Sankey Commission 46
Schonfield, Andrew 76
Scotland
  Act of Union 12, 164
  Assembly for 123, 138, 193
  Secretary of State for 122
Scotland & Wales Bill 124
Scottish Council of Labour 110–11
  Executive of 117–19, 120, 135
Scottish Labour Movement 57
Scottish Office 107
SDA 124
SDP 183, 191
Sedgemore, B. 143–4, 149, 157
Self, P. 148
Shaw, G. B. 30
shop stewards movement 49
Shore, Peter 126, 187, 190
Short, Edward 119
Sillars, Jim 113, 123, 138
Sinn Fein, 171
Smith, Geoffrey 124
Snowden, Philip 51, 52
SNP 110, 120, 136
social contract 81, 195
Social Democratic Federation 32–3
social democratic state 3–4
Socialism
  in France & Germany 25
specialist select committees 153–5, 157
Spence, Thomas 16, 18–20
Stafford Cripps, Sir 61
state
  and collectivisim 24
  and conservative ideology 21–5
  and democracy 199–201
  in European tradition 10–11
  and laissez-faire economics 22–3
  and middle class morality 20–1
  and theories of 3–7
Stewart, Michael 107–8

STUC 111, 115
STV 55
syndicalism 33

Taff Vale Judgement 28
Tatchell, Peter 197
Tawney, R. H. 13, 43, 51, 58
Thatcher, Margaret 7, 68, 82, 136, 198
Thomas, George 112
Thomas, Hugh 145
Thomas, J. H. 45, 48, 52, 172
Thompson, E. P. 19
Thomson, George 181
Trade Unions 44
  and EEC 184, 189
  and incomes policy 69–70, 100–1
  and Liberalism 28
  and Northern Ireland 167–8, 176, 179–80
  and parliamentary action 48–9
  and public corporations 60
  and state intervention 28–9
  and state planning 92, 94
Trades Disputes Act 29
Trevelyan, G. M. 18
Tribune Group 184
Triple Alliance 45–6
TUC
  and incomes policy 74, 77–9
TUC/Labour Party Liaison Committee 102

Ulster *see* Northern Ireland
Ulster Workers' Strike 176–7

Victory for Socialism 184

Wales
  Assembly for 120, 122
  and Labour movement 57
  Secretary of State for 122
Wales TUC 115
Walker, W. 170
Webb, Sidney and Beatrice 29, 30, 42–3, 49, 54, 63, 83
Welsh Council of Labour 111–12, 117–19
Welsh Office 107
Wheatley Commission 105–6
Wheatley, J. 49
Whig tradition 17
Wilkes, John 18
Wilson, Harold 87, 125, 141, 152, 181, 195
  and civil service reform 86, 145, 147

and devolution/regionalism 116,
    118–19, 127
and EEC 185, 187
and incomes policy 73, 76

and nationalization 90–1
and Northern Ireland 174, 176–7, 192
Winkler, J. T. 4
Woodcock, George 74, 77